ZOMBIE HOLOCAUST

ZOMBIE HOLOCAUST

How The Living Dead Devoured Pop Culture

DAVID FLINT

Plexus, London

Published by Plexus Publishing Limited
25 Mallinson Road
London SW11 1BW
First printing 2009
www.plexusbooks.com

British Library Cataloguing in Publication Data

Flint, David
Zombie holocaust : how the living dead devoured pop culture
1. Zombies 2. Zombie films - History and criticism
I. Title
398.4'5

ISBN-10: -0-85965-397-8
ISBN-13: 978-0-85965-397-8

Cover design by Coco Wake-Porter and Rebecca Longworth
Book design by Coco Wake-Porter
Cover images and all photographs from David Flint Collection
Printed in Great Britain by Cromwell Press Group

Acknowledgements

I would like to thank Paul Woods and Dick Porter for the title
and the structure of this book; Dick Porter and Adrian Smith for their corrections,
additions and suggestions; Sandra Wake, my patient publisher who came up with the idea;
Coco Wake-Porter, who designed the book without complaining about the revolting illustrations;
Carl Daft, David Moody and Tony Leathers for expanding my zombie collection in various ways;
and my parents, for letting my fourteen-year-old self rent *Zombie Flesh Eaters* all those years ago.

This book is dedicated to the various young ladies I've forced to
sit through badly dubbed, cheaply made, gore-soaked zombie films over the years. I apologise to you all.

Thanks to all the film producers, distributors, video companies and Zombie film-makers.
Every efffort has beeen made to acknowledge and trace copyright holders and to contact original sources, and
we apologise for any unintentional errors which will be corrected in any future editions of the book.

Contents

Introduction

Zombies. The living dead. Flesh-eating ghouls who must be destroyed. These shambling, emotionless abominations are perhaps the ultimate horror icon. Everyone can do a zombie impression; shuffling along with arms outstretched, hungry for brains. Everyone knows that to kill a zombie you have to shoot it in the head. The zombie has become the archetypal horror character – the star of countless low-budget movies, comic books, toys and games, from the multi-million-dollar *Resident Evil* franchise to self-consciously trashy efforts like *Zombie Strippers*. As many a movie suggests, zombies are taking over through sheer weight of numbers.

Yet it wasn't always so. For years, the zombies were the great unwashed; B-movie bottom-feeders. Hapless, not particularly scary or threatening and often the lackeys of a wealthy, power-crazed villain, zombies were as low as you could go in the horror hierarchy. Audiences chilled to Dracula, Frankenstein and the Wolfman. Zombies just didn't cut it.

Not that the living dead didn't dominate the horror genre. After all, vampires, Frankenstein's Monster, the Mummy and other assorted creatures all rose from the dead in one way or another. And pseudo-zombies chilled sci-fi audiences as sinister alien invaders took over the minds of the living and resurrected the dead in movies as diverse as *Invaders from Mars* and *Plan 9 from Outer Space*. But the traditional zombie was seen as the also-ran of the horror world, relegated to the cheapest B-movies and gory horror comics from publishers such as EC – highly regarded now, but seen at the time as the lowest of the low. Horror in general has rarely been the critic's choice, but zombies in particular seemed wholly without merit, even for genre fans.

The rebirth of the zombie, which began in 1968 with *Night of the Living Dead*, reflected changes in society. 1968 was, after all, the year of revolution – student uprisings in Paris and anti-war protests in the USA and UK as ascendant youth culture began to sweep away old attitudes. The spate of political assassinations in America (both Robert Kennedy and Martin Luther King were murdered in 1968), the brutal Vietnam War being beamed into homes across the world, and the rise of the sniper, the mass murderer and the serial killer at the end of the decade made the old monsters seem dated. The traditional horror figures began to seem as out of touch with the *zeitgeist* as the political and social establishment. After all, how could an aristocrat from Transylvania or a crazy scientist be much of a worry when petrol bombs were exploding in the street and madmen were picking off civilians from tall buildings?

The zombie rose to prominence during these turbulent years because zombies – at least Romero's zombies – represented modern fears. A truly 20th century horror figure, the zombie – alongside the psycho killer – spoke directly to audiences who felt that civilisation was collapsing around them. The apocalypse seemed close, and zombie movies, with their unstoppable, expanding army of monsters who couldn't be reasoned with and who acted without feeling or emotion, seemed to capture a feeling of mass helplessness.

Certainly, the rise of the zombie film at the end of the 1970s reflected the decline of the more

A Reissue poster for Lucio Fulci's 1981 cult classic *The Beyond*.

traditional horror characters. Too over-exposed and corny to frighten anyone, Count Dracula and Doctor Frankenstein have had a tough time of it over the last thirty years or so, at least theatrically (the vampire in general maintains a literary following as a romantic figure, but Dracula movies in a similar vein have generally been unsuccessful both financially and creatively, and only pop culture reinventions like *Buffy the Vampire Slayer* have brought anything fresh to the genre).

Despite periodic attempts at revivals, the day of the traditional gothic horror icon seems to have passed. Notably, the influence of the zombie is strong in recent movies such as *30 Days of Night*, where animalistic vampires roam in packs and have none of the panache of their noblemen forefathers.

Of course, audiences are in danger of becoming inured to the zombie menace. Zombies are increasingly used for comic effect now, and a plethora of amateurish video productions have considerably devalued the sub-genre. Yet the recent success of revisionist films such as the *Resident Evil* series, *28 Days Later*, *Dawn of the Dead* and *I Am Legend* suggests that the zombie holocaust is still something that speaks to audiences on a very primal level. Even the parodic *Shaun of the Dead* managed to provide moments of genuine horror – unlike allegedly 'serious' productions such as *Zombie Chronicles* (to choose just one of hundreds of shot-on-video efforts) that threaten to drown the genre in a sea of mediocrity, juvenile humour and cheap gore.

On a more personal level, for myself and just about every other horror-movie fan that reached their teens at the end of the 1970s, zombie movies were a pivotal part of growing up. The UK cinema releases of *Dawn of the Dead* and *Zombie Flesh Eaters* – and a timely re-release of *Night of the Living Dead* – came alongside the launch of *Fangoria* magazine and the birth of fanzines like *Gore Gazette* and *Splatter Times*, bringing a new and visceral flavour to the sub-genre. Even for the youngest zombie fans, the films may have been out of reach, but now at least they could read about them, and gasp at the gory illustrations that *Fangoria* revelled in publishing. The old school of critics – who sneered at exploitation movies and dismissed the likes of *Night of the Living Dead* as 'minor films' – now seemed wholly out of touch.

The development of a mass market for home video a year or so later finally opened the floodgates. All those movies we thought we'd never see – the ones too nasty, too trashy and too obscure to ever turn up on TV – were now there for the taking. It's worth pointing out to younger readers that, in the early 1980s, horror ruled the video charts – it seemed that more or less everyone who owned a VCR was watching splatter movies, and the zombie films were huge hits.

This book aims to explore the rise of the zombie within popular culture, not just in the world of cinema but also in literature, comic books, video games, music and beyond. I hope to show that the zombie has increasingly dominated the horror genre, becoming its pre-eminent archetype.

All opinions expressed are those of the author, and I make no apology for rattling a few cages along the way – no one is beyond criticism, and that includes the genre's sacred cows. I don't make any claims for exhaustiveness: the amateur-hour zombie film is now so prevalent that I doubt anyone could – or would want to – see them all. But hopefully I can shine a light on the development of zombie culture – a phenomenon that shows no sign of abating at the time of writing, with George Romero's *Diary of the Dead* and the remake of *Day of the Dead* recently on release. The living dead, it seems, are still capable of striking fear into the hearts of movie fans *everywhere*.

1. The Magic Island
The Hard-Working Dead of Haiti

Zombies existed long before they first shuffled their way across the silver screen. The fear of the dead – of death itself – is a universal one, and myths have long existed about the unquiet departed. Be it ghosts, vampires, the revenants of medieval Europe or any number of supernatural beings from around the world, the idea that the dead can rise again has always been a potent one.

The zombie, however – at least the word 'zombie' – is specific to Haiti, where, even into the 20th century, it wasn't simply a supernatural myth, but a reality that was generally accepted as fact without question. The fears surrounding the zombie were not so much that you might become a victim of such a creature, but rather that you yourself could end up in this pitiful state.

Emerging as part of the voodoo religion, the zombie was said to be a recently dead corpse that had been reanimated by voodoo practitioners – not to wreak havoc on the local population, but for the rather more prosaic task of providing cheap labour for plantation owners, who – according to writers like William Seabrook – would pay such practitioners to revive the 'dead'.

We should, however, take all such stories with a pinch of salt. While there is plenty of evidence to show that 'zombies' did indeed exist in one form or another, to suggest that they were an integral part of the voodoo religion would be as inaccurate as claiming that all Catholic priests are child molesters. For the most part, voodoo was – and is – a fairly benign mish-mash of traditional African religions and Catholic symbolism, and any tales of voodoo curses, dolls with pins stuck in them and so on, are more the result of fevered imagination and Western religious propaganda than fact.

Just as today's 'mainstream' religious leaders routinely identify Pagans and Wiccans as devil worshippers, so they would twist the truth about voodoo to portray the competing faith in the worst possible light.

As a religion, Voodoo originated in Africa, and was transplanted to Haiti with the slaves that were brought over by European traders, who effectively repopulated the island in the 15th and 16th centuries after wiping out the indigenous population. The island – and its now mostly black population – finally gained independence after a revolt led to the abolition of slavery in 1793, and the final withdrawal of the French colonials in 1804.

In the ensuing years, Haiti has faced violent political upheaval on a fairly regular basis, with corrupt politicians and dictators frequently ruling the island, and civil unrest a constant threat. It is unsurprising then that, in such an atmosphere of political instability, any attempts to stop the practice of voodoo have failed.

Although ostensibly a Catholic country, many of Haiti's Catholics also still practise voodoo. In fact, Haitian *vodou* rituals incorporate many elements that were originally adapted from Catholicism as a means of disguising the continuation of voodoo practices from slave masters who had forbidden them. These included saints who have been assimilated into the pantheon of voodoo gods as part of a largely benign religion that is heavy on symbolism and steeped in spiritualism. Using the power of persuasion, drugs and the unshakable devotion of the faithful, voodoo's drum-laden rituals may not be the sex-crazed orgies as imagined by many Western writers and filmmakers, but do nonetheless incorporate a heady mix of animal sacrifice, magic and 'possession'.

For many, the zombie has come to represent an important part of the voodoo belief system. A supernatural creature that is not simply a figure of fantasy, but a genuine, omnipresent threat for many believers, who live in fear that the bodies of relatives will be revived and used as slave labour.

Popular voodoo mythology asserts that corpses can be reanimated by a 'bokor' or sorcerer, who achieves this by taking astral control of their victim. In reality, it would seem that the 'zombie' is not, in fact, dead, but under the influence of powerful drugs that place them into a trance-like state and make them highly susceptible to the will of others. These drugs also have the effect of placing the person into a death-like coma, which can last for several days.

Such victims have often been declared dead and then buried, making their subsequent resurrection seem as though the deceased really have returned to life. Anthropologist Wade Davis has claimed that the drug tetrodotoxin is responsible, though this claim remains contentious, and other researchers maintain that zombification is an entirely psychological phenomenon.

However, voodoo followers also believe that the soul can be taken from the body, allowing a god to take over the person. When this happens, only a priest can return the soul, and if this fails to take place, the vacated shell will become a zombie.

Inevitably, there have been those who have chosen to use the threat of voodoo to gain power and instil fear in others. Corrupt criminal gangs have been known to employ the services of bokors, while others formed secret societies that aimed to gain power through magic or ritual (such secret elites are hardly unique to Haiti – take a look at the symbolism and rites associated with the Rosicrucians, Freemasons or Bavarian Illuminati).

Then, of course, there are the voodoo priests who are said to have used their powers to settle scores. Their success in doing so might be more to do with the influence of suggestion than any actual magical ability, but the results are often the same. Cursed people 'die' and then 'return to life' as zombies.

As recently as the 1970s, Haitian dictator Francois 'Papa Doc' Duvalier exploited voodoo and the threat of the zombie to keep the entire nation under his control. A known practitioner of voodoo, he surrounded himself with bokors and used witchcraft rather than more traditional strong-arm tactics to prevent rebellion.

On the whole, though, zombies were traditionally created for the rather more basic need of providing free labour. Bokors would be paid by plantation owners to supply a steady stream of zombies to work the fields or perform other manual labours. Plenty of eyewitnesses have attested to the existence of these slaves – who, we must remember, were not actually dead but instead most likely drugged and captured – throughout the 20th century.

Just how dead bodies were supposedly revived by bokors remains a secret, although varying stories have emerged. The most frequently described method involves marking a living man for zombification. After gaining the permission of Baron Samedi – the spirit of the dead who rules

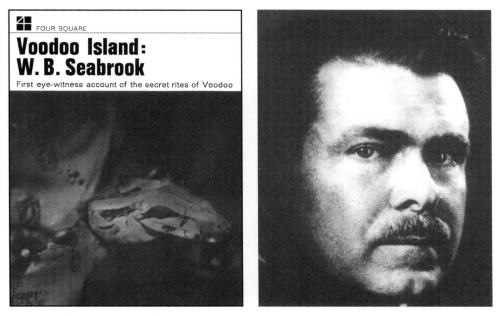

Writer William Seabrook (right) first brought the zombie to the attention of the masses in *The Magic Island*, later republished as *Voodoo Island*.

over all zombies – the bokor will saddle up a horse in the hours of darkness, mounting it back to front before riding to the proposed victim's home. He then makes a slit in the door, presses his lips against it and sucks out the soul of the victim, which he then traps in a bottle. Within days, the victim will have died.

The bokor will then wait until midnight on the day of the funeral, at which point he will visit the grave, disinter the body and call to the corpse by its name. As the corpse responds, the bottle holding the soul is held under the would-be zombie's nose, thus enslaving him. The victim is then chained and dragged away, while the grave is re-covered to hide any trace of the act. The zombie is then given a secret concoction that ensures his obedience, and kept 'alive' with a bland soup called *bouillie*.

The revived corpse will stay enslaved unless it is fed salt or meat. Should this happen, the zombie's consciousness will return and it may well take revenge on those who had induced the zombified state. Witnesses of such moments have stated that the zombie regains the power of speech and reasoning. It can remember who he or she is – or was. The unfortunate individual can then be reunited with their family, although folklore states that most are more inclined to seek a return to the grave.

For those outside Haiti, zombies were little known to the general public until anthropologist and writer William Seabrook published his sensational book *Magic Island* in 1929. Seabrook wasn't the first person outside Haiti to write of zombies. The term had, due to slavery, entered the *Oxford English Dictionary* as early as 1819.

Eighty years later, journalist Lafcadio Hearn briefly wrote about zombies in *Harper's* magazine. On visiting Martinique, Hearn had been told various tales of the walking dead – though he never saw any evidence himself. Still, it made for an intriguing travel article.

But Seabrook had the populist touch to take this one aspect of an exotic religion and make it a sensation. He was very much in the tradition of the 'gonzo' journalist, long before Hunter S. Thompson popularised the term – not content to merely observe, he threw himself headlong into his subject.

He claimed once to have eaten human flesh as part of his research into cannibalism, and his books included studies of Africa, the occult – a subject he had a more than casual interest in – and his own struggles with alcoholism. Seabrook also had a decidedly kinky side to him, his taste for sado-masochism playing a part in his 1941 divorce. A friend of artists like Man Ray and occultist Aleister Crowley, Seabrook was clearly a man who liked to live life to the full.

In the case of *The Magic Island*, this meant delving deep into the world of Haitian voodoo. Seabrook attended – and participated in – several voodoo rituals, and at one point actually meets a group of 'zombies' – who he eventually concludes are simply mentally impaired men who have been forced into slavery.

In the chapter entitled '…Dead Men Working in the Canefields', Seabrook recounts a meeting with Haitian farmer Polynice, something of an expert on local superstitions. After some conversation about werewolves, fire-hags and vampires, Seabrook asks about the Zombie, a creature seemingly exclusive to the island. Polynice responds:

'Superstition? But I assure you that this of which you now speak is not a matter of superstition. Alas, these things – and other evil practices connected with the dead – exist. They exist to an extent that you whites do not dream of, though evidences are everywhere under your eyes.'

He continues with an offer that Seabrook can hardly refuse. 'If you will ride with me tomorrow,' he states, 'I will show you dead men working in the canefields.'

Sure enough, Seabrook saw his zombies. Not at night, but in broad daylight. Encountered on the road, a woman overseeing three male zombies who are labouring is stopped. Seabrook describes the experience:

'My first impression of the three supposed "zombies", who continued dumbly at work, was that there was something about them unnatural and strange. They were plodding like brutes, like automatons. Without stooping down, I could not fully see their faces, which were bent expressionless over their work. Polynice touched one of them on the shoulder, motioned him to get up. Obediently, like an animal, he slowly stood erect – and what I saw then, coupled with what I had heard previously, or despite it, came as a rather sickening shock. The eyes were the worst. It was not my imagination. They were in truth like the eyes of a dead man, not blind, but staring, unfocused, unseeing. The whole face, for that matter, was bad enough. It was vacant, as if there were nothing behind it. It seemed not only expressionless, but incapable of expression.

'…I had a sickening, almost panicky lapse in which I thought, or rather felt, "Great God, maybe this stuff is really true and if it is true, it is rather awful, for it upsets everything."'

Seabrook is brought back to reality when he recalls the face of a dog he had once seen; the animal had undergone a lobotomy, and its eyes stared like the eyes of the zombie. He realises that the zombies are not supernatural beings, but simply brain-damaged individuals, forced to work as slave labour. However, Polynice is unconvinced, and points out that many people have recognised zombies as relatives who had died.

Later, Seabrook meets with Doctor Antoine Villiers, who offers a less magical, but equally sinister solution. He shows Seabrook the official Criminal Code of the Republic of Haiti, which includes the following:

'Article 249. Also shall be qualified as attempted murder the employment which may be made against any person of substances which, without causing actual death, produce a lethargic coma more or less prolonged. If, after the administering of such substances, the person has been buried, the act shall be considered murder no matter what result follows.' The implications are clear – the authorities were well aware that criminals were drugging people in order to create 'zombies'.

The Magic Island is a remarkable work – unlike many books of the period, it still feels fresh today, and is notable for the respect that Seabrook shows for Haiti, its people and culture – to him, these are not the primitive savages that amused so many other writers and filmmakers during the first half of the 20th century, but well-rounded individuals. Seabrook's account opens up a whole new world of magic, superstition and strange ritual for the reader that even now seems fascinating and alien.

Unsurprisingly, the book caused something of a sensation when first published, and became an instant best-seller. However, it was Seabrook who opened the floodgates for the zombie. His literary success not only led to a stream of other anthropological studies of voodoo and the zombie phenomenon, but also brought the zombie to the attention of Hollywood, where a new horror boom was about to get under way.

While the original horror icons were born from literature, European folklore and the current fascination with all things Egyptian (and its accompanying curses), zombies were new, exotic and scary. It would only be a matter of time before Seabrook's lurid tales would make their way into the world of the moving picture.

2. Drums of Voodoo
Bad Juju at the Movies

Two years after the publication of *Magic Island*, big-screen adaptations of *Dracula* and *Frankenstein* made stars of Bela Lugosi and Boris Karloff, and kick-started a horror-movie boom. Not only was Universal Pictures quick to exploit the success of its two hits with numerous sequels, imitations and spin-offs, but other studios and independent producers also jumped aboard the bandwagon with supernatural haste.

One of the first independent horror films of the period was *White Zombie* (1932), produced by Victor and Edward Halperin. Made for less than $50,000, the movie took Seabrook's stories of zombies and wove them into a melodrama that, even today, has much to admire. More significantly, it brought the zombie to the screen for the first time, creating a new monster for audiences to fear.

Bela Lugosi played the sinister zombie master and sugar-mill owner Murder Legendre, hired by a jealous and wealthy American, Charles Beaumont (Robert Frazer), to help him lure Madeleine Short (Madge Bellamy) away from her fiancé, Neil Parker (John Harron). This he does by zombifying her on her wedding night using a magical potion supplied by a voodoo priest that causes her to seem dead, and later taking her from her grave.

Like Seabrook's zombies, Madeleine is not really dead – just placed in a trance by Legendre. When Beaumont realises that a brain-dead Madeleine is no substitute for the 'living girl', he attempts to force Legendre to reverse his spell, but instead is himself dosed with zombie poison and forced to watch as Legendre takes Madeleine as his own slave (though what he does with her is left to the imagination).

Meanwhile, Neil – who has spent much of the film drinking, stumbling about and bemoaning his fate – manages, with the help of missionary Doctor Bruner (Joseph Cawthorn), to reach Legendre's castle, where Madeleine is finally dragged out of her stupor and Legendre and his zombies meet their end.

Like many low-budget films of the period, *White Zombie* suffers from creaking sets and wooden acting. When ham actor Bela Lugosi gives the best performance of the film, it's always a bad sign, and the romantic leads are possibly the most insipid in the history of the genre, with Bellamy and Harron being equally characterless. But the positive elements of the film more than outweigh the negative.

With sets borrowed from Universal (if you've seen Lugosi's *Dracula*, you'll recognise the interior of Legendre's castle immediately) and some eerie scenes of zombies walking through the night-time forest, the film has a chillingly distinctive atmosphere, particularly during the opening scenes where the happy couple's coach arrives upon a roadside burial and encounters Lugosi and his zombies. It's not hard to imagine this having 1932 audiences glued to the edge of their seats, and it remains an influence today, with a devoted cult following (including musician/filmmaker Rob Zombie, who named his band after the film).

The cadaverous creatures from Hammer's *Plague of the Zombies* remain among the most iconic of horror images.

The living dead reach the big screen in the seminal *White Zombie*.

In fact, *White Zombie* managed to be so creepy that it isn't until afterwards that you realise the essential flaw in the idea of the zombie as a horror character – they are not very scary. Invariably the stooges of a villainous character like Legendre, the zombies don't have any malicious intent. They don't attack anyone, but instead carry out mundane tasks. The only scary element of the zombie is the prospect of becoming one and, as horror films of the time made clear, that would only happen if you ventured to Haiti or some other exotic locale. This failure to evoke a genuine sense of peril would relegate the zombie to the bottom of the horror bucket for the next thirty years.

Nevertheless, *White Zombie* raked in an astounding $8 million at the box office, meaning that the walking dead had scored a guaranteed place in the monster-movie pantheon. Unfortunately, the films that followed over the next two decades were a pretty depressing bunch.

The rot set in almost immediately, with the Halperins' follow-up film, *Revolt of the Zombies* (1936). The action is transposed from Haiti to First World War Cambodia, and the central idea is interesting enough – antiquarian scholar Armand Louque (Dean Jagger) is investigating the mind-control methods known to Cambodian priests, in the hope that an army of powerful zombies can be created to help win the war.

Once Louque has discovered the secret of the zombies, he uses the power to enslave his own private army and exact petty vengeance against former colleagues who had scoffed at his interest in the arcane. In a plot turn resonant of *White Zombie*, Louque blackmails a young woman (Dorothy Stone) into breaking off with her fiancé (Robert Noland). But once Louque discovers that Stone will never love him, he relinquishes his power over the zombies, who then storm his villa and exact deadly revenge upon their creator.

Revolt of the Zombies suffers most acutely from an incoherent story, wooden acting (the main cast seem no more animated than the zombies) and a distinct lack of thrills. With the zombies being nothing more than living men under a form of mind control, there is no supernatural horror element to thrill audiences. Instead, much of the film is taken up with the tedious love triangle. For the zombie film, it represented a creative descent from the terror of *White Zombie*.

The zombie was spoofed for the first time in 1940's *The Ghost Breakers*, a Bob Hope comedy thriller that aimed to capitalise on the success of the previous year's box-office hit *The Cat and the Canary*. *The Ghost Breakers* reunited the wisecracking Hope with his *Cat...* co-star Paulette Goddard and transplanted the then-popular 'old dark house' formula (inheritance, murder and malice) to a small Cuban island.

The film mixed sharp comedy and thrills pretty effectively, as Hope and butler Alex (Willie Best, mugging and eye-popping furiously) join Mary Carter (Goddard) as she claims her inheritance – a spooky, and apparently haunted, house. As with *Cat...*, the sinister goings on are eventually revealed to be all too human in origin, but not before Hope has had a run-in with a

The meagre thrills of *Revolt of the Zombies* are summed up in this poster.

'zombie' (Noble Johnson) – though, to be fair, the role was little different to the typical henchman/thug parts that turned up in other comedy thrillers of the time.

The Ghost Breakers was a brief moment of quality for the zombie film – solid production values, a good script and recognisable stars. After that, it was back to basics.

1941's *King of the Zombies* saw the living dead being dragged firmly into the world of poverty-row filmmaking, as the infamously cheap Monogram Studios set about cynically pumping out a flimsy tale of terror. Although the studio cut every conceivable creative and technical corner, much of the Monogram output remains surprisingly entertaining when viewed today – *The Devil Bat, Invisible Ghost, The Corpse Vanishes* and others (more often than not, starring a down-on-his-luck Bela Lugosi) are a lot of fun to watch. But the fun stopped

Mantan Moreland scoring cheap laughs in *King of the Zombies.*

when the studio set its sights upon the zombie sub-genre. Notably, even Lugosi passed on *King of the Zombies,* even though the lead villain was written with him in mind.

The inaction begins when a light aircraft is blown off course and crash-lands on an uncharted Caribbean island. There, Bill Summers (John Archer), who had taken the doomed flight in search of a missing admiral, his valet Jeff Jackson (Mantan Moreland) and their pilot James 'Mac' McCarthy (Dick Purcell) seek shelter in an old mansion inhabited by sinister scientist Doctor Miklos Sangre (Henry Victor).

As evidence of various experiments in zombification are unearthed, it is clear that the doctor is up to no good. It transpires that he has captured the missing admiral, and is trying to use voodoo to force him to unveil his military secrets. Doctor Sangre, unsurprisingly, is in cahoots with the Nazis.

King of the Zombies is something of a low point for zombie cinema in particular, and the horror genre as a whole. Slow-moving, anything but scary, and with the wholly ineffectual zombies pretty much irrelevant to the plot, the film has little to offer anyone who isn't enamoured with Mantan Moreland's wild mugging – a display that made Willy Best's performance in *The Ghost Breakers* look positively restrained.

As his 'wacky' antics take up much of the running time – the two male dramatic leads having little to do but stand around looking confused for most of the movie – watching the film becomes something of an endurance test.

Several critics have subsequently sought to extrapolate some racist subtext from *King of the Zombies*. It's true that the Doctor Sangre character is openly hostile to the black Moreland – an element that briefly seems to give the film a certain *frisson*. However, Moreland's character and performance are simply the result of a less enlightened era, and if anything are representative of a specific racist comedy stereotype that was popular at the time.

Despite this casual racism, the novelty of a black actor being afforded a prominent role ensured that the movie was a hit with black audiences. The studio was quick to exploit this phenomenon and, when *King of the Zombies* played black neighbourhoods, Moreland was given top billing.

Monogram followed up *King of the Zombies* with *Revenge of the Zombies* in 1943, bringing back Mantan Moreland and drafting in John Carradine to retread much of the previous film. This time, Carradine plays the fittingly named Doctor Max Heinrich von Altermann – a Nazi agent who is trying to develop an army of zombies (represented onscreen by a handful of shuffling extras – hardly the invincible *übermensch* promised by their goose-stepping creator), while coping with the very specific demands of his surprisingly wilful zombie wife.

Even more lowbrow than its predecessor, *Revenge of the Zombies* is little more than a hastily produced retread of *King of…* aimed at scraping in a few more dollars from unwary thrill-seekers.

Increasingly bad though these movies were, there was still enough box-office life in the dead

Cheap thrills – and precious few of them – in *Revenge of the Zombies*, an early addition to John Carradine's lengthy career in schlock.

Poverty Row of the Dead — two Bela Lugosi cheapies.

horse for Monogram to keep flogging it – though the company increasingly hedged its bets by splicing zombies with whatever genre seemed to be making money at the time.

The studio again disinterred the living dead for 1942's *Bowery at Midnight*, where the luckless Lugosi again appears, this time as Professor Frederick Brenner – a criminal who uses his soup kitchen as a front for the activities of a gang of hoodlums and ne'er-do-wells. After murdering his lackeys, Brenner receives his comeuppance at the film's conclusion, when they re-emerge as zombies and wreak their vengeance on him.

A weak crime flick, *Bowery at Midnight* appears to have had the zombie element grafted on as an afterthought in the hope of adding some spark to an otherwise leaden hour of viewing.

Voodoo Man (1944) again cast Bela Lugosi in the role of a mad doctor, this time abducting young women in order to transfer their souls to his zombie wife. This fails, leaving the now zombified girls stashed upright in coffins at his home.

Relatively big names such as John Carradine and George Zucco joined the action, but even by Monogram's low standards *Voodoo Man* was pitiful stuff, failing to offer even a modicum of entertainment and with the glassy-eyed zombie girls being decidedly unscary. After this weak effort, the studio finally allowed the undead to rest in peace.

1943 saw the release of what was to become one of the most critically acclaimed zombie films. Val Lewton's production of *I Walked with a Zombie* was among the first in his series of horror films for RKO.

Lewton hated horror, and had nothing but contempt for the Universal films of the time, considering himself above their crass commercialism. He was, however, not above accepting the job of heading RKO's horror division. His rather arrogant reasoning was that, if he were to be forced to make horror movies, he would undermine his backers and his audience and shoot the films he wanted to see, rather than those requested by the studio and enjoyed by the public.

Directed by Jacques Tourneur – who had made the classic *Cat People* a year earlier – *I Walked with a Zombie* tells the story of Betsy (Frances Dee), a young nurse who travels to the island of San Sebastian in the West Indies on holiday, only to land the job of looking after Jessica Holland (Christine Gordon), the catatonic wife of plantation owner Paul Holland (Tom Conway). The locals believe Jessica to be a zombie, and Betsy is increasingly drawn into the world of voodoo, as she attempts to find a cure for her patient. At the same time, she is caught in a love triangle with Paul and his brother Wesley (James Ellison).

The critical reputation of *I Walked with a Zombie* has long been considered unassailable – mainstream critics have frequently expressed their admiration for the relaxed pace, lack of overt horror and alleged sophistication found in Lewton's production. Yet most horror-movie fans, if they were brutally honest, would have to concede that the film is less than satisfactory.

This is unsurprising: it is very much a critic's film – praised by people who generally treat the genre with contempt because, despite the catchpenny title (designed with mass appeal in mind), it is unquestionably a serious and subtle work. Horror fans, on the other hand, might feel justified in arguing that *I Walked with a Zombie* is fatally flawed because, despite a great title, the film itself is not only slow-moving (an achievement in itself for a movie that is barely an hour long) but also fails to deliver the visceral goods.

Overall, *I Walked with a Zombie* has many admirable qualities, not least of which is the fact that the film looks beautiful – it's one of the most strikingly visual films of the period. The examination of Haitian voodoo is surprisingly sympathetic and thoughtful. The religion is not depicted as particularly sinister or dangerous – a rarity among voodoo-themed movies.

Taken for what it actually is (a melodrama, rehashing *Jane Eyre* in a tropical location) rather than what it claims to be (a horror movie), the film is an effective, if minor production.

Despite the critical plaudits, *I Walked with a Zombie* can be viewed as one of Val Lewton's lesser efforts, and knowing the contempt felt by Lewton for the studio's target audience – something he shared with critics who believe that they are above such low-brow fare – tends to leave a sour taste, regardless of the quality of the film itself

Horror-movie fans who feel compelled to praise Lewton's work should perhaps bear in mind his abhorrence of the genre, and remember that his films are lauded primarily because many film critics share his disdain.

Nonetheless, *I Walked with a Zombie* was successful enough for RKO to return to the undead. But, for reasons unknown, it was decided that the best way to follow up this quiet, subtle movie would be a crass comedy.

1945's *Zombies on Broadway* cast vaudeville comedy team Wally Brown and Alan Carney as publicists for a new nightclub, The Zombie Hut. The duo, a poor man's Abbott and Costello,

Val Lewton's production of *I Walked with a Zombie* offers sumptuous visuals but few thrills.

are tasked with finding a real zombie for the club's opening and set off for the island of San Sebastian where they meet mad doctor Bela Lugosi, who is experimenting with zombification. Unsurprisingly, given the already hackneyed nature of the plot, the ensuing action is short on laughs and even shorter on shocks and suspense.

The final 'zombie' movie of the 1940s was also the most forgettable. Republic Pictures' 1946 production *Valley of the Zombies* had a rather misleading title. This story of a mad scientist using blood transfusions to come back from the dead had more to do with both vampirism and the spate of 'Mad Doctor' films (often starring Boris Karloff) that proliferated

Excitement galore – or perhaps not – from *Zombies on Broadway*.

throughout the decade. The 'valley of the zombies' is mentioned in passing, but at no point are any actual zombies (or valleys) in evidence.

If the development of the zombie movie during the 1940s was sporadic, things were about to get worse. The entire horror genre was in decline during the first half of the Fifties, with science fiction having a greater impact on post-atomic audiences. Concerns over 'reds under the bed' and the Cold War hotting up – not to mention worries about juvenile delinquents, rock'n'roll and social upheaval – were more immediately worrying than fiendish aristocrats in East European villages.

It was science fiction, with its alien invaders (UFO sightings first began in earnest during the Fifties), atomic mutants and mad scientists (a close relation of, but distinct from, the mad doctor) which was providing the chills during much of the decade. Ironically, this gave the zombie a new lease of life, as revived corpses and mind control would be increasingly grafted on to sci-fi plots about mad scientists and alien invaders, taking the living dead galaxies away from their Haitian roots.

Saturday-morning serial *Zombies of the Stratosphere* had plenty of action but no actual zombies.

The Sputnik decade's first 'zombie' presentation was *Zombies of the Stratosphere* (1952). This twelve-part serial is again notable mainly for having nothing – aside from a mention in the final episode – to do with zombies, instead being a cheaply churned-out rehash of earlier Saturday-morning kids fare involving Martian invaders.

The 1953 Dean Martin/Jerry Lewis vehicle *Scared Stiff* was a pointless retread of *The Ghost Breakers*. Despite being a hit with audiences who came to see the popular comedy duo making what the lobby posters described as 'a spook-tackle of themselves', the ham-fisted comedy made even the worst of Abbott and Costello's 'Meet the Monsters' films seem like the height of subtle wit.

In 1955, zombies crashed headlong into the brave new world of science fiction in Edward L. Cahn's *Creature with the Atom Brain.* The plot centres upon a gangster and a former Nazi scientist who team up to revive the dead and use them as a radio-controlled avenging army against the pair's rivals.

Structurally, this may have been similar to the zombie films of the 1940s, but the feel of the film was very much science fiction, and Cahn – a director who could be relied upon to make the most of low budgets and threadbare material – delivers a fast-paced saga of radioactive mayhem and science gone awry.

Two years later, Cahn took on more traditional zombie fare with *Zombies of Mora Tau.* The film tells the story of an expedition of diamond hunters determined to find the fortune supposedly lying in a shipwreck off the titular island. However, tragedy strikes as the undead captain and crew of the sunken vessel – doomed to guard the treasure as the result of a voodoo curse – strike, forcing the scavengers to choose between wealth and the possibility of death.

Cahn does his best with the low budget, though his 'underwater' scenes are less than convincing. However, the film contains the first portrayals of underwater zombies, which would return to haunt audiences two decades later in *Shock Waves* and *Zombie Lake.*

Voodoo Island (1957) was something of a disappointment. Boris Karloff plays Professor Philip Knight, a sceptic who is sent to a Pacific island to debunk claims that voodoo practices are responsible for the disappearance of several workers building a new hotel. The lone surviving worker has returned home as an apparent zombie.

The living dead rise from the sea in *Zombies of Mora Tau.*

Boris Karloff unsuccessfully battles boredom in *Voodoo Island*.

Once on the island, Karloff and his team wander about aimlessly waiting for something to happen, before they encounter several man-eating plants and eventually discover a lost tribe. The film limps to a frustratingly flaccid climax, and the usually reliable Karloff seems to be treating the material with thinly disguised contempt.

While the 1950s saw the advent of a number of films such as *Invsisble Invaders* and *Invasion of the Bodysnatchers*, in which visitors from outer space enslaved humanity, Ed Wood's infamous *Plan 9 from Outer Space* upped the ante – his film featured alien invaders actually raising the dead to do their bidding.

Plan 9 is hard to write about objectively, given its undeserved reputation as The Worst Film Ever Made. The temptation is to heap praise upon the movie in order to redress a perceived imbalance, but the truth is *Plan 9...* is pretty shoddy. However, it's no worse than many other low-budget science-fiction films of the time and, in its own limited way, it's a great deal more entertaining than many overblown big-budget sci-fi movies of recent years.

Sure, it replaces the dead Bela Lugosi with an actor (Wood's dentist, allegedly) who is considerably taller than him and tries to hide the switch by repeatedly covering his face with a cape. Certainly, the flying saucers are wobbly hubcaps on wires, the acting is weak, the dialogue bizarre and the sets are beyond basic.

However, such flaws should not be seen as wholly bad. Regardless of kitsch appeal, the fact is that *Plan 9...* moves at a steady pace, packs plenty of incident into the eighty-minute running time and has an infectious sense of enthusiasm about it. No film with all that going for it could possibly be the worst ever made.

During the same year, Edward L. Cahn attempted another variation on the increasingly

Ed Wood's much maligned but always entertaining *Plan 9 from Outer Space* saw aliens resurrecting the dead to do their bidding.

UNSPEAKABLE HORRORS FROM OUTER SPACE PARALYZE THE LIVING AND RESURRECT THE DEAD!
PLAN 9 FROM OUTER SPACE
with
BELA LUGOSI
VAMPIRA
LYLE TALBOT
A J. Edward Reynolds Production
Produced and Directed by
Edward D. Wood, Jr.
DCA

Aliens possess the dead in the effectively creepy *Invisible Invaders*.

mutable zombie theme with *Invisible Invaders*. This time, the zombies are dead bodies that have been taken over by previously invisible, moon-based aliens intent on conquering the world. They are eventually defeated when sound waves are employed to destroy their flying saucer.

This cheap but effective shocker features some of the most sinister zombies of the decade – the scenes of the walking dead advancing with eerie menace clearly had some influence on George Romero, who duplicated some of the imagery in *Night of the Living Dead*.

Hack director Jerry Warren's *Teenage Zombies* was shot in 1957, though it didn't see release until 1960, by which time its already hackneyed teens must have seemed even more incongruous.

This mercifully brief movie has a bunch of rather aged teenagers head to a supposedly deserted island, only to be captured by a mysterious *femme fatale*, who is working (for 'the enemy') on a nerve agent to turn people into mindless slaves. Her plans are foiled by a gormless friend of the teens (who looks about twelve), and a marauding gorilla is crowbarred into the story too for no good reason other than the fact that gorillas were box-office dynamite at the time (see *Gorilla at Large*, *The Bride and the Beast*, *Konga* and others).

Like much of Warren's chamber of directorial horrors – *Man Beast*, *The Incredible Petrified*

The 'awful secret' of *Doctor Blood's Coffin* was hardly worth the effort of sitting through this dull British shocker.

World, The Wild, Wild World of Batwoman – *Teenage Zombies* was badly acted, poorly plotted and thrown together with a distinct lack of interest in anything other than getting the film in the can. Unsurprisingly, the movie did little to enhance the sub-genre, and even when viewed with irony is a fairly tiresome experience.

After a decade where the zombie had almost sunk into creative oblivion, the 1960s ushered in something of a revival. As low-budget exploitation films became more prevalent and increasingly graphic, zombies slowly began to shuffle out of the shadows and back into the limelight. The Sixties would culminate in the most important zombie film ever made, but, before then, the decade of revolution produced a decidedly mixed body bag of living-dead movies.

Britain hopped aboard the creaking zombie bandwagon with *Doctor Blood's Coffin* (1961), although the film owed more to the Frankenstein mythos than any voodoo-inspired living-dead saga. Like many of the horror films that emerged in the initial post-Hammer period, this is a low-budget, low-thrill imitation with Irish heroic lead Kieron Moore as the eponymous Doctor.

Blood has set up shop carrying out heart-transplant experiments in a Cornish village. As this involves killing 'useless' locals to remove their hearts and revive corpses, his actions understandably cause some distress amongst the villagers. When the nurse he's been romancing (Hammer scream queen Hazel Court) discovers his actions, she launches into a hissy fit comprised of the sort of religious hysteria that anyone who has followed embryology research will be only too familiar with. Blood responds – somewhat understandably – by reviving her long-dead husband. Unfortunately, this touching gesture fails to win her over and the film ends, like so many British horror movies, in flames.

Doctor Blood's Coffin has its moments, but is woefully lacking in action. Early efforts to create a degree of mystery about the identity of the killer are somewhat undermined by the title, and are soon dropped, while the zombie finale comes too late to revive audience interest.

Ultimately, the only (unintentional) legacy to be drawn from this film is as a guide to how

The Dead One delivers on all the gaudy promises made in this garish double-bill poster. (Its support feature *The Monster of Piedras Blancas* sadly does not.)

not to be a mad scientist – from the start, Doctor Blood blunders, leaves clues, and generally messes up everything he turns his hand to. Had the filmmakers picked up on this and turned it into a study of a hapless fool's life spiralling out of control, *Doctor Blood's Coffin* might have been more fun.

1961's *The Dead One* (also issued on video as *Blood of the Zombie*) is something of a curio. Written and directed by legendary softcore filmmaker Barry Mahon, it tells the story of John Carlton (John MacKay), who travels with his new bride Linda (Linda Ormond) to his ancestral plantation mansion in New Orleans to take up an inheritance.

His arrival comes much to the chagrin of his cousin Monica (Monica Davis – we can assume the cast didn't have much trouble remembering their characters' names), who has been running the estate for years and sees it as her home. Fortunately for Monica, she's been practising voodoo rituals with the local African workers, and soon raises her dead brother Jonas whom she despatches to kill Linda, thus invalidating the will, which states that the estate passes to John only when he is married.

It's pretty crude stuff – the production values and acting are all notably threadbare – but not without its charms. Viewers with no interest in early-Sixties New Orleans jazz and burlesque might find the opening section a little dull, as it takes in lengthy travelogue footage of the city's clubs, but once the action starts the film trots along at a decent pace.

Mexican wrestling superhero El Santo battled every monster imaginable during his lengthy career, including the living dead.

There are plenty of unintentional laughs – Carlton is supposed to be an upright hero, yet seems to leer at every woman he meets, while the presence of astonishingly wooden belly dancer Bella Bella (Darlene Myrick) raises many a chuckle. That said, the voodoo sequences are effectively staged and Mahon succeeds admirably in making the best of the low budget by creating some genuinely atmospheric moments.

More significantly, the zombie takes another step towards actually being scary. He might still be the slave of a living puppet master, but here the walking corpse looks impressively decayed. This is unlike the living dead of earlier films – notable solely for their wide-eyed stares and stiff gait. The shots of him slowly emerging from the tomb are unexpectedly chilling, even by modern standards. *The Dead One* may have quickly vanished into obscurity, but it nevertheless pointed the way forward for the zombie sub-genre.

Zombies frequently cropped up in the bizarre Mexican films starring masked wrestler El Santo (The Saint). Masked wrestling was huge in Mexico during the late-1950s and Sixties, though the films rarely travelled well at the time (they have subsequently accrued something of a global cult following).

The most notable example of this incongruous genre splicing is *Invasion of the Zombies* (1962). In this Spanish-language film, dead criminals are revived by a masked mastermind to carry out robberies on his behalf. Luckily, El Santo and his wrestling skills are on hand to defeat the threat. Over his lengthy career, El Santo would battle everyone from Dracula and

Cash Flagg, a.k.a. Ray Dennis Steckler, becomes an Incredibly Strange Creature in a film that is more fun to read about than watch.

Frankenstein's Monster to aliens and werewolves until well into the 1970s, and the living dead were regularly revived to make cameo appearances in his adventures.

Ray Dennis Steckler's *The Incredibly Strange Creatures Who Stopped Living and Became Mixed-Up Zombies* (1963) has long amused film buffs with its ridiculous title, and helped Steckler become something of a cult figure in the early 1980s, with interviews and lengthy articles appearing in magazines such as *Fangoria* and Re/Search's influential book *Incredibly Strange Films*.

This cult following endured right up until people finally got to see his movies, which – unlike the works of many other 'trash' directors who were equally lauded at the time – proved to be almost universally terrible. A few of his movies – *Wild Guitar*, *The Thrill Killers*, *Rat*

Pfink a Boo Boo – have a certain mad charm, but never passed the point of broad kitsch appeal.

Despite its notoriety, *The Incredibly Strange Creatures...* is actually one of Steckler's less interesting efforts. Steckler (as Cash Flagg) plays Jerry, a misunderstood youth who takes his girlfriend to the carnival where he is hypnotised into becoming a deranged killer by Madame Estrella the fortune teller. Eventually, the conniving clairvoyant worries that Steckler is escaping her control and so mutilates him with acid and cages him alongside her previous victims. Finally, the 'zombies' escape and terrorise the midway.

With lengthy musical numbers padding out the carnival footage, incoherent dialogue, terrible acting and ham-fisted direction, the film is certainly something to behold. However, the sense of novelty soon wears off and is replaced by a dull sense of *ennui*. But, thanks to

The living dead battle the Roman Empire in the Italian production *War of the Zombies*.

Steckler's Barnumesque showmanship – the poster screamed, 'See: The dancing girls of the carnival murdered by the incredible night creatures of the midway! See: The hunchback of the midway fight a duel of death with the mixed-up zombies! See: The world's first monster musical!' – the film played for years.

Subsequently seeking to slice yet another round of sandwiches out of this particular turkey, the director then re-titled the film *Teenage Psycho Meets Bloody Mary* and hired people to dress as monsters and jump into the audience at screenings

Italy's first zombie film appeared in 1964, though it had little in common with the gore-drenched films that would flood the market in the early 1980s. Rather, *War of the Zombies* (*Roma contro Roma*) was part of the popular 'peplum' genre (sword and sandal epics) that were churned out in the wake of *Hercules'* international success in 1958.

John Drew Barrymore was the imported US star brought in to play Aderbal, a sorcerer who leads an army of the dead in a battle against the Roman Empire. Whereas Monogram's movies had failed to deliver effective zombie armies, *War of the Zombies* does at least provide convincing battle scenes, with decent production values. The film was a welcome – if eccentric – development in the lineage of zombie cinema.

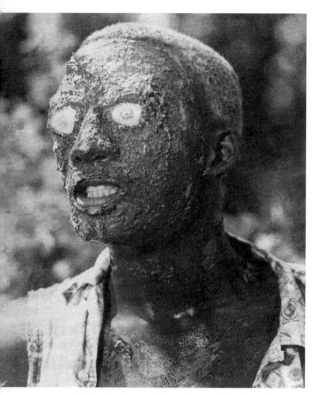

Oddly effective zombies can't save *I Eat Your Skin*.

Alien body snatchers returned in the 1964 British film *The Earth Dies Screaming*, directed by Terence Fisher. A gas attack wipes out much of the Earth's population, and a small band of survivors gather together in a small English village, where they try to avoid detection by a robot army who are reviving the dead to work as slaves.

The film has some effective scares and moments of unease, but Fisher seems uncomfortable with science fiction and – always a director who was only as good as his source material – struggles without the writing and production team that helped make his Hammer Horror films so successful. The low budget also shows, never more so than at the film's end, when cars can be clearly seen speeding down the motorway of the 'dead' Earth.

American B-movie maven Del Tenny's *I Eat Your Skin* was announced as *Invasion of the Zombies* in 1963, and shot as *Zombie* a year later. It wasn't until 1971 that the film finally saw release, however, retitled and teamed with *I Drink Your Blood* to form perhaps the most viscerally named double-feature ever. It's hard to imagine what audiences made of this unlikely pairing, as *I Eat Your Skin* was a creaky black and white effort that would have looked decidedly dated on its own, let alone when teamed with an ultra-violent Seventies shocker like *I Drink Your Blood*.

The film opens promisingly enough, with a frenzied voodoo ritual and decent opening title sequence. But it's all downhill from here, as a publisher, his brassy wife and a playboy author travel to the imaginatively named Voodoo Island to research a new novel. Once there, they encounter strange-looking zombies with festering skin and eyes that resemble fried eggs. While it seems that these zombies are the result of voodoo, it soon transpires that they are scientifically created – a scientist looking for a cure for cancer stumbled upon the zombification formula and has been forced to create an army of them for his insane employer.

With bad acting, slow pacing and irritating characters, *I Eat Your Skin* is pretty awful stuff, and the fact that it stayed unreleased for so long is no real surprise.

In 1968, audiences were presented with a choice of fresh zombie entertainments – *Night of the Living Dead* or *Astro Zombies*. Thankfully, it was the former film that ultimately influenced the direction of the genre.

An Astro Zombie lurches into action in Ted V. Mikels' camp classic.

Ted V. Mikels was a contemporary and colleague of Ray Dennis Steckler, the two filmmakers often collaborating on projects. Like Steckler, Mikels was elevated to cult status in the early Eighties and, like Steckler, his work only occasionally justified such attention. While his better efforts such as *The Doll Squad* and *The Corpse Grinders* at least provided a degree of entertainment, much of his work is shockingly bad.

In fact, *The Doll Squad* is actually quite good, and Mikels may have a point when he claims the film was copied by the *Charlie's Angels* TV show – the concept and characterisation are remarkably similar, right down to the inclusion of a character named Sabrina.

Astro Zombies sits somewhere in the middle of Mikels' range – amateurish and clumsy, yet harmlessly trashy fun for the more kitsch-orientated viewer.

Co-written by *M.A.S.H.* star Wayne Rogers, *Astro Zombies* stars John Carradine as a mad scientist, Doctor DeMarco, who creates an 'Astro Man' from the dead body of a criminal. However, he can't control his creation, which takes to the streets armed with a machete. All this activity attracts the attention of the government and a spy ring, who battle to control the secret of the Astro Zombies.

The zombie design is genuinely laughable – a poor-quality skull mask with glued-on reflectors. The action is murky and the pacing leaden. The acting, on the whole, is terrible – cult icon Tura Satana does her best with the dialogue, but Carradine sleepwalks his way through scenes, and the supporting cast are extraordinarily wooden.

But none of this stops the film being entertaining – in fact, it all seems to help. And how can you not love a film where the zombie recharges himself by holding a flashlight to his forehead?

Astro Zombies subsequently spawned such a cult following that a 2002 sequel, *Mark of the Astro Zombies*, was commissioned. The straight-to-video 'reinterpretation' was again directed by Mikels, and despite a quarter-century of technical development had production values that were no better than the original.

Nevertheless, *Astro Zombies* seemed to sum up a decade where the zombie milieu had become entirely populated by low-budget, low-talent exploitation filmmakers.

The zombie movie was now dismissed, denigrated and ignored by genre commentators and fans alike. As *Monster Times* commented in their 'Zombie Special', 'nobody likes zombies… they're not really monsters. They're not really even dead. They're not really alive. Nor particularly bright. Nor are many of their films any good.'

But there were exceptions – films which showed the living dead some respect and which pointed the way towards an unlikely resurrection in fortunes for the sub-genre over the following two decades.

It took Hammer Films to breathe some life back into the undead during the 1960s. *Plague of the Zombies* (1966) was unquestionably the best outing the living dead had been given since *White Zombie*, and also turned out to be one of the company's better films of the period.

Ironically, the picture had started out with modest ambitions – Hammer had shot *Plague of the Zombies* and *The Reptile* back-to-back as supporting features for *Dracula: Prince of Darkness* and *Rasputin: The Mad Monk* respectively, and both were made with lower than usual budgets. But given the bottom-of-the-barrel nature of most previous zombie films, *Plague…* shone out as a classy, stylish effort. More significantly, it still holds up well today.

Like *Doctor Blood's Coffin*, *Plague of the Zombies* is set in Cornwall and opens with a voodoo ritual, this time taking place in an apparently disused tin mine. In the nearby village, people have been mysteriously dying, and the local doctor Peter Thompson (Brook Williams) desperately calls on his old teacher Sir James Forbes (Andre Morell) for help.

It transpires that the local squire (John Carson) is using voodoo to raise the dead and force them to work as slave labour in his tin mine, previously closed due to dangerous working conditions. In trademark Hammer style, the film ends with a fiery conflagration as the zombies turn on their master.

Like most Hammer films, *Plague of the Zombies* has a lush look, solid performances from the leads (including Diane Clare, who plays Sylvia Forbes, the feisty heroine – often the area that Hammer would fall down in casting) and several good horror set-pieces. The scene in the graveyard, where Thompson's wife Alice (Jacqueline Pearce) returns from the dead and is decapitated by a shovel, remains a classic shock scene, and the dream sequence which follows is impressively eerie, as several zombies claw their way from the grave and advance menacingly on the heroes.

Hammer Films brought some much needed class to the genre with the masterful *Plague of the Zombies*.

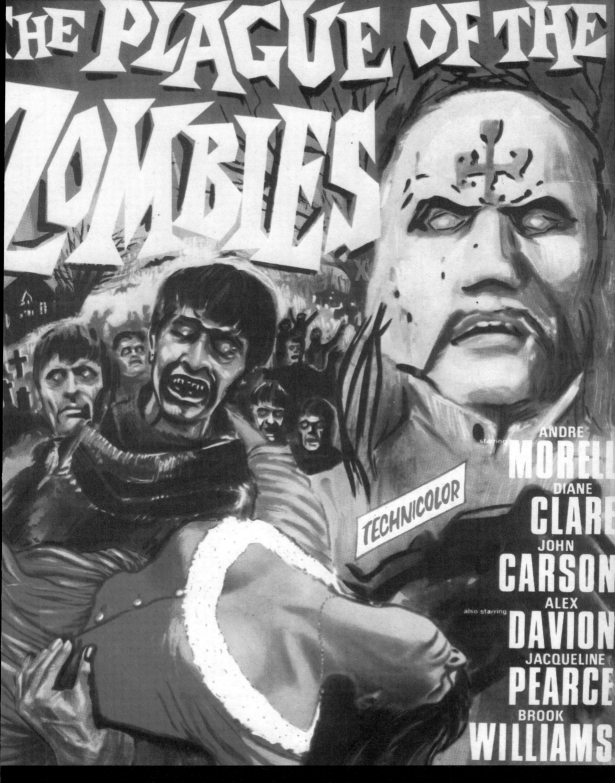

Vincent Price battles the living dead in the first – and best – movie version of Richard Matheson's novel *I Am Legend*.

Plague of the Zombies demonstrated what the zombie film could be, given the right combination of talent and care. However, it was another film, made in Italy around the same time, which provided the template for the sub-genre's future direction.

Generally ignored at the time, *The Last Man on Earth* (1964) set the scene for George Romero's groundbreaking work a few years later. The film would become the first of three movies based on Richard Matheson's 1954 novel *I Am Legend*, which Hammer had initially optioned for filming in 1959.

However, when the company submitted the screenplay to the British Board of Film Censors – common practice at the time – they were advised that the resulting film would almost certainly be banned in the UK, and the project was dropped. With no screenplay to consult, it's hard to say what Hammer's approach to the project would have been.

The Last Man on Earth is a pretty effective shocker, helped by an unusually restrained performance from Vincent Price as Robert Morgan – seemingly the only survivor of a plague that has turned the human race into vampires. By day, Morgan travels the city destroying the sleeping creatures; by night, he cowers in his house as the living dead besiege him, baying for his blood.

Although identified as vampires, these slow-moving monsters are clearly what would subsequently become recognised as archetypical zombies. The scenes where the mindless horde gathers outside Morgan's home are instantly recognisable to anyone who has seen *Night of the Living Dead*, and the idea of humanity being wiped out by a plague of the undead would become a zombie film cliché.

Directors Ubaldo Ragona and Sidney Salkow did a fine job emphasising Morgan's isolation, though a flashback sequence to the days before the plague goes on a little too long. Where *The Last Man on Earth* is most interesting is in the characterisation of Morgan. We are initially encouraged to see him as a heroic figure – a last survivor struggling to stay alive in the face of overwhelming odds. But when Morgan discovers another survivor, Ruth (Franca Bettoia), who – unlike him – is not immune to the infection (but has not succumbed to vampirism), everything changes. She tells him that there are others like her, and that some of them are the people Morgan has been driving wooden stakes into during his daylight raids. 'Many of the people you destroyed were still alive,' she tells him. 'You're a legend in this city.' With this revelation, we see that, to the other survivors, Morgan is as much a monster as the vampires.

When he discovers that they intend to kill him, Morgan makes a futile break for freedom. In the end, as he is gunned down, he cries out defiantly, 'I'm the last man!' And indeed he is. But in this new world, Morgan represents the old order, and is no longer relevant.

The film has its faults – the Italian-US co-production suffers from the Italian actors being dubbed rather flatly into English, and the aforementioned flashback slows things down somewhat – but remains a surprisingly potent movie.

Remade twice (1971's tedious *The Omega Man* dispenses with the vampire element, instead having the survivors chasing Charlton Heston in the guise of 'mutants', while 2007's *I Am Legend* sees Will Smith do battle with hordes of pale-skinned CGI creations in a deserted New York City), this first adaptation – which Matheson disliked – remains the definitive version to date, and its significant influence on *Night of the Living Dead* distinguishes the movie as a groundbreaking work.

TOMB OF A THOUSAND TERRORS!

They dared the curse of the ancients... to solve the most amazing mystery ever encountered by mortal man!

THE MUMMY'S HAND

with

DICK FORAN • **PEGGY MORAN** • **WALLACE FORD**
CECIL KELLAWAY • **EDUARDO CIANNELLI**
GEORGE ZUCCO • **TOM TYLER**

3. Horror Rises from the Tomb
Mummies, Ghouls, Brainwashing and Other Quasi-Zombies

If we are to be pedantic about what a cinematic zombie is, then we must accept that he (or she) is a living corpse – or at least the apparently dead victim of a fiendish voodoo priest, mad doctor or other deviant hell-bent on world domination or fulfilling his own carnal lusts.

However, a line has to be drawn somewhere – and so, dead or not, the supernatural vampires are clearly not zombies, nor are vengeful ghosts. Largely by dint of their scientific means of creation, the assorted Frankenstein's Monsters also seem a little too removed from true zombiedom.

Any attempts at codifying what constitutes a cinematic zombie can be undermined by the way in which elements of the zombie canon often cross over into other movies that do not fit into the traditional idea of the sub-genre, yet can still be viewed as closely relating to the zombie archetype.

Take the Mummy – there is a strong argument for saying that he is little more than an Egyptian zombie. Then we have the mind-controlled victims of assorted alien invaders, who always seem eager to enslave humanity (and sometimes revive the dead) to do their dirty work.

And what of the various *Night of the Living Dead*-inspired apocalypse movies that began to appear in the early 1970s? In the latter case, it's a conundrum that vexes zombie fans even now thanks to *28 Days Later* – a zombie film in every sense save for the inclusion of the living dead.

Films featuring Mummies, alien imperialists and zombifying infections have developed into divergent strands of the zombie canon, enhancing and expanding upon the original archetype to add depth and variety to the sub-genre.

'Beware the Beat of Cloth-Wrapped Feet!'

While the zombie languished at the bottom of the horror hierarchy, his Egyptian relative the Mummy somehow managed to get into the top four, alongside Dracula, Frankenstein's Monster and the Wolfman. This despite being quite possibly the dullest monster ever to totter across the silver screen.

The Mummy's elevated status was due entirely to luck. When Universal Pictures were inventing the horror film, they followed up the success of *Dracula* and *Frankenstein* with *The Mummy* in 1932, forever cementing the bandaged Egyptian corpse in the public consciousness as one of the original stars of the genre.

Ironically, *The Mummy* didn't feature much in the way of mummified action. After an impressive opening, where Boris Karloff's disinterred Im-Ho-Tep revives and – as Bramwell Fletcher memorably declared – 'went for a little walk', the film rapidly went downhill. Karloff re-emerged ten years later as wizened but unbandaged Ardet Bey, helping archaeologist David Manners find the tomb of Princess Anck-es-en-Amon.

The Mummy – the living dead of Egypt – has proved to be an enduring horror staple,
despite most of the movies being extraordinarily dull. *The Mummy's Hand* was an early addition to the series.

KARLOFF *The UNCANNY* *in* *The* MUMMY

The only scene in 1932's *The Mummy* to actually feature the traditional bandaged corpse was also the only memorable moment in the whole film.

In what would become a tiresomely repeated plot technique in Mummy films, it turns out that the Princess' reincarnation just happens to be a member of the archaeological team, and Bay/Im-Ho-Tep is determined to join their souls.

All of this takes an age to happen, and the film fails to develop any clear sense of purpose. Karl Freund's direction is weak, the plot feeble and the action non-existent. But, riding on the coattails of the horror boom, *The Mummy* was successful enough to launch a series of sequels, remakes and imitations.

In *The Mummy's Hand* (1940), Im-Ho-Tep has become Kharis, and cowboy star Tom Tyler has replaced Karloff. Using magical tana leaves to stay alive, Kharis has guarded the tomb of Princess Ananka. When those pesky archaeologists open the tomb, High Priest George Zucco revives Kharis – who, unlike his predecessor, stays fully mummified throughout – and sends him hobbling off to seek revenge.

This established a format for future Mummy movies. Tana leaves, tomb desecration, reincarnated princesses and footage lifted from earlier movies to pad out the scant running times. Such exotic elements were simply not enough to prevent these being amongst the most

Tom Tyler took on the role for *The Mummy's Hand*, the first film to feature the Mummy as audiences would grow to know and 'love' him.

tedious horror films ever made, but the formula was repeated until even the most rabid Mummy fan lost interest.

During the 1940s, the character was again revived for a trio of B-movies starring Lon Chaney Jr. *The Mummy's Ghost*, *The Mummy's Tomb* and *The Mummy's Curse* were all pretty interchangeable, and all shockingly bad. Despite only running for an hour apiece, all three are tedious, with seemingly endless scenes of Chaney ambling slowly across the screen to pad out the inaction. After this, it only took a 1955 encounter with an equally inert Abbott and Costello to kill off any lingering interest in the Mummy.

Chaney's films did at least show that the Mummy was a flawed concept when it came to

A rare moment of excitement in *The Mummy's Tomb*.

scaring audiences. Shuffling along s-l-o-w-l-y, this single creature was probably the easiest movie monster to escape from – like the zombie, walking at a brisk pace would have kept you safely ahead of him; unlike the zombie, he didn't have strength in numbers.

Things picked up considerably in 1959, when Hammer Films added *The Mummy* to their roster of horror remakes. After the success of *The Curse of Frankenstein* and *Dracula*, the film again teamed Peter Cushing and Christopher Lee, and once more managed to breathe a new sense of excitement into a familiar story.

The plot is closer to the *Mummy* sequels than Universal's original. Lee is Kharis, and French siren Yvonne Fureaux is Isobel, the reincarnation of Ananka – who just happens to be married to tomb plunderer John Banning (Cushing). But good performances (Lee is truly frightening as the bandaged, decaying Mummy) and some impressive fight scenes combine with solid direction from Terence Fisher to create an exceptional effort. As far as regular Mummy movies go, this is probably the best.

Unfortunately, Hammer found the character just as hard to do anything else with as Universal had. 1964's *Curse of the Mummy's Tomb* saw Prince Ra shipped to England from

Despite his slow shuffle and feeble appearance, the Mummy
always got his man, as in this scene from *The Mummy's Ghost*.

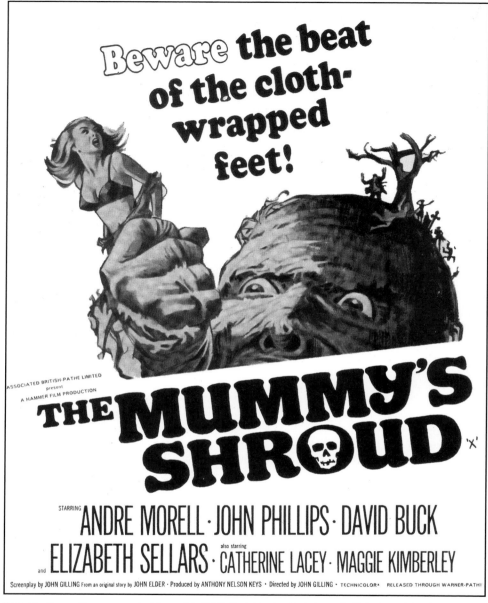

Beware the beat of the cloth-wrapped feet!

ASSOCIATED BRITISH-PATHE LIMITED
present
A HAMMER FILM PRODUCTION

THE MUMMY'S SHROUD 'X'

STARRING ANDRE MORELL · JOHN PHILLIPS · DAVID BUCK
and ELIZABETH SELLARS · also starring CATHERINE LACEY · MAGGIE KIMBERLEY

Screenplay by JOHN GILLING From an original story by JOHN ELDER · Produced by ANTHONY NELSON KEYS · Directed by JOHN GILLING · TECHNICOLOR* RELEASED THROUGH WARNER-PATHE

Hammer's Mummy films were a mixed bag — this 1967 effort tries hard but shows the limitations of the character.

Egypt by an exhibitor, only for him to revive and go on an incongruously dull killing spree, while 1967's *The Mummy's Shroud* was slightly better, with another revived Mummy being used as an instrument of vengeance by a Bedouin who resurrects him using a sacred oath found on the eponymous shroud.

While this film moves at a better pace than its predecessor and includes some inventive slaughter – this Mummy isn't satisfied simply with strangling his victims, and at one point throws acid in the face of one unfortunate – the predictable script fails to engage the viewer.

Hammer's final Mummy film is their most interesting, if only because it doesn't actually feature a Mummy. 1971's *Blood from the Mummy's Tomb*, based on Bram Stoker's *Jewel of the Seven Stars*, instead tells the story of Margaret Fuchs (played by Bond Girl Valerie Leon) who is possessed by the spirit of Queen Tera after her father leads an expedition to unearth the queen's tomb.

The film had a troubled production – director Seth Holt died midway through and Hammer head Michael Carreras had to complete the film, while Peter Cushing was compelled to drop out of the movie at the last minute after his wife died.

Like many of Chris Wicking's screenplays, the film is complex and often hard to follow, yet it has an undeniable quality to it that overrides this. Gory (most people die by having their throats torn out) and with a heavy emphasis on Leon's impressive cleavage, *Blood from the Mummy's Tomb* seemed to point the way forward for Mummy movies – namely, drop the Mummy. The novel would be filmed again in 1980 as *The Awakening*, with Charlton Heston struggling through a series of *Omen*-inspired deaths.

Outside the Universal and Hammer axis, the Mummy proved popular in Mexico – or at least a variant on the theme did. The Aztec Mummy made appearances in several 1950s and Sixties films, most notably *Wrestling Women vs. the Aztec Mummy* (1964), which took the character into the strange world of Mexican horror wrestling cinema. Not to be outdone, the legendary El Santo took his shot at the Mummy in 1971's *Santo En La Venganza de la Momia*.

Actor and director Paul Naschy (real name Jacinto Molina) was Spain's biggest – in fact, Spain's *only* – horror star, and made his name with a series of cheap, trashy movies that usually delivered enough nudity and gore to keep less discerning fans happy, but rarely had much artistic merit.

His series of werewolf films – where he played the unfortunate Waldemar Daninsky in a string of unrelated lycanthrope adventures – remains his best known work, but Naschy ran the classic horror gauntlet, playing Dracula, the Mummy, Frankenstein's Monster as well as Jack the Ripper and other assorted anonymous villains.

Naschy added the Mummy to his resume in 1973's *Venganza de la Momia* – which, like most of Naschy's films, takes a 1930s plot and adds liberal quantities of gore and nudity. In this film, he plays both the Mummy and Assad Bey, the High Priest who is using young virgins as sacrifices in London. Even by Naschy's standards, the film is quite poor, with an unconvincing monster (Naschy was too portly for many roles, and this is one of them), dismal production values and a sluggish pace that no amount of sleaze can compensate for.

By the beginning of the 1980s, the zombie revival launched by George Romero's *Night of the Living Dead* and – more recently – the 1978 sequel *Dawn of the Dead* was in full flow, and the new, visceral style of horror meant gore, nihilism and apocalyptic themes.

The Mummy film entered this new era in 1981 with Frank Agrama's cheekily titled *Dawn of the Mummy*, in which a group of American fashion models visiting Egypt fall foul of a whole army of flesh-hungry Mummies. The film piles on the gore during the climactic attack, but is so dull until that point that only the most dedicated viewer will have stuck around. Agrama's previous film had been the little-seen and thoroughly terrible *Queen Kong* in 1976, suggesting that the flaws in *Dawn of the Mummy* couldn't be ascribed to bad luck.

After this, it was slim pickings for Mummy watchers, with just the odd comedy and kids' films like *The Monster Squad* (1987) to suggest that the genre wasn't as dead as an ancient Egyptian. But just when it seemed that the Mummy was buried forever, a slew of movies emerged.

1990's *Tales from the Darkside: The Movie* was a mixed bag, as tended to be the case with such portmanteau offerings, most of which failed to provide a full set of entertaining tales. Nobody had been crying out for the lacklustre anthology show to transfer to the big screen, and the results were in keeping with the inconsistent TV series that spawned it.

The opening segment loosely adapted 'Lot 249' – an Arthur Conan Doyle short story in which a resurrected Mummy is used by a student to gain vengeance over a wealthy rival. George Romero wrote the screenplay for the second of *Darkside*'s trilogy, 'Cat from Hell', an adaptation of a Stephen King short story that recounts the tale of a hitman who is hired to rub out a malevolent moggie.

1993 saw ageing heartthrob Tony Curtis show up in the title role of *The Mummy Lives*. Again, the Mummy is obsessed with a woman who is the reincarnation of his lost love. The film is not exactly Curtis' finest, as both he and the movie as a whole shuffle around to no great effect in this uninspired low-budget effort.

The Jewel of the Seven Stars was dusted off again for another rehash, though Jeffrey Obrow's *Legend of the Mummy* (1997) was no closer to the original story than either previous version.

This time, a Mummy is revived after Queen Tera's tomb is excavated, and sets out seeking vengeance, resulting in some minor gore, gratuitous nudity and little else to hold the attention. However, the film sold well enough on video to justify a 'sequel', which – in typical fashion – has nothing to do with the original. *Legend of the Mummy 2* (2000) started out as *Ancient Evil Scream of the Mummy*. Directed by B-movie regular 'Disco' David DeCocteau, the film sees a bunch of archaeology students battling a revived Mummy to no great effect.

Russell Mulcahy's *Tales of the Mummy* a.k.a. *Talos the Mummy* (1999) has Christopher Lee and his archaeological team unearthing the tomb of Talos, only to become entombed themselves. Years later, his granddaughter opens up the tomb and unleashes the curse. Quite how Lee ended up in this feeble effort is hard to imagine – it sits alongside *Funny Man* and *Howling II* as something of a blemish on his later career.

1998's *The Eternal* (also known as *Trance*, *The Eternal: Kiss of the Mummy* and *Michael Almereyda's The Mummy*) saw the director of revisionist vampire film *Nadja* once again taking an arthouse approach to the gothic, with little success. More concerned with style than content, Almereyda's film is too slow, pretentious and self-conscious to make much impact.

The less said about *The All New Adventures of Laurel and Hardy in 'For Love or Mummy'* the better. This 1999 movie saw a couple of impersonators playing the much-loved comedy team protecting a professor's daughter from a revived Mummy. The results are so bad that you could have forgiven Stan and Ollie if they rose from the dead to take revenge on those responsible.

Lust in the Mummy's Tomb (2002) is mercifully brief at forty minutes, and, while fans of soft-porn scream queen Misty Mundae might find this erotic film stimulating, for anyone else it is painfully dull, being neither sexy, silly nor scary.

This post-Romero effort has rampaging Mummies tearing apart and eating their victims, but still manages to be depressingly dull.

The same could be said for former musician and comic-book writer Don Glut's *Th*
Mummy's Kiss (2003), which unsuccessfully tries to mix a traditional Mummy story with horn
college girls. Incredibly, in 2006, the film spawned a sequel – *The Mummy's Kiss: 2nd Dynasty*
More recently, aghast DVD viewers have sat ashen-faced through 2005's *The Kung Fu*
Mummy (a Mummy is resurrected in modern-day Hollywood), suggesting that bad Mummy
films could start to rival bad zombie films in quantity. Predictably, the post-modern, camp titl
is better than the movie, which features little in the way of horror or martial arts. The film wa
supposedly shot for a mere $500, and so the very fact that it exists at all is some sort of
achievement for writer/director Randy Morgan – but such prudence hardly represents
compelling reason to seek it out.

Bucking the trend, Don Coscarelli's *Bubba Ho-Tep* (2002) was an unexpected hit. Based on
a short story by Joe Lansdale, the film has Elvis Presley (Bruce Campbell), still alive and living
in a nursing home. There, the ageing King teams up with fellow resident Ossie Davis, who
despite being black – thinks he's John F. Kennedy. Together, they battle an Egyptian Mumm
who is sucking the souls from their fellow residents.

Charming, funny, sometimes creepy and always unique, *Bubba Ho-Tep* came as a rea
surprise to audiences, and quickly established a cult following, playing as much on a share
cultural experience among its fans – who are all familiar with the Hollywood Mummy *and*
Elvis Presley archetypes – as with its unquestionable qualities as a film.

From the end of the 1970s, Universal made several efforts to revive the Mummy, seemingl
oblivious to existing horror trends that favoured family-sized helpings of gore or heavy satani
elements. In 1979, *Animal House* director John Landis was lined up to helm a series of remake
of the classic Universal titles, starting with *Creature from the Black Lagoon* and then moving on
to *The Mummy*.

However, the director and studio had different ideas about the project – Landis wanted th
film set in the 1920s while Universal wanted a contemporary visualisation. In the end, no
agreement was reached and the entire remake project was abandoned.

A decade later, Clive Barker was placed at the helm of *The Mummy* remake, fresh from th
success of *Hellraiser*. But his subsequent cinematic excursions had considerably less impact
and *The Mummy* was eventually dropped. The remake's case was scarcely helped by a Mich
Garris screenplay that Barker told *Fangoria* was 'undiluted horror'. It also contained element
of transsexuality – this before *The Crying Game* proved that such themes were not necessaril
box-office poison – but no shuffling, bandaged corpses.

George Romero also turned in a screenplay in the 1990s before Universal decided that the
didn't want a horror film after all, but a family-orientated blockbuster.

In 1999, a new version of *The Mummy* would be filmed by Stephen Sommers. This remak
had little in common with its predecessors – or, indeed, with the horror genre. Instead
Sommers came up with a CGI-heavy, family-friendly action adventure that had more to d
with Indiana Jones than the walking dead.

Given how difficult filmmakers had found it to inject any sense of excitement, terror or eve
interest in previous Mummy movies, it's hard to complain too much about this radica
reinvention, and the box-office success of the film seemed to justify these innovations. Two mor
films – *The Mummy Returns* and spin-off *The Scorpion King* – followed, along with an animate

TV series. In 2008, *The Mummy: Tomb of the Dragon Emperor*, hit the screens to demonstrate that Sommers' retooling of the Mummy mythos was proving enduringly popular.

'They're Coming!'

The idea that your community could be taken over by invaders, that your friends, colleagues and even family might not be who they seem to be, and that sinister forces were subverting society was clearly very much on the minds of many Americans during the Cold War, and never more so than during the 1950s.

Senator Joseph McCarthy's notorious anti-Communist witch hunts ended careers and ruined reputations in Hollywood and elsewhere, while the belief that Russians – or their sympathisers – were plotting against the American people through subversion (Frederic Wertham's attacks on horror comics were laced with suggestions of a 'Red' conspiracy to corrupt American youth) or invasion were stoked by a cynical media and politicians.

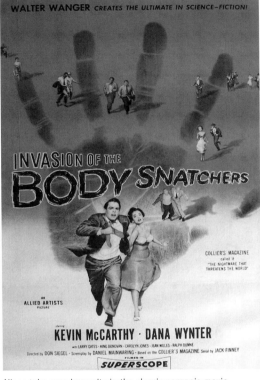

Aliens take over humanity in the classic paranoia movie *Invasion of the Body Snatchers*.

The threat of nuclear annihilation was established and only served to add to the pervasive climate of paranoia. It's unsurprising then that many science-fiction films of the period played on this paranoia. The most obvious question about such movies being: were they stoking these fears or attacking them?

The most famous – and ambiguous – of the Fifties mind-control films was *Invasion of the Body Snatchers*, made in 1956 and based on a story by Jack Finney. Kevin McCarthy stars as Doctor Miles Bennell, who finds that strange things are happening in his hometown – people who claimed to be ill suddenly can't recall their ailments, while others insist that friends and relatives are 'not themselves'.

Slowly, the doctor realises that people are being replaced as they sleep by alien duplicates, which are growing in giant pods. As the town is slowly taken over, Bennell finds himself increasingly isolated amid the growing numbers of extraterrestrial doppelgangers.

Invasion of the Body Snatchers starts slowly, but once the truth is revealed, the levels of paranoia and terror are cranked up to great effect. McCarthy does an impressive job of transforming Bennell from self-assured professional to raving paranoid as his life literally falls

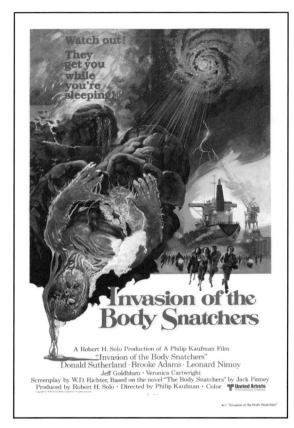

Watch out! They get you while you're sleeping!

Invasion of the Body Snatchers

A Robert H. Solo Production of A Philip Kaufman Film
"Invasion of the Body Snatchers"
Donald Sutherland · Brooke Adams · Leonard Nimoy
Jeff Goldblum · Veronica Cartwright
Screenplay by W.D. Richter, Based on the novel "The Body Snatchers" by Jack Finney
Produced by Robert H. Solo · Directed by Philip Kaufman · Color ⊤⊤ United Artists

The *Body Snatchers* story was injected with a dose of 1970s angst in this superior remake.

apart, and Don Seigel's direction is equally sure-footed.

But the film has a subtext that is hard to pin down. Is this a warning about the threat of Communism, or attacking the McCarthyism of the time, which hounded anyone suspected of left-wing sympathies? Or, for that matter, is it simply a scary movie? Opinions remain split.

The story was potent enough to be remade no less than three times. 1978's version, directed by Philip Kaufman, has all the paranoia and edginess of the best Seventies political conspiracy thrillers and an apocalyptic vision in keeping with the finest horror movies of the period.

This time around, Donald Sutherland is excellent as Bennell, making a heroically doomed attempt to save humanity. The shots of the Pod People pointing and screaming as they spot someone who hasn't been assimilated are amongst the most evocative moments of the genre.

Abel Ferrara's 1993 *Body Snatchers* is less effective. One of the maverick director's less personal works, the film transfers the action to a military base and fails to provide any sense of paranoia – instead playing very much like a by-the-numbers sci-fi horror movie of the period. Given that the writers include heavyweights such as Larry Cohen, Stuart Gordon and regular Ferrara collaborator Nicholas St. John, the film is wholly disappointing.

The most recent version of the film, 2007's *The Invasion*, dumbs things down further, seemingly happy to try to cash in on the recent zombie/infection film boom rather than offer anything new. The only innovations evident are that the alien virus changes DNA while people sleep, while Doctor Carol Bennell (Nicole Kidman) finds that her son is immune to the infection and may hold the key to humanity's salvation. The bleak feel and ending of the original versions is noticeably absent here.

The roots of *Invasion of the Bodysnatchers*' evil seed can be found in 1953's *It Came from Outer Space*. Directed by Jack Arnold, the movie featured alien invaders taking over human beings, launching the motif with a literal bang when a meteor lands in the desert, only for

Nicole Kidman stars in yet another version of *Body Snatchers* – the ill-conceived 2007 film *The Invasion*.

Richard Carlson to discover that it was, in fact, a spaceship.

At first, his attempts to alert the authorities fall upon deaf ears, but suddenly, the locals start to act strangely. Eventually, the powers that be take notice and the aliens reveal themselves as massive, jelly-like masses with a single huge eyeball.

Shot in 3-D, the film manages to keep the paranoid mystery going just long enough before revealing the truth, and has a surprisingly upbeat ending – the aliens are not here to conquer the world, but simply to get their crashed spaceship operational again.

The aliens in the same year's *Invaders from Mars* are less friendly. Again, they crash into the desert, but this time they are set on conquering the planet. As they take over the minds of anyone who goes out to the crash site to investigate, the only person who knows what is happening is a kid, David MacLean (Jimmy Hunt – who subsequently appeared as a Police Chief in Tobe Hooper's ill-considered 1986 remake). He realises that anyone venturing into the desert returns profoundly altered. Eventually, the authorities are alerted, and an all-out attack on the Martians commences.

Weird and surreal, *Invaders from Mars* (again shot in 3-D) is a crude but effective movie, with some impressive dream-like moments, set design that emphasises the child's perspective and one of the more bizarre alien creatures to emerge at the time (no mean feat in itself).

I Married a Monster from Outer Space (1958) was hampered by a tacky-if-memorable title,

It Came from Outer Space — and outta the screen in 3D — in the classic 1950s alien invasion film.

but this is actually a pretty serious, well-made shocker. New bride Marge Farrell (Gloria Talbott) starts to realise that her husband has become a changed man, seemingly without emotion. She soon discovers that he, alongside other men in the town, have been taken over by aliens from a dead planet who want to breed with Earth women as all the female aliens had been wiped out in an explosion that destroyed their homeworld.

Quatermass 2 (1957) had a more political flavour than most alien assimilation films. The follow-up to Hammer's *Quatermass Xperiment* (which itself sought to extend the franchise begun with the 1953 BBC TV series *The Quatermass Experiment*), it again starred Brian Donleavy as Professor Quatermass.

The plot concerns the discovery of an alien conspiracy to seize control of the army and usurp positions of power throughout Britain. The aliens infect their prey using a gas, which escapes from small meteors that have landed across the country.

A fast-paced, highly paranoid and chilling movie, *Quatermass 2* is one of the best – and most underrated – science-fiction films of the decade.

'You Can't Trust Your Mother… Your Best Friend… The Neighbour Next Door'

The influence of *Night of the Living Dead* expanded beyond the zombie film in the 1970s, and helped spawn a short-lived sub-genre of apocalyptic horror, in which society is taken over by an outside infection, turning the populous into crazed killers who spread their disease rapidly across the country. The infection was often a blood disease, and more often than not spread through biting. While these killers may not have been dead, they were unquestionably the spawn of Romero's zombie archetype.

Romero himself was at the forefront of such films with his hugely underrated *The Crazies*

Lynn Lowry succumbs to the effects of infection in *The Crazies*. She was equally unfortunate in two other viral classics from the same period, *Shivers* and *I Drink Your Blood*.

(1973). Briefly known as *Code Name: Trixie*, this represented the director's return to the visceral, apocalyptic horror of *Night of the Living Dead*, as he had dabbled unsuccessfully outside the genre during the intervening years. This time, Romero had colour on his side, and the result is a more polished, if slightly less potent movie.

The film starts brutally – a couple of children are awoken by the sounds of destruction in their home, only to discover that the man smashing up furniture and setting the house ablaze is their father. He's already killed their mother.

This act of madness – and the others that follow – are the result of a biological weapons toxin that has seeped into the local water supply after a military plane crash. Soon, the local population are becoming increasingly demented, while the army struggle to maintain control.

The Crazies is bleak stuff. No one comes out of this film with much credit – the local officials are petty-minded hicks, more concerned with maintaining their authority than anything else, while the military – clad in white chemical suits and gas masks – are a literally faceless occupying force, out of control and given to looting.

The scientist struggling to find a cure is hamstrung by bureaucracy and inefficiency, and the leading characters seem set on a doomed mission to escape the military cordon, as they slowly succumb to infection. The result is Romero's most cynical film, and one of his best.

Interestingly, *The Crazies* star, Lynn Lowry, also appeared in two other early-Seventies infection films. Both *Shivers* and *I Drink Your Blood* dealt with a rapidly spreading disease that took over the mind of the victim, though in very different ways.

Shot in 1970, *I Drink Your Blood* is a remarkably gory movie – allegedly the first film to be rated X for violence by the MPAA. It tells the story of a group of Manson-inspired hippy Satanists, who arrive in a small town and start to terrorise the locals. When they spike an old man with LSD and rape a young woman, a boy takes revenge by feeding them pies that have been injected with the blood from a rabid dog. Soon, the infected hippies are on an even more bloodthirsty rampage, as they foam at the mouth and bite locals, spreading madness and mayhem far and wide.

While clearly not the most accurate depiction of the effects of rabies (the victims not only foam at the mouth, but also seem to have increased strength), *I Drink Your Blood* is a pretty relentless movie. David E. Durston directs efficiently and the extreme violence is brutally effective.

This is also the reason why the film is so hard to pin down to a definitive version, as the cuts were not only made to secure an R rating, but also to satisfy the whims of local councils. It is said that no two prints of the film are the same, though the Grindhouse DVD would seem to be the most complete version currently in circulation.

David Cronenberg's *Shivers* (1975) was the director's first commercial movie, after his experimental features *Stereo* and *Crimes of the Future*, and set a new standard for what would become known as Body Horror. Mixing sex and graphic gore, Cronenberg's film is a rollercoaster of excess. It's also one of the best horror films of the decade.

Set entirely in a huge apartment block (the opening titles play over a hard sell for the self-contained building), *Shivers* takes a cheesy sci-fi ploy – a mad scientist creates a new 'super bug'

A suitably lurid poster for a legendary double-bill.
I Drink Your Blood lives up to the hype; *I Eat Your Skin* does not.

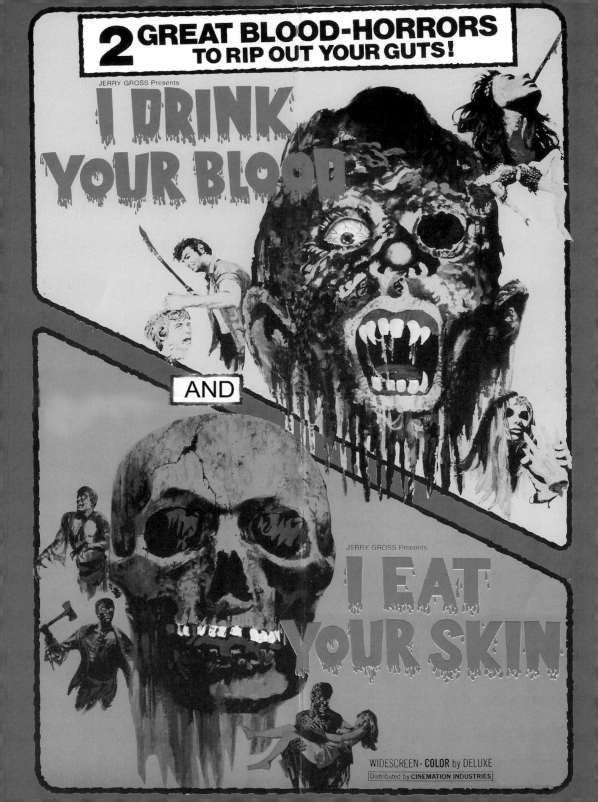

The parasites attack in David Cronenberg's visceral *Shivers*.

that infects the local population – and gives it a kinky twist. The effect of the slimy, phallic bug – which literally crawls into its victims – is to unleash the libido, and transform the infected into ravenous nymphomaniacs.

Shivers is a daring film. Cronenberg has stated that he is on the side of the infected, and he has a point – the only violence in the film is the result of resistance from the 'unliberated', and when the film ends with the infected setting out, calmly, to spread their love to the wider community, it doesn't seem such a bad thing.

Cronenberg's next film had a similar theme, but was less confrontational and contentious. *Rabid* (1977) starred porn actress Marilyn Chambers as a young woman who unwittingly becomes the carrier of a new strain of rabies after being subjected to experimental surgery following a road accident. Unable to retain normal food, Chambers drinks blood through a phallic siphon that emerges from a vaginal opening in her armpit (for those of you who haven't seen the film, this is not as silly as it seems on paper). But while she is not infected, her victims

Marilyn Chambers is the unwitting Typhoid Mary in Cronenberg's unique take on the vampire film, *Rabid*.

develop a violent need to bite others, becoming crazed, foaming at the mouth and rapidly spreading the infection.

As a modern take on the vampire legend, *Rabid* is a powerful, brutal movie. It's less effective than *Shivers*, mainly because the story takes place in the wide-open spaces of Montreal, rather than the confines of Starliner Towers, and enables Cronenberg to depict action-orientated set-pieces such as car crashes.

Where *Rabid* improves on *Shivers* is in its characterisation. The characters in *Shivers* seem detached and emotionless – almost dead inside, which is why their infection represents a kind of liberation. In *Rabid*, Chambers assumes the role of an emotional focal point as she struggles with her need for blood and the realisation of what she has unleashed. Good performances from Chambers and Frank Moore as her helpless boyfriend give the film much of its edge. But once the gas-masked troops arrive, it starts to resemble *The Crazies* a little too much.

This poster makes *Nightmare City* look rather more stylish than is actually the case, but does capture the frenetic thrills on offer.

1976 saw a novel variation on the infection movie with the rarely seen *Blue Sunshine.* The ultimate warning against drug use, the film tells the story of a group of college kids who took an experimental batch of LSD during the 1960s. Ten years later, they've grown up and have respectable lives, but then the side effects of the drug start to kick in – their hair falls out and they become homicidal maniacs.

With a cast headed by Zalman King (the producer of numerous softcore thrillers in the 1980s and Nineties) and directed by Jeff Lieberman (better known for *Squirm* and *Just Before Dawn*), the film is not quite as good as the premise (and the lobby stills) would suggest.

The bald-headed, zomboid maniacs are pretty startling, but too much of the film is taken up with King trying to prove his innocence when he's mistakenly accused of the killings. While not exactly a wasted opportunity – the film still has plenty to offer – this should be a lot better than it actually is.

Bad drugs turn up again in 1980's *Forest of Fear* (a.k.a. *Bloodeaters, Toxic Zombies*), when a bunch of hippies become infected after their marijuana harvest is sprayed with herbicide by a government crop duster, and turn into flesh-eating maniacs.

Despite the reissue title, they're not quite zombies, but behave in much the same way – attacking anyone they come into contact with. Charles McCrann (who died in the 2001 attacks on the World Trade Center) directs, writes, stars, edits and produces – and sadly is not particularly good in any role. With just a modicum of gore, *Forest of Fear* is tame and poorly made. How it found itself banned in the UK as a 'Video Nasty' is indicative of the moral panic of the period.

1980 also saw the release of Umberto Lenzi's hysterical (in every sense of the word) *Nightmare City.* Appearing in the midst of the Italian zombie-movie boom, Lenzi's film offered a slight variation on the theme – his bloodthirsty monsters are not zombies, but rather cannibalistic radioactive maniacs, who emerge from a plane after an onboard radiation leak and set about murdering and devouring everyone in sight.

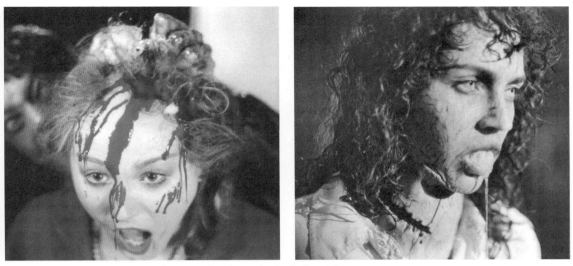

Gruesome moments from Lamberto Bava's ambitious but fatally flawed *Demons*.

These 'zombies' are fast (whoever retitled this *City of the Walking Dead* for the US market clearly hadn't seen it), intelligent and use weapons, making them rather livelier than the average re-animated corpse.

Lenzi directs with his usual disinterested efficiency, and ladles on gore and sleaze – when the mutants invade a TV station, they take care to rip the clothes off the women before eating them. As you'd expect from any film starring the notoriously wooden Mexican star Hugo Stiglitz, there's little in the way of subtlety and sophistication evident, but the whole trashy affair moves at such a fast pace and has so much action that this hardly matters. *Nightmare City* is an underrated gem of Italian trash cinema.

Better known, but far less entertaining, is Lamberto Bava's *Demons*. This 1985 production was one of the last Italian horror films to have any global impact (and was shot specifically to break into the US teen market), but also indicates the manner in which the sub-genre was in terminal decline. Alongside Dario Argento's unsatisfying *Phenomena*, it marked the beginning of the end for Italian horror as a creative force.

Demons starts well – a group of people are invited to a horror-movie premiere in an old theatre. When a prostitute cuts herself on a prop from the film (a mask resembling the one used in *The Mask of Satan* – which was directed by Bava's father), the wound quickly becomes infected. She subsequently becomes a hideous demon, drooling green slime, and sets about attacking the other moviegoers, thus spreading the demonic bug. To make things worse, the cinema doors are locked and no one can get out.

So far, so good. But then Bava and co-writer/producer Argento effectively destroy the atmosphere of terror by suddenly cutting away from the claustrophobic action to unrelated events outside the theatre, to feature a bunch of irritating coke-snorting characters whom we haven't met before. The film never recovers from this incongruous digression, and things get

THE BIGGEST MASS SLAUGHTER IN STUDENT HISTORY...

Ghoul School was a typically shoddy Eighties video production with sloppy gore and crass attempts at humour.

worse as Bava piles on spectacular but empty moments – like a helicopter crashing through the roof.

The final scenes – with the survivors driving through the city as the infection spreads – are pretty good, but come too late to salvage the film. With poor performances (not helped by terrible dubbing) and a clumsy soundtrack (the original Claudio Simonetti compositions are excellent, but the grafted-on heavy-rock tracks by the likes of Accept and Saxon don't fit), *Demons* feels like another wasted opportunity.

Still, it's a masterpiece compared to the sequel, which is one of the shoddiest horror films ever made. *Demons 2* (1986) delivers more of the same, this time set in a tower block, where a demon outbreak – via the TV – spreads from apartment to apartment.

None of this makes much sense – the infection in the first film didn't stem from watching a movie, as seems to be the case here.

There's little to recommend in this sequel – the demons look terrible (particularly the embarrassing 'demon birth' scene where a shoddy puppet emerges from someone's back) and the story is pretty much non-existent, the film simply moving from incident to incident without any attempt to establish a solid narrative. Worse, it doesn't even follow on from the original, but instead simply rehashes the same ideas, badly.

Despite the dreadfulness of the first sequel, the series was popular enough for international distributors to try to pass off a welter of unrelated films as 'Demons 3'. Bava's forgettable TV movie *The Ogre* (1988) was one such example, and Michele Soavi's ambitious but flawed *The Church* (1989) was also retitled for some markets. To be fair, the project had begun life as a third Demons film before being revamped as a separate entity. Umberto Lenzi's *Black Demons* (1991) also tried to pass itself off as the third instalment of the franchise in some countries, but was in fact a *bona fide* – if pretty dull – zombie film.

The zombie-infection film craze seemed to peter out during the 1980s. Only the odd offshoot like *Ghoul School* – where an infected swimming team go on the rampage after coming into contact with toxic chemicals – kept the sub-genre clinging to a form of life.

But recent movies such as *28 Days Later* and *I Am Legend* suggest that a post-millennial appetite for such movies is alive and well.

4. 'Scenes Dealing with, or Instruments Associated with, Walking Dead...'

US and UK Zombie Comics

Horror comic strips began to appear during the 1930s, at the very birth of the comic book in America, and by the end of the war, the first dedicated horror comic books hit the newsstands.

These were largely inspired by pulp magazines like *Weird Tales*, which mixed horror, adventure and mystery tales (including work by H.P. Lovecraft, Robert E. Howard and others). The pulps were cheaply produced and often packaged with salacious cover art. The crucial difference with comic books was that they were aimed at a younger market.

Amongst the first horror-comic publishers were Marvel/Atlas, who re-titled their flagging superhero series *Marvel Mystery Comics* as *Marvel Tales* in 1949, setting writer Stan Lee to work on a series of short shock stories. Zombies were a popular staple of these early comics, sitting alongside more prosaic tales of wartime adventure.

Lee's work was pretty basic – most of his horror stories are only of interest now because of his subsequent career, and perhaps as rather camp terror tales. For instance, 'A Living Corpse for the Zombie' – concerns a talkative living corpse's attempts to recover his missing face, which had been stolen after he fell in wet concrete. Or, as the zombie explains (merrily rewriting living-dead mythology as he goes):

'There is only one thing a zombie must avoid… having his features trapped in a lifelike image! When that happens, he loses both his face and his control over the undead he commands… unless he finds and destroys the image before the break of dawn!'

1949 also saw the start of the most significant era in horror-comic history. EC Comics had started out as Educational Comics before the death of founder Max Gaines in 1947 saw the business taken over by his son. William Gaines subsequently renamed the line 'Entertaining Comics' and moved away from dull-but-worthy historical and biblical tales to feature crime, war and other sensationalist themes. It would not be long before he noticed the popularity of the burgeoning horror market.

Late in 1949, Gaines added a new, horror-themed story to EC's *Crime Patrol* and *War Against Crime* anthologies, and asked for readers' reactions. Clearly, the response was positive, as, just two issues later, *Crime Patrol* was rebranded *The Crypt of Terror* (soon to be renamed again as *Tales from the Crypt*) and *War Against Crime* became *The Vault of Horror*.

Although EC had published a zombie story before launching their horror series – 'Zombie Terror' appeared in a 1948 issue of superhero book *Moon Girl*, the story in *Crime Patrol* that had launched EC's horror boom was called 'Return from the Grave', written and drawn by Al Feldstein – one of EC's best horror-comic creators. It set the scene for several other zombie-themed stories that would appear in EC's expanding range, which went on to include *The Haunt of Fear*.

EC's horror comics subsequently featured several zombie tales during the early 1950s. Two decades later, *The Monster Times* declared that 'Horror We, How's Bayou?' from *Haunt of Fear* was 'the greatest zombie comic story of all time'.

Certainly, this tale of two brothers – one a maniac, the other luring victims to keep him satisfied – is pretty juicy stuff. The victims' remains are tossed into a nearby bog, but eventually the cadavers rise from the dead – their bodies fused together – to take revenge. With its mix of wit and gruesomeness, the story is vintage EC.

Other EC zombie tales included 'The Living Corpse', 'Zombie', 'Voodoo Death', 'Poetic Justice' (later filmed as part of *Tales from the Crypt*) and 'Voodoo Horror'. Vengeful corpses often appeared on comic-book covers (for example, *Tales from the Crypt* issue twenty-four features a particularly cadaverous corpse dragging a hapless victim into a pit of quicksand).

The success of the EC line inspired a deluge of horror-themed comics from rival publishers. By 1953, some seventy-five different titles – many admittedly short-lived – were fighting for space on the newsstands. Titles such as *Forbidden Worlds*, *Weird Thrillers*, *Eerie Adventures* and *Black Magic* vied for the horror fan's two bits. As the competition hotted up, ever more sensational covers and stories were produced, often featuring zombies, ghouls and other walking corpses.

Avon Comics even produced the one-shot *The Dead Who Walk*, while Farrell Publications brought out *Voodoo*; clearly, zombies were more popular in print than on film, where the horrors of the living dead were still fairly tame – no movie could hope to match the gruesomeness found within many 1950s horror comics.

Amid such competition, there was no room for subtlety in the horror comic. The covers were vivid, gory, lusty and creepy, and the contents rarely failed to live up to the hype. It would not be long before these gruesome comics were attracting unwelcome attention on both sides of the Atlantic.

In Britain, the backlash began as early as 1949, when the Reverend Marcus Morris railed against crude American imports. A year later, he launched that most bourgeois of British comics, *The Eagle*, to counteract this influence with a selection of wholesome strips featuring stiff-upper-lipped heroes like Dan Dare and decidedly middle-class *Boys' Own*-style adventure stories.

By 1952, an unlikely alliance of churchgoers, moralists, the National Union of Teachers, members of the Communist Party and politicians saw capital to be made. The Comics Campaign Council was formed in 1952 to seek a ban on 'horror' and 'crime' comics. In 1954, the CCC submitted a draft bill to the Home Secretary.

Within a year, the Children and Young Persons (Harmful Publications) Act came into force, making it an offence to publish comics featuring 'the commission of crimes, acts of violence or cruelty, or incidents of a repulsive or horrible nature' – a vague set of all-purpose guidelines that today's moral legislators would be proud of. The act is still in force – if not actually enforced – today (the handful of prosecutions against 'offensive' comic books like *Lord Horror* in more recent years have relied on the Obscene Publications Act).

In America, disquiet over the content of horror comics was stoked by the publication of Doctor Frederic Wertham's *The Seduction of the Innocent*, which argued, via a series of false

A classic moment of EC Comics horror, from *Tales from the Crypt* issue twenty-four.

Marvel Comics' *Tales of the Zombie* was a superior horror series, later reprinted in the UK as *Tales of Terror*.

syllogisms (e.g. the majority of juvenile delinquents read comic books – therefore comic books cause juvenile delinquency), that crime and horror comics were destroying America's youth. He also accused Superman of fascism, said Batman and Robin were homoerotic and insisted that Wonder Woman was into sado-masochism.

When Congress set up the Joint Legislative Committee to Study the Publication of Comics, publishers could see the writing on the wall and, in a bid to stave off punitive legislation, set up their own censorship body – the Comics Code Authority. The code came into force in September 1954.

The establishment of the US Comics Code didn't, as many believe, kill off horror comics completely – it simply emasculated them. Among the rules laid down were bans on stories featuring vampires, ghouls – and, of course, zombies. Artists couldn't show 'scenes of horror, excessive bloodshed, gory or gruesome crimes, depravity, lust, sadism, masochism' or 'scenes dealing with, or instruments associated with, walking dead, torture, vampires and vampirism, ghouls, cannibalism and werewolfism'. Comics were likewise banned from using words such as 'horror', and 'terror' in their titles. All of which didn't leave much creative leeway for comic-book publishers.

EC dropped their horror line – the company later became better known to the general public for *Mad* magazine. Other publishers, mostly the fly-by-nights cashing in on a boom, folded entirely, while others managed to maintain a lacklustre 'horror' assortment, usually featuring insipid ghost stories. The horror comic had been stripped of its fangs.

However, there was a get-out clause. The code only covered comics – digest-sized, full-colour comics. It didn't cover magazines. And this allowed horror comics to rise again, like the now-forbidden zombie.

James Warren, publisher of *Famous Monsters of Filmland*, had long been a horror-comic fan, and, in January 1965, he broke new ground with the publication of *Creepy* – followed a year later by *Eerie*, and in 1969 by sex-kitten space vampire *Vampirella*.

These three black and white magazines would set the standard for 'mature' horror comics over the next two decades (*Vampirella* in particular led to a whole series of supernaturally-themed, scantily clad horror sirens). In reality, they were aimed at precisely the same audience as the colour comics, but their exemption from the Comic Book Code meant that they could up the horror levels (as well as the sex, which became increasingly graphic during the 1970s). The taboos that were strangling their colour cousins could now be gleefully transgressed.

Warren's biggest rival of the early 1970s was Skywald, who used many of the artists and writers from the Warren bullpen (often working under pseudonyms to avoid contractual clashes). Skywald's stories were gruesome, witty and intelligent – at their best, much like EC's finest comics. Their starkly titled magazines *Nightmare*, *Scream* and *Psycho* only occasionally featured zombie-themed tales, and the company was edged out of the horror field in 1975, when the market became inundated by derivative variations on the Warren/Skywald template.

By the start of the 1970s, the Comic Book Code had begun to lose its influence (not helped when the Code refused to approve several issues of *Spider-Man* in the late Sixties because of drug references – even though the story was a result of a government request to Stan Lee to help push an anti-drug message) and public attitudes had relaxed enough for the colour horror comic to make a comeback, albeit not a full-blooded one.

This was partly due to the success of Warren's black and white books, as well as a relaxation of the Code itself, which allowed horror comics a little more leeway, giving the green light to previously banned characters and themes – though still in a considerably less gruesome fashion than before.

The two leading comic-book publishers in America took advantage of this new age of openness with a series of horror-themed output. DC comics produced a stream of generally interchangeable anthology titles during the 1970s – *House of Secrets* and *House of Mystery* (both of which had been around since the 1950s, having been bland enough to survive the purges) were joined in the late Sixties and early Seventies by *Secrets of the Haunted House*, *Ghosts*, *Unexpected*, *Weird War Tales* and others.

Inevitably, standards began to slip as quantity outpaced quality. Several titles merged and then quietly vanished and, by the early 1980s, the DC horror boom was over.

The Comic Book Code ensured that zombies only rarely made an appearance in these titles – the most frequent stories dealt with 'vengeful ghosts' – though suitably decaying corpses did shuffle through their pages from time to time. They just had to avoid the 'Z' word. Marvel would sometimes refer to its walking dead as 'zuvembies', while other publishers simply fudged the issue.

'Night of the Voodoo Curse', published in DC's *Unexpected* in 1979, is a prime example of the manner in which zombies were represented in all but name. The story brought the zombie back to its voodoo roots, but oddly referred to its clearly rotting monster as a 'spirit' or 'ghost' throughout, the only nod towards the living dead being a reference to his 'zombie-like' walk. Yet the artist's rendition of the character clearly depicts a decaying corpse. Evidently, publishers were still taking the restrictions seriously, worried about losing sales for the lack of having the Comics Code seal on their cover.

Marvel also brought out several horror titles during the Seventies, though these were split between black and white anthology books and character-led colour comics. The latter followed the Marvel superhero tradition, with its monsters being presented as outsider heroes rather than traditional horror figures.

The long-running – and excellent – *Tomb of Dracula*, for instance, had the Count caught up in a mix of soap opera and vampiric conspiracy. Other horror series in the Marvel line included *The Frankenstein Monster*, *Man-Thing* (a scarier-looking contemporary of DC's *Swamp Thing*), *Werewolf by Night*, *Ghost Rider* and *Tigra, the Were-Woman*. In typical Marvel style, most of these characters would also pop up in their other titles, battling – or assisting – characters like Spider-Man.

Marvel's black and white magazines suffered in the same way as DC's colour anthologies – there were simply too many all at once. In a one-year period during the mid-1970s, Marvel brought us *Monsters Unleashed, Dracula Lives, The Haunt of Horror, Vampire Tales* and others, most of these titles only having short runs.

A pity, as the magazines were surprisingly excellent on the whole. Freed to tell more mature tales – and seemingly inspired by the black and white format which suited horror far more than colour – Marvel's writers and artists mixed one-off stories with continuing series, featuring more mature versions of the characters found in their colour comics.

To their credit, Marvel did try several times to revive the adult horror comic, but all efforts seemed doomed. A 1979 'mature' version of the successful colour monthly *Tomb of Dracula* was produced to cash in on an expected boom in interest in the Count thanks to the big-budget *Dracula* remake of that year. However, both film and comic were less successful than expected. Similarly, a one-shot revival of *Haunt of Horror* and specials for *Satana* and *Blade* also failed to spawn an ongoing series.

One magazine, *Tales of the Zombie*, featured the first living-dead superhero – so to speak. *Simon Garth: Zombie* was a serial in which the eponymous character sought vengeance on those who had killed him and then dragged him from the grave. Garth predictably became caught up in other people's dramas, saving them from evil only to be shunned in return. Marvel were doing much the same thing with *Frankenstein's Monster* and *Werewolf by Night*, though, and *Simon Garth* never really caught on with enough comic-book fans to ensure its survival.

Tales of the Zombie was one of the more interesting Marvel horror series, and one that told a complete story, unlike many from the company. This was latterly due to the efforts of Tony Isabella, who took over the scripting chores for the final instalment when regular writer Steve Gerber was unavailable. Marvel executives had originally announced that the magazine would be cancelled with issue nine, and so Isabella – assisted by long-standing *X-Men* scribe Chris Claremont – crafted a story that neatly wrapped up Simon Garth's adventures.

When the magazine was subsequently given a one-issue stay of execution, Garth appeared

Clockwise from top left – Stan Lee's *A Live Corpse for the Zombie*, 1988's *Taboo*, an ad for *Tales of the Zombie*, Uncanny Tales' *When Walks the Zombie*, House of Hammer's comic version of *Plague of the Zombies* and Simon Garth's first appearance from 1954.

on the cover, but not inside. A new Simon Garth adventure was announced, but the magazine never made it past issue ten, and so the zombie was left to rot.

Interestingly, the origins of Simon Garth lay in a Stan Lee/Bill Everett story from 1954, entitled 'Zombie', and reprinted in the first issue of *Tales of the Zombie*. Set in the Louisiana swamps, Simon Garth is a zombie when the tale begins – a former 'captain of industry' and now the slave of his former gardener (a spectacularly unpleasant-looking character), who uses 'the amulet of control' and a voodoo doll to send his undead lackey out on petty mugging errands.

Everything goes wrong when he sends Garth to get a woman, 'When you get her here I'll pretend I'm rescuing her from you… I'll save her an' take her back home! She'll be grateful to me… an' gratitude ain't far from love!' The zombie returns empty-handed and strangles his oppressor. As he returns to the grave, we discover that the woman in peril was his daughter.

A tightly written seven-page tale, it set the scene for the later stories – a zombie without a mind, but still with a spark of humanity somewhere (a theme that ran through many of Marvel's horror characters, from *Man-Thing* to *The Frankenstein Monster*).

Beyond Simon Garth, *Tales of the Zombie* featured Brother Voodoo, a rather lacklustre character from Marvel's colour range, and filled out its pages with one-off zombie/voodoo-themed tales, as well as occasional movie reviews (a six-page piece on *Night of the Living Dead* in issue three was one of the earliest published pieces on the film).

Tales of the Zombie ran for ten issues (and one annual) before being cancelled in 1975. Simon Garth made a one-off comeback in 1982 when he joined other renegades from Marvel's horror series in a belated (and unsuccessful) attempt to revive the range, in *Bizarre Adventures* (an anthology magazine used as a market-tester by the company) for a story that chronologically fitted into the middle of his previously published saga. The series is now available in a tread paperback format.

Other publishers were also quick to leap aboard the 1960s and Seventies horror-comic bandwagon. Gold Key specialised in TV spin-offs, such as *Boris Karloff's Tales of Mystery* (inspired by the TV series *Thriller*) and *The Twilight Zone* – neither of which lived up to their source material. Both titles ran from the early 1960s until the beginning of the Eighties.

Elsewhere, Charlton Comics had the long-running *Ghostly Tales* (which began in 1966 and lasted until the company's demise in 1985) and others such as *Ghostly Haunts*.

The early 1970s saw a new kid on the block; Atlas Comics (not to be confused with the Fifties publisher of the same name) weighed in with *Weird Tales of the Macabre*, *Tales of Evil*, *Fright* and the *Vampirella*-inspired *Devilina*. Unfortunately, due to poor distribution and low sales, Atlas came and went within a year, and none of their publications lasted more than five issues.

None of these Code-governed comics featured zombies, of course – at least not by name. The living dead were still *persona non grata* in the world of the colour comic book.

In Britain, horror comics also remained technically illegal. But by the 1970s, no one really cared any more. US imports were readily available in newsagents across the country, and in 1974, Marvel UK were even able to publish a weekly UK edition reprinting *Dracula Lives* without any outcry.

Homegrown comics of the period were still very much either juvenile humour strips or *Boys' Own* adventures, usually based around the Second World War (and it wasn't until the infamous *Action* in 1976 and its hugely popular sci-fi-themed follow-up *2000AD* that things began to change).

The odd horror title did slip through – *Chiller Library* was a cheap and cheerful pocket-book series that featured a macabre tale each issue. However, true crime and vampires seemed more popular than zombies. 1984's *Scream* was an attempt to do for horror what *2000AD* had done for science fiction, but despite featuring talent such as future *Watchmen* and *V For Vendetta* writer Alan Moore, the comic only lasted fifteen issues. There were no zombie stories in the comic, though that didn't stop at least one cover – issue six – featuring a dead hand bursting from the ground.

More significant was *House of Hammer* magazine, which had an occasionally uneasy mix of film features and comic strips. The magazine struggled to satisfy two distinct markets – the comic fans wanted more comics while the movie fans wanted less and vice versa – but, at its best, the magazine excelled in both areas. The main comic strip of each issue was an adaptation of a Hammer Horror movie, and issue thirteen featured *Plague of the Zombies*, illustrated by future *Judge Dredd* artist Brian Bolland.

The strip doesn't add much to the film, but nevertheless is one of the tighter, more effective adaptations, with some striking compositions by one of Britain's best comic-book illustrators.

The end of the horror boom came quickly. The comic-book industry as a whole was suffering from declining sales and a shift in the market, and horror comics – often without a continuing character to hold on to the readership – were hit especially hard. DC dropped its titles in 1982.

Marvel's final attempt at a black and white horror comic, the relaunched *Tomb of Dracula*, had gone a year earlier after just six issues. Warren's magazine empire collapsed in 1983 and, although his titles were sold to Harris Publications, his anthology titles *Creepy* and *Eerie* were rapidly consigned to the comics crypt (happily for the vampire/cheesecake demographic, *Vampirella* was revived in the 1990s and enjoyed several years of renewed popularity).

Yet just as the mainstream horror comic was breathing its last, a new generation of underground, small-press publications began to appear, inspired by Romero and the new visceral horror of the time. The age of the adult comic book and the graphic novel was about to begin. And eventually, the zombie would start to shuffle into the comic-book spotlight.

1987 saw the publication of *Deadworld*, written by Stuart Keer and drawn by Vincent Locke. In this series, the dead were revived by alien invaders to pave the way for the colonisation of Earth. Stylishly produced in black and white, the strip featured plenty of graphic violence and quickly became a cult favourite. The original series ran until 1992, with a short-lived revival a year later, and was subsequently revived again in 2005.

A year after *Deadworld* began, *Swamp Thing* art-team Steve Bissette and John Totleben launched *Taboo*, an ambitious series of comic books (with the emphasis on *book* – issue one clocked in at 160 pages) that took the approach of the 1970s horror-anthology comics and gave them a new, more visceral feel. Pulling in the likes of Alan Moore, Clive Barker and Charles Burns, the book featured some high-quality material, and Bissette's own 'Cottonmouth' was a gruesome zombie story.

Rather less significantly, 1990 saw *Biohazard*, an independent publication that lasted a mere two issues. The crude style and basic story saw this Romero-inspired book fail to find an audience. But with the enduring popularity of zombies in movies – albeit to a less-than-mainstream audience – it was only a matter of time before the genre would rise once more.

There have been several movie-inspired zombie comic books and graphic novels, including (left) *28 Days Later* and (right) *Night of the Living Dead*.

By the beginning of the new century, zombie comics were starting to emerge in their own right, as a solid market for horror comics finally developed. The last decade has seen a significant number of zombie-themed comic books appear.

These have included movie-related books that either adapt or expand films such as *28 Days Later*, *The Evil Dead*, *Night of the Living Dead*, *Dawn of the Dead* and *Shaun of the Dead*. These books are, like the Marvel movie adaptations of the 1970s, aimed primarily at fans of the original films, and the new material tends to be fairly throwaway, at best offering little beyond the original story and at worst bastardising it. John Russo has milked his *Night of the Living Dead* connection further with *Escape of the Living Dead*, set in 1971 and mixing zombies, mad scientists and bikers in an ineffective grab-bag of clumsy ideas.

Other, more original material has included Jerome Gaynor's *Bogus Dead*, an anthology title bringing together several cartoonists and writers around the theme of a zombie apocalypse (Gaynor had previously used the same format to tackle alien invasion in 1995 with *Flying Saucer Attack*), and *Fleshrot*, another anthology of zombie tales (often with a darkly humorous bent) that came complete with an introduction from George Romero.

The zombie anthology soon became a popular format, with the likes of *Zombie Tales*, *Zombies* and others vying for space on the racks.

Romero undertook a direct involvement in the comic-book world in 2004 when he was hired by DC to write *Toe Tags*, a six-part series that took his zombie universe and added a sexy, ass-kicking heroine, a robo-zombie and an intelligent elephant into the mix. Reaction from fans was mixed – many felt horrified at what he'd done while others took it for what it was – a lightweight romp.

Soon, zombies were cropping up all over the place. Oddball efforts like *Zombies vs. Robots* and *Jesus Hates Zombies, Lincoln Hates Werewolves* were overly gimmicky. Mike Richardson's *Living with the Dead* mixed horror and humour fairly effectively, and *Hellboy* creator Mike Mignola's *Zombie World* was an impressive mini-series, more influenced by H.P. Lovecraft than George Romero.

General horror anthology series *Carnopolis* offered a Warren magazine-style mixture of black and white nudity and violence in a series of impressive strips. These included the brilliantly titled 'Zombies of the SS' by 'Marco Polo'. And the living dead were soon cropping up in the oddest places, including mainstream superhero titles such as *Wonder Woman* and *Wolverine* – a far cry from the days when they were the unmentionable.

This trend came to a head with the *Marvel Zombies* mini-series. Set in an alternative Marvel Universe, the book features just about every Marvel superhero infected with a zombie virus, turning them into cannibalistic killers. Their superpowers make them an unstoppable force – and these zombies maintain their intelligence and reason – soon they have eaten the whole population. After feasting on the planet-eating demigod Galactus, the hungry zombies set off across the universe – even spanning dimensions – and devouring planets as they go.

Frenetic, amusing and surprisingly gory, *Marvel Zombies* is ideal for anyone who wondered if Spider-Man would be more fun if he ate the bad guys, and the story crossed over with several regular Marvel books. The series also spawned a collaboration with Dark Horse Comics, where *The Evil Dead's* Ash battled the costumed zombies.

The most successful ongoing zombie series to date is *The Walking Dead*, written by Robert Kirkman. It began publication in October 2003 and has – at the time of writing – reached fifty-three issues. Although not overly original – its tale of a world devastated by a zombie outbreak is pure Romero, and much of the characterisation and style is clearly influenced by *Night of the Living Dead* and its sequels – the ongoing story has been able to develop various strands and explore depths that a single film cannot match. The main protagonist is cop Rick Grimes, who struggles to survive in his hometown of Cynthiana, Kentucky, as the dead rise across the world.

The success of *The Walking Dead* suggests that the future is bright for zombie-themed comic books, and crossovers like *Marvel Zombies* serve to breathe new life into the genre and also make the zombie more accessible to mainstream comic readers. It's been a long, hard road back to acceptability for the comic-book zombie, but with a higher profile than ever, and an increasingly mature readership, it looks as though the living dead are becoming an unstoppable force in the comics world.

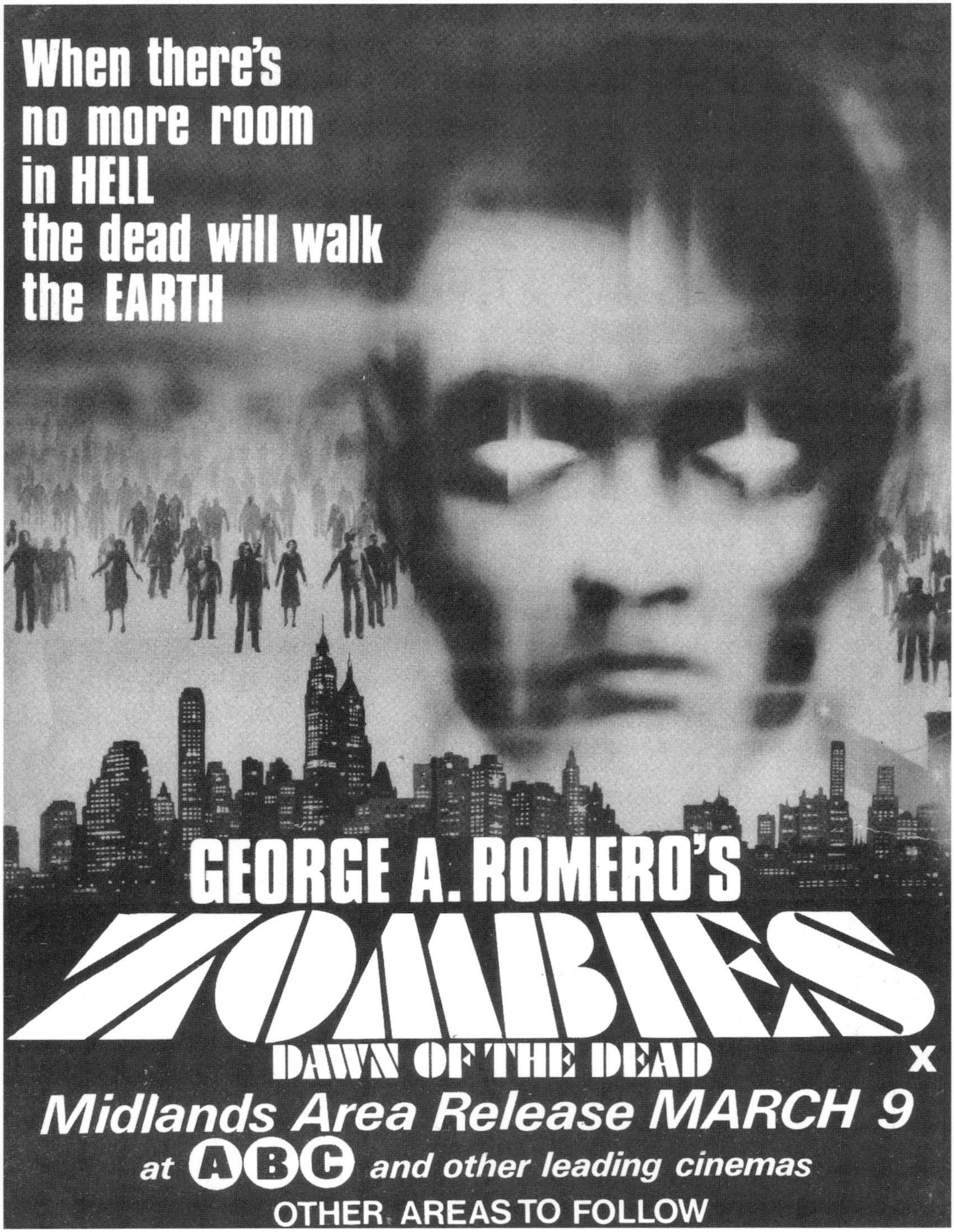

When there's no more room in HELL the dead will walk the EARTH

GEORGE A. ROMERO'S

ZOMBIES

DAWN OF THE DEAD

x

Midlands Area Release MARCH 9

at ⒶⒷⒸ and other leading cinemas

OTHER AREAS TO FOLLOW

5. 'They're Dead. They're All Messed Up'

George Romero Reinvents the Zombie Movie

1968 was a year of turmoil. Political riots rocked Paris, London and Chicago as young people took on the establishment. In Czechoslovakia, workers fought against Communist rule. The Vietnam War rumbled on with no end in sight. All across the globe, things were changing.

The same year saw the release of three horror movies that would have a significant impact. *Rosemary's Baby* brought a new, restrained realism to the genre that made the period gothics of Hammer suddenly seem rather contrived, while *Witchfinder General* ushered in a new wave of gritty realism and downbeat brutality. Most significant – in terms of impact and artistic innovation – was a low-budget black and white film emerging from the unlikely locale of Pittsburgh. *Night of the Living Dead* crept out without fanfare, but its release ensured that horror films would never be quite the same again.

Night of the Living Dead was the creation of a group of advertising filmmakers who wanted to break into feature production. George Romero, John Russo and Russell Steiner had been working on TV commercials and corporate films since 1957.

Russo and Steiner's business, The Latent Image, was ticking over, but they were finding it hard to attract lucrative accounts. Frustrated with commercials, and owning all the necessary equipment, they decided to make a feature film and, like many first-time filmmakers, figured a horror film had the best chance of commercial success on a low budget. Specifically, a contemporary horror film that didn't need much in the way of special effects, period costumes, sets or anything costly.

Begging investment from friends and saving money through utilising their business contacts (Karl Hardman not only took a major acting role in the film but also owned a recording studio), they scraped together enough to begin shooting the untitled project, which would eventually cost $114,000. Romero was determined to shoot on 35mm, which meant that the film had to be made in black and white – a rare occurrence in an age of widescreen colour blockbusters.

Romero and Russo wrote the screenplay, though Russo's contributions were mostly to earlier drafts, which bore little resemblance to the finished film. Romero wrote the bulk of the final script, borrowing heavily from Richard Matheson. '*The Night of the Living Dead* thing, though, I basically ripped off from Richard Matheson's *I Am Legend*, which is really the "Man Alone",' he admitted to *Ainitcool.com*.

Throughout the shoot, the film was simply titled *Monster Flick* – the name given to the job envelope by company treasurer Vince Survinski. When completed, the film was initially called *Night of the Flesh Eaters* before they discovered the 1964 movie *The Flesh Eaters*

A UK press ad for George Romero's seminal *Dawn of the Dead*.

already had claim to the title. Romero suggested *Night of Anubis*, named after the Egyptian god of death, but this was rejected as too obscure a reference. Eventually, they settled on *Night of the Living Dead*.

NOTLD set itself apart from most horror films from the outset. On a brightly lit day, a car drives up to a cemetery. The occupants, a brother and sister, bicker about having to drive two hundred miles to visit their father's grave. The brother, Johnny, starts to tease his sister with one of the most portentous lines in film history – 'They're coming to get you, Barbra.' A shambling passer-by suddenly attacks Barbra, and then kills Johnny. Barbra flees to a nearby farmhouse, where she finds a mutilated corpse and little else. And more shuffling figures are approaching.

Matters are marginally improved when fellow refugee Ben arrives at the farmhouse and assumes control, boarding up the windows and doors. It's then that we discover the house's other occupants – Harry and Helen Cooper, their injured daughter Karen and teenagers Tom and Judy – all of whom have been hiding out in the cellar. Cooper insists that they all retreat back there, but Ben argues against this, seeing the one-exit basement as a potential death-trap. Cooper, on the other hand, points out that the makeshift barricades won't hold out against a major attack. It's Ben who wins the argument.

Finding a television, the group tune into emergency broadcasts, which initially state that the unknown assailants are eating their victims, and then reveal that it is, in fact, the dead coming back to life. The causes are unknown, though there are suggestions that it is caused by radiation from a returning Venus space probe.

After Tom and Judy are killed in an abortive escape attempt, Ben and Cooper fight it out for supremacy as the zombies attack. Ben shoots Cooper as Helen breaks free, only for her to be murdered by her zombie daughter. As the living dead break into the farmhouse – including Johnny, who drags Barbra away – Ben retreats to the cellar. The next morning, he emerges from his hideout, only to be shot down by a posse that mistake him for a zombie.

Forty years on, *NOTLD* still holds up remarkably well. The tiny budget adds an element of *verité*, with the gritty black and white photography and naturalistic look giving the film a documentary feel. The performances are, on the whole, pretty good – Wayne Keith and Judith Ridley are pretty inconsequential, but the rest of the cast are impressive – not something you could always say about a Romero zombie film.

Romero has admitted that the casting of Duane Jones had nothing to do with his colour – insisting that the actor 'simply gave the best reading', so it's perhaps sensible not to read too much into it, but clearly his presence would have been significant for 1968 audiences, who were unused to seeing black male leads in films – particularly black male leads who beat up white characters. Ben is such a strong character that audiences don't immediately realise that he's utterly misguided in all his decisions.

The 'cowardly' Cooper (cowardice in this instance being the desire to survive and protect your family, it seems) is right when he says that the boarded-up windows won't keep out the dead and that the cellar is the safest place – a fact borne out when Ben has to retreat there at the film's climax. Ben is also complicit in the deaths of Tom and Judy (who would attempt to

A Spanish poster for *Night of the Living Dead*.

POR FIN EN VERSION ESPAÑOLA LA OBRA MAESTRA
DEL CINE DE
TERROR

LA NOCHE
DE LOS
MUERTOS
VIVIENTES

(NIGHT OF THE LIVING DEAD)

Jose Esteban Alenda / distribución

Un film de GEORGE A. ROMERO · Guión de JOHN A. RUSSO y GEORGE A. ROMERO
Producida por RUSSEL W. STREINER y KARL HARDMAN
JUDITH O'DEA · DUANE JONES · MARILYN EASTMAN · KARL HARDMAN · JUDITH RIDLEY · KEITH WAYNE

An iconic publicity shot from *Night of the Living Dead.*

shoot the locks off a petrol pump after laying a flaming torch on the ground?) and his spiteful murder of Cooper hardly covers him in glory.

Interestingly, Romero's zombies – or 'ghouls' as they are referred to here – haven't yet learned the rules. Prominent ghoul Bill Hinzman virtually *runs* around the car that Barbra has locked herself into, and then chases her. The zombies routinely use rocks and clubs as weapons, and the zombie child murders her mother with a trowel in a move that is more *Psycho* than *Living Dead.*

NOTLD was an immediate success. At least so far as paying audiences were concerned. The critics were split between those who were repulsed by the graphic nature of the film (and the scenes of the ghouls gnawing on body parts must have been shocking at the time) and those who recognised its visceral impact. The most famous critique at the time was not of the film itself, but rather its exhibition.

In 1968, the films ratings system had not come into play in the US. Monster movies were seen as kiddie fare and, amazingly, *NOTLD* often played Saturday matinees to theatres full of children. *Chicago Sun-Times* critic (and Russ Meyer screenwriter) Roger Ebert attended such a screening and was horrified at what he saw. 'The kids in the audience were stunned. There was almost complete silence. The movie had stopped being delightfully scary about halfway through, and had become unexpectedly terrifying. There was a little girl across the aisle from me, maybe

The dead attack in the startling opening scene of *Night of the Living Dead*. Horror movies would never be the same again.

nine-years-old, who was sitting very still in her seat and crying.'

Night of the Living Dead had made over $10 million by 1978; it's currently estimated to have made around $30 million overall. Unfortunately, none of the people involved saw much of that.

Having sold the distribution rights to the Walter Reade Organisation, the producers discovered that the company had 'forgotten' to add a copyright notice to the film when changing the title – something the law at the time required for a work to maintain sole rights. This effectively placed the film in the public domain. At any given time there are several versions of *NOTLD* in distribution on video, DVD and online from a variety of sources.

Still, it seemed that the success of the film would ensure a healthy career for its director. Romero's post-*NOTLD* work, however, failed to find anything like a similar-sized audience. His immediate follow-up was a romantic comedy, *There's Always Vanilla* (1971), suggesting that he didn't see his future as a horror director.

The film sank without trace, as did his next movie, a suburban witchcraft film called *Jack's Wife* (1972) (later re-titled *Hungry Wives* and now better known as *Season of the Witch*). This was hardly surprising, as it's a pretty awful mix of the supernatural and feminist politics in which nothing happens. 1973 saw him return to *NOTLD* territory with *The Crazies*, which again failed to make much of a box-office impression. It wasn't until 1976, with his post-modern vampire film *Martin*, that he had some success – at least critically.

Martin put Romero back on the map as a horror filmmaker, and brought him into contact with Italian director Dario Argento. The two of them agreed to collaborate on a sequel to *NOTLD*, financed by Argento's producers. Romero holed up in a Rome hotel room to write the first draft of *Dawn of the Dead*.

Under the terms of their agreement, Romero would write and direct, while Argento acted as a consultant and would produce his own edit of the film for the European market. Argento also hired a rock band, Goblin, who had scored his films *Deep Red* and *Suspiria*, to produce the music.

However, Romero was apparently unhappy with Goblin's excellently evocative score,

replacing large chunks of it in his final film with library music similar to that used in *NOTLD* (there's more of this in the 139-minute cut which was rushed to completion for the 1978 Cannes Film Festival).

Chronologically, *Dawn of the Dead* takes place straight after *NOTLD*, though it was updated to the then-present day. The zombie apocalypse is in full swing, as society begins to collapse. In a TV studio, producer Fran (Gaylen Ross) watches in despair as outdated rescue station information is pumped out (because a ratings-obsessed station head worries that, without any information onscreen, 'people will tune out'). With helicopter-pilot boyfriend Stephen (David Emge), she decides to make a run for safety.

The couple are joined by SWAT team members Roger (Scott H. Reiniger) and Peter (Ken Foree), who have also decided to flee after taking part in a bloody assault on a tenement building where the local Puerto Rican population are holed up, refusing to hand the bodies of the dead over to the authorities. Using the TV station helicopter, the four of them take off, and eventually arrive at a sprawling shopping mall.

Left and above: *Dawn of the Dead* combined the apocalyptic vision of *Night of the Living Dead* with extraordinary full-colour gore and helped launch a new generation of horror fans and splatter cinema.

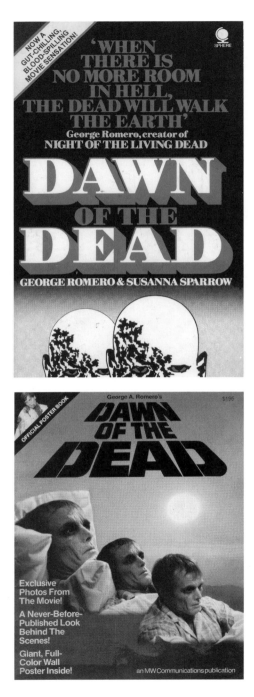

Breaking in through the roof, they initially plan to hoard supplies, but quickly realise that the building – with its well-stocked shops – is an ideal place to take shelter. After ridding the building of zombies and securing all the doors – during which time Roger is fatally bitten – the three survivors settle into an artificial normality. But their safety is shaken when a marauding gang of bikers invade the mall, letting the zombies back in.

Subsequently, Stephen is killed as Fran and Peter climb to the roof and take off into the night – their chances of survival being as limited as the fuel in the chopper. (The original script had Peter shoot himself and Fran stick her head into the helicopter blades, but Romero later decided this was too bleak. The scenes were at least partially shot, but have yet to emerge in public.)

If *Night of the Living Dead* was a revolutionary statement in horror cinema, then *Dawn of the Dead* is its *Never Mind the Bollocks* – a work that sat at the forefront of a new era for the genre and its fans. Prior to *Dawn...*, horror fandom was dominated by the past, with crusty old critics and magazines like *Famous Monsters of Filmland* still writing about the days of Bela Lugosi and Boris Karloff, dismissing the by-then decades-old Hammer films as tasteless modern imitations and completely ignoring the likes *of Last House on the Left* and *The Texas Chain Saw Massacre*.

The few magazines that *did* acknowledge the fact that horror had moved on generally deplored this new breed of violent, visceral terror. Yet within a year of *Dawn of the Dead's* release, *Fangoria* magazine had appeared and, by the beginning of the 1980s, fanzines like *Gore Gazette* began to emerge, speaking for

Dawn of the Dead merchandise – the novelisation (above) and the rarely seen poster magazine (below).

horror fans who no longer found Dracula and Frankenstein's Monster all that scary. Romero's film was at the eye of this revolutionary storm.

The director's unwillingness to compromise did nothing to harm his reputation with fans. Realising that the gore in his film would almost certainly see it branded with the dreaded 'X' rating by the MPAA – which by 1978 had become entirely synonymous with porn – Romero decided to release the picture unrated.

It was a gamble – some cinemas and newspapers were as reluctant to screen or publicise unrated films as they were X-rated movies, and there was inevitable distributor pressure to make cuts and secure the much more commercial 'R' rating. Romero held firm, and the gamble succeeded – *Dawn of the Dead* made over $55 million from a production budget of just $650,000.

Dawn of the Dead certainly starts with a bang. The opening ten minutes are a fairly relentless assault on the senses, with graphic gore (including the notorious exploding head)

Tom Savini's spectacular gore effects included this horrific exploding head – much imitated but never equalled.

The zombies attack in *Dawn of the Dead*.

that was unlike anything audiences had seen before. There's no build-up, no explanations – it simply hits the ground running.

In a message lost on most of the film's imitators until the *Dawn...* remake in 2004, Romero establishes that there is no necessity to underscore horror with explanations – the audience will accept the idea of cannibalistic zombies without any medical/scientific/religious explanations if the film works (and equally, won't accept *any* explanation if it doesn't).

The ambition of *Dawn...* is also reflected in Romero's confident direction of the movie. It remains his best work by a long way, and the style and look of the film is impressive. There are no zombies leaping out from the shadows here – everything is bathed in bright light, natural or otherwise, giving the film a unique feel. And Romero's action sequences are excellent, managing to be both exhilarating and tense. *NOTLD* was crudely visceral, but this presentation is sophisticated and slick.

However, it's not entirely perfect, and *Dawn of the Dead* struggles on several levels. Even if we are to ignore the terrible zombie make-up – the corpses here turn a blue-grey colour that looks ridiculous – there are a number of faults with the film.

The most notable flaw is the dialogue. Watching the movie, it's hard not to recall Harrison Ford's alleged comments to George Lucas during the shooting of *Star Wars* – 'You can write this crap but you can't say it.' Fans faithfully quote Romero's screenplay, but his dialogue is little more than a series of sound-bites that at no point sounds like authentic speech. The cast do their best, but fail to construct a silk purse out of this particular sow's ear.

The film also suffers with poor pacing. Between the action-packed first and third acts, very little happens. It's true that Romero was trying to convey the sense of boredom felt by the besieged characters, but he did so a little too effectively. Argento's cut – dismissed by Romero and his cheering section for removing much of the 'social commentary' – works much more effectively as a horror film (the 139-minute edition – not Romero's preferred version which, despite often being sold as the 'director's cut' – is even more torpid).

And it's this 'social commentary' that is the biggest problem in the film. For all the praise heaped upon Romero for his insight, you have to wonder why the suggestion that people in shopping malls are just like zombies seemed so revelatory.

And, for that matter, why is it so readily accepted? Certainly, if you believe that people wander through shopping centres with empty brains and dead eyes, you might sympathise with that idea – a popular one these days with anti-globalisation, anti-consumerist groups. But it's an elitist concept, and – unless Romero doesn't buy food, clothes, electrical goods or anything else sold in such places – a bit of a hypocritical one too. Most people use shopping centres to buy the things they need – that hardly makes them consumerist zombies.

The main problem – and it's one that would continue to dog him throughout the remainder of his

Two alternative posters for Romero's *Day of the Dead*.

zombie-movie career – is that Romero approaches his subject matter in a black and white, one-dimensional manner. The opening SWAT assault is a case in point: in Romero's eyes, the soldiers are the bad guys, and he hammers the point home in the way he has continued to use since – having one character spout a stream of racist comments to show what a bad guy he is (Tom Savini's biker character later on is also a racist) before embarking on a killing rampage. It's a cheap way of manipulating the audience to condone the director's sympathies, rather than simply allowing the story to establish characterisation.

Considered rationally, it doesn't seem all that unreasonable of the authorities to take action against a building where people are refusing to hand over the dead for incineration, given the nature of the disaster. If flesh-eating zombies were real, I imagine most people would demand that strong action be taken against anyone exacerbating matters.

Faults aside, *Dawn of the Dead* represents a watershed for the sub-genre and includes some of the most

Whatever faults *Day of the Dead* has, Tom Savini's special effects remain gruesomely impressive.

iconic images in cinema. Romero would never better it, and eventually, it effectively sealed his destiny as a filmmaker: he was 'Mr. Zombie'.

After *Dawn of the Dead*, Romero had plenty of ambitious ideas. Alongside a third zombie film – planned for around 1988 and epic in scale, with zombie and human armies battling it out – Romero shot the non-horror *Knightriders* in 1981.

He also announced a series of collaborations with Stephen King, including a film adaptation of his epic apocalyptic novel *The Stand*. While this project proved just too ambitious to get off the ground, 1982's *Creepshow* would become Romero's biggest box-office hit.

Creepshow was a portmanteau film, based on several King short stories – some published, some original. It was inspired by the EC comics of the Fifties, and combined horror with dark humour in a series of tales that – much like the Amicus anthology films of the Sixties and Seventies – were something of a mixed bag.

The zombies shuffle into action in *Day of the Dead*.

Two of the stories featured zombies, though not in the traditional Romero style. The opening tale, 'Father's Day', had a tyrannical old patriarch returning from the grave to take vengeance on his murderous daughter and her family. The gruesomely rotting corpse (Tom Savini's make-up being far superior to his work on *Dawn…*) demands his Father's Day cake – which he ultimately prepares for himself, employing a severed head as its centrepiece.

Less interesting is 'Something to Tide You Over', where jealous husband Leslie Nielsen buries his wife and her lover up to their necks on the beach and then watches as the tide rolls in, drowning them. That night, they rise from the grave to exact revenge.

Creepshow was a fun film, if somewhat inconsequential, and its success could have taken Romero into the mainstream. However, he was determined that his next outing, the third part of his zombie trilogy, would – like *Dawn of the Dead* – be unrated, effectively scuppering any chance of major studio backing.

Although *Dawn of the Dead* had shown that a film could be successful while avoiding the

The dead wander the streets of a deserted city in *Day of the Dead*.

MPAA, times had changed by 1985, with waves of censorious conservatism sweeping America and the UK during the Reagan/Thatcher era. A clampdown on pornography and graphic violence, and the rise of the religious right in the US made it harder for films to buck the system.

While unrated movies began to face the same struggles as X-rated films when it came to distribution. Fewer cinemas and newspapers were willing to promote X-rated movies, and many saw unrated releases in the same light. Sinking several million dollars into a film that would have limited advertising and distribution opportunities didn't seem like a sound investment, particularly in the days before unrated video releases became profitable.

Offered $7 million to make an R-rated version or half that amount to go unrated, Romero chose the latter. A bad move that, ironically, killed the film artistically. If – as Romero's fans claim – his work is not simply about the gore, why compromise your ideas and reduce your potential audience just to indulge yourself via a few disembowellings? It seems perverse.

The completed version of *Day of the Dead* tells the story of a ragbag band of scientists and soldiers, holed up in a massive underground bunker while the dead have overrun the cities. Helicopter forays to find other survivors are unsuccessful, and the tensions between the scientists – who are charged with finding an answer to the zombie outbreak – and the military quickly deteriorate.

The demented Captain Rhodes (Joe Pilato) is no longer willing to support the research and threatens to flee the bunker, taking his men with him and leaving the scientists behind. But Doctor Logan (Richard Liberty) has made some progress, training a zombie he names Bub (Sherman Howard) to 'behave' and even speak. Eventually, the zombies break into the bunker, leading to a (long-overdue) action-packed, gore-drenched finale.

Almost from the moment that *Dawn of the Dead* hit the screens, the idea of *Day of the Dead* had horror fandom slavering with expectation. However, when finally released, the film was widely viewed as a disappointment, and, although some of Romero's supporters have since engaged in a spot of revisionism to proclaim the film another classic, in reality it has not aged well.

There are many problems with this film that go beyond the lack of narrative ambition. Like *Dawn...*, it is full of terrible dialogue and poor performances, but, unlike its predecessor, there is little going to mitigate against these flaws. Instead, much of the film is taken up with Joe Pilato's one-note performance, Richard Liberty's ridiculous mugging and Lori Cardille, who is simply not up to the task of engaging the audience as the one character we are presumably supposed to root for.

Once again, Romero takes a simplistic approach to characterisation; his bad guys are all thoroughly horrible, prone – as always with Romero – to racist comments just to emphasise their rottenness. But while the one-dimensional bikers of *Dawn...* were a minor part of the film, these characters are ubiquitous.

To make matters worse, even his 'sympathetic' roles are poorly realised and unappealing. *Day of the Dead* marks the point where

Romero and Dario Argento collaborated on the uneven Poe adaptation *Two Evil Eyes*.

Romero lost interest in his human cast and opted to re-posit the zombies – who, lest we forget, are brain-dead, reanimated, cannibalistic corpses and not some oppressed minority – as his sympathetic leads.

Of course, underdeveloped characters wouldn't be so bad if the film delivered as a horror movie, but for much of the running time, very little happens other than people shouting at each other. The climactic zombie attack is too little, too late. By the time it happens, all but the most blinkered Romero fan will have given up.

Further hampered by a genuinely awful music score from Jim Blazer, John Harrison and Sputzy Saracino (including a particularly excruciating number over the closing credits) and a final scene which – based on the reactions of the audience I first saw the film with – confuses viewers into thinking the whole movie has been a dream. It's little wonder that the movie was so roundly rejected by 1985 audiences, who generally preferred Dan O'Bannon's less pompous and more entertaining *Return of the Living Dead*.

Admittedly, Romero's screenplay went through major changes before production, cutting back on the scale of the film considerably – most notably reducing his trained zombie army to just one (other aspects of the story would later make their way into *Land of the Dead*). But claims that the 'original' screenplay would have produced a masterpiece seem a little fanciful, at least if the version available online is authentic.

The differences are significant enough, but all the faults that eventually undermine the final film are present and correct. Much of the screenplay is embarrassing to read, with the author writing 'Bullamm! Bullamm! and 'Phoooooomph!' to denote gunfire and explosions, and giving an oriental character unenlightened dialogue like, 'Doc Logan! Doc Logan! Dere's a lady dead out dere! Gotta hurry! Gotta hurry! Dunno how long she been dat way! Maybe she gettin' ready to come back.' It's dreadful stuff, and we can only hope the version available is fraudulent – always a possibility with material available from the internet.

More positively, the film does feature the most convincing zombies to be found in any of Romero's work. Thankfully rejecting the blue corpse paint of *Dawn…*, Tom Savini's make-up provides a series of gruesome cadavers that avoid the masked effect found in the subsequent *Land of the Dead*, as well as some effectively gory set-pieces.

However, it was never the gore that made Romero's earlier films work – a point that sometimes seemed to elude the director. When the gorehounds praised Romero for sticking to his guns, it was hard to equate their insistence that his works had social significance with their predilection for graphic violence. After all, if the films were more than simple gross-out spectaculars, they would be just as effective with less graphic scenes of horror.

Several of the most visceral scenes in *Day of the Dead* – although probably the best thing about the film – are entirely gratuitous. None more so than the moment when a semi-eviscerated zombie breaks free from its restraints simply to facilitate a contrived shot of its entrails dropping to the ground.

Two decades later, Romero's most devoted fans – and Romero himself – would happily discard their commitment to hardcore horror, when the director finally had the chance to expand his zombie epic further – this time with major studio backing and with the stipulation of the R-rating. It speaks volumes that none of his fans cried 'sell-out'. But then again, they have proven themselves to be *very* forgiving.

Tom Savini turned director for the 1990 remake of *Night of the Living Dead*, written by George Romero.

In the years after *Day of the Dead*, Romero moved into the Hollywood mainstream, albeit with limited success. As a producer and writer, he contributed to *Tales from the Darkside* (both the movie and the TV series) and *Creepshow 2* (1987), while as a director he shot the lacklustre *Monkey Shines* (1988).

In 1990, he collaborated with Dario Argento on *Two Evil Eyes*, based on a pair of Edgar Allan Poe tales. Romero's segment of the movie – 'The Facts in the Case of Mr. Valdemar' – saw him once again in the realm of the living dead, as the titular character rises from the grave to take revenge on his wife and her lover. It was, until recently, notable as being Romero's worst work by far – even though it comprises only half a feature film, 'Mr. Valdemar' manages to be crushingly slow and devoid of any directorial passion, playing like an extended episode of the *Tales from the Darkside* TV series. While there were many criticisms that could be levelled at Romero, blandness had never been one of them, but there was no other way to describe this insipid effort.

The zombies take their revenge in *Land of the Dead*.

The same year, Romero oversaw a remake of *Night of the Living Dead* (something fans hypocritically always manage to avoid mentioning while criticising other remakes), writing the screenplay but handing the directorial reins to Tom Savini, whose previous experience in that capacity amounted to a couple of *Darkside* episodes. The film was made solely for financial reasons – none of the people involved in the original film had made much money from it, and most of them were on board as producers for the remake.

Other, cynical attempts to make money from the first film have included a shockingly bad colourised edition, and a pointless 30th Anniversary edition version that has clumsy additional scenes shot in 1998, adding an unnecessary backstory to the Bill Hinzman zombie (now named Abbott Hayes and revealed to be a child murderer) and placing a religious slant upon proceedings, suggesting that a Christian belief can somehow cure the infected. With lengthy new sequences both opening and closing the film, terrible acting, awful new synthesizer muzak and the unmissable fact that Hinzman looks nothing like he did thirty years earlier, this version is an embarrassment.

The 1990 *NOTLD* is little more than a slicker, revisionist version of the original film which follows the same story fairly closely. However, the storyline incorporates changes that reflect Romero's emerging philosophy – namely that mankind (as opposed to *woman*kind) isn't worth saving.

This time around, Barbara (Patricia Tallman) swiftly emerges from her traumatised state to become the film's focal point and voice of reason, while Ben (Tony Todd) – the politics of gender now seemingly more important to the director than matters of race – spends most of his time bickering and fighting with Cooper (Tom Towles). In turn, Cooper is presented not only as a coward, but also as a villainous incompetent. When Ben meets his inevitable end, it is not at the hands of the posse, nor is he devoured by zombies, but as the result of a petty shoot-out with Cooper.

The most significant – and unnecessary – changes are at the film's conclusion. Barbara (now transformed into a typical action heroine) escapes, while Ben locks himself in the cellar to die and Cooper scrambles into the attic. After meeting a bunch of typical Romero rednecks, Barbara gets to see the zombies hung from trees to be used as target practice while the good ol' boys whoop with delight – both images something of a Romero motif.

His belief that society would react to a zombie attack as if it were some kind of owlhoot jamboree with rednecks running around whooping as they shoot the dead runs through his work, and he relentlessly hammers home his concepts of humanity losing itself and being no different from the flesh-eating corpses who are attacking them.

A pity then that, once you think about it, it makes no real sense. It hardly justifies his heroine killing Cooper in cold blood at the end of the film. Some critics have suggested that she is symbolically killing the patriarchal cause of humanity's problems, which at least explains why Romero has been able to impress so many reviewers with his repetitive social commentary – some of them are only slightly more perceptive than the zombies, it seems.

There are a few decent moments in the movie: the idea that the sound of the survivors boarding up the farmhouse is what actually attracts the zombies is a neat twist, as is the play on the original film's legendary opening sequence, which uses audience familiarity with the scene to create a fresh shock. But it's a generally flawed update, which – although apparently set in 1989 – maintains its devotion to the original film to the extent of looking as though it's taking place during the 1960s.

Despite the combination of Romero and Savini, the film lacks any significant gore. Admittedly, cuts were made to secure an R rating, but this in itself is telling, given that only five years earlier, Romero had refused to compromise his bloody vision. Clearly, the failure of *Day of the Dead* had been sobering. From now on, all Romero's zombie films would have an R rating, no matter what cuts were asked for.

After 1990, Romero's career hit something of a slump. 1993's *The Dark Half* failed to impress audiences, and it would be seven years before he directed again, with 2000's disastrous *Bruiser*.

Between and beyond those lacklustre, bland movies, he suffered with aborted and failed projects, including a version of *The Mummy*. But in 1998, he briefly returned to zombie filmmaking with a thirty-second commercial for the video game *Resident Evil 2*. The *Resident Evil* games had been inspired by Romero and, although the ad wasn't seen outside Japan and is little more than a live-action taster, it impressed game makers Capcom enough to ask Romero to consider shooting a movie based on their product.

Initially, the director seemed reluctant to return to the world of the living dead and also apparently expressed an antipathy towards video games, but eventually turned in a screenplay for the film after having his secretary play the game and record the gameplay for him to study. His screenplay – also available online – stuck closely to the game's plot and notably eschews social commentary for wall-to-wall action.

How the finished movie would have turned out is anyone's guess, as the screenplay failed to impress Capcom, who promptly fired Romero from the project. A very different version by English director Paul W.S. Anderson was released in 2002.

By the time the remake of *Dawn of the Dead* was in the works, Romero seemed to have overcome his reluctance to revisit his zombie-film past. In fact, the director seemed to be proposing zombie projects at a rate of knots, possibly due to the realisation that no one was likely to hire him to shoot anything else at this point.

One ludicrous idea was *Diamond Dead*, a horror-comedy about a zombie rock band. Originally written by Brian Cooper, the film seemed closer to a gross-out Troma comedy than a traditional Romero zombie film, and left most sensible fans aghast at the thought of it. Worse still, the project is still on the cards as this book goes to press, scheduled for a 2009 release.

The other Romero zombie film announced at the time was *Dead Reckoning*, which was picked up by Universal in the wake of *Dawn of the Dead's* success in 2004. Expanding on the original trilogy and using elements from the unfilmed version of *Day of the Dead*, the movie would be the first Romero zombie feature to benefit from major studio backing, and as such, the director was contracted to deliver an R-rated movie. Unlike in 1985, when he turned down a bigger budget to deliver the gore, this time Romero agreed.

Retitled *Land of the Dead*, the resulting film was a considerable improvement on *Day of the Dead*, and suggested that the constraints of the studio system were good for Romero, compelling him to be less self-indulgent.

Land of the Dead is set in Fiddler's Green, an elite fortress in Pittsburgh that seems to be a functioning version of the shopping mall in *Dawn of the Dead*. While the rich can live a life of safety and luxury, the rest of the survivors live a run-down, *Mad Max*-style existence on the streets, while outside the heavily fortified city the zombies are in control. Supplies are secured by teams who venture outside the city in a heavily armed vehicle called Dead Reckoning, using fireworks to distract the zombies while they scavenge for food and luxuries.

When Fiddler's Green's leader Kaufman (Dennis Hopper) refuses to allow Cholo (John Leguizamo) to join the elite in the fortress, the disgruntled trooper steals Dead Reckoning and threatens to shell the city. Kaufman sends Riley Denbo (Simon Baker) and his team to recapture his $2 million vehicle, but Riley has his own plans. Meanwhile, the zombies are gaining self-awareness, and under the leadership of their zomboid leader, Big Daddy, are advancing on the city.

Land of the Dead is shorter and tighter than Romero's previous two zombie movies, and progresses at a decent pace, mixing plot development and action quite well. Romero's negative view of humanity still shines through though – in his world, money equals power (though with no banks and an economy built on scavenged goods, it's unclear how exactly) and the survivors, rather than rebuilding society, are content to ignore the problem and live off the leftovers. But at least this time Romero's social commentary remains low-key – by his standards at least.

With better actors than his earlier films and less cumbersome dialogue for them to wrestle with, Romero also manages to deliver some effective action scenes. The use of CGI splatter

Diary of the Dead – a depressing low point in George Romero's career.

effects is distracting, though there are plenty of visceral organic gore moments (at least in the unrated cut) to keep fans happy.

Unfortunately, it's not all good. The zombies themselves are unimpressive, looking far too prosthetically enhanced to be convincing, and Romero's positing of them as the real heroes of the film is misguided – these are, after all, aggressively cannibalistic corpses and hardly an oppressed minority as the film seems to suggest – though not unexpected.

Dennis Hopper was charged with the thankless task of trying to bring Kaufman to life. The veteran cult icon is hamstrung by the worst dialogue of the film, being used as Romero's evocation of human evil. Kaufman spouts capitalist rhetoric and indulges in casual racism.

Romero claims the character and performance were based on notorious US Secretary of Defense Donald Rumsfeld, though it's unlikely that many people would have picked up on that particular nugget. In reality, it's simply a case of Hopper phoning in his performance, and adds nothing to the film.

As the film's eponymous centrepiece, Dead Reckoning is not that impressive. Together with the mean streets of the city – where survivors live a virtually lawless existence – it seems like a leftover from some late-1970s/early Eighties post-apocalypse film like *Damnation Alley*.

Faults aside, *Land of the Dead* represented something of a return to form for Romero. Unfortunately, despite generally positive reviews, the film was not a box-office success and effectively ended any chance of the director enjoying any kind of long-term mainstream comeback.

Not that Romero seemed too bothered, as he began to plan yet another zombie film. This time, he was going back to his roots, shooting independently on a low budget – and taking his zombie saga back to the beginning.

Diary of the Dead was shot on video for just $2 million, and used the 'video diary' format seen in films such as *The Blair Witch Project*. The story is told from the perspective of a group of student filmmakers who are attempting to get home as reports of the dead rising start to emerge. Keeping their cameras rolling, the students capture the horror of what is happening, and the resulting footage is edited into the film presented here – entitled 'The Death of Death'.

Diary of the Dead is without question Romero's worst film to date, outdoing even his risible contribution to *Two Evil Eyes*. All the progress made during *Land...* is discarded as the director once again opts to indulge himself. No longer content to allow his message to simply filter through the story or be bellowed at the audience by his main characters, Romero this time uses a narration by Debra (Michelle Morgan) to sledgehammer the point home. And by now, it begins to feel like the bitter rantings of an old man.

One of his new motifs – alongside the usual 'they are us and we are them' dynamic (now stated bluntly at the end of the film just in case the point hadn't been clear, even though his zombies have no individual personalities to sympathise *with*) – is an overt disdain for the online media. For Romero, developments such as YouTube, blogs and websites do not represent an opportunity for more voices to be heard. For him, this explosion in communication is a bad thing – 'More voices. More spin. Truth becomes noise.'

All this would be tolerable if the film delivered on any other level, but it doesn't. There's no plot as such – just a series of incidents. The gore – always a cornerstone of Romero's zombie canon – is reduced to ineffective CGI blood effects, while the action sequences are conspicuous by their absence.

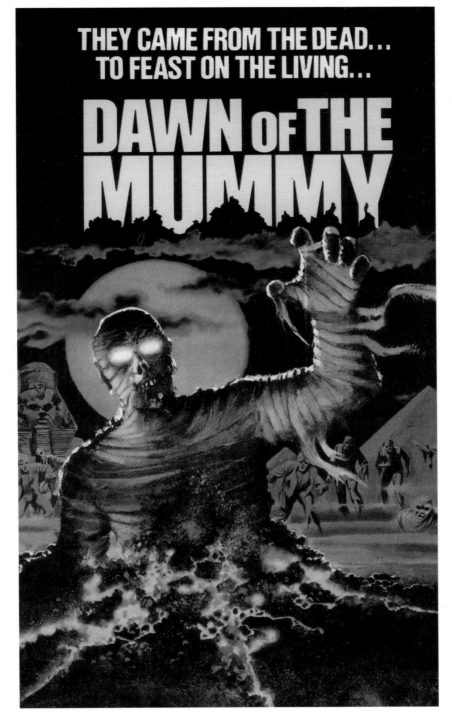

Dawn of the Mummy.

UK video sleeve for *Astro Zombies*.

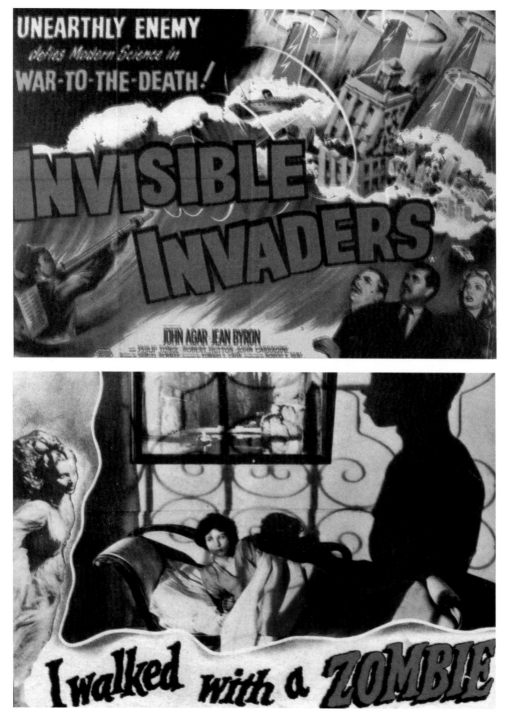

UK poster for *Invisible Invaders* (top); lobby card for *I Walked with a Zombie* (bottom).

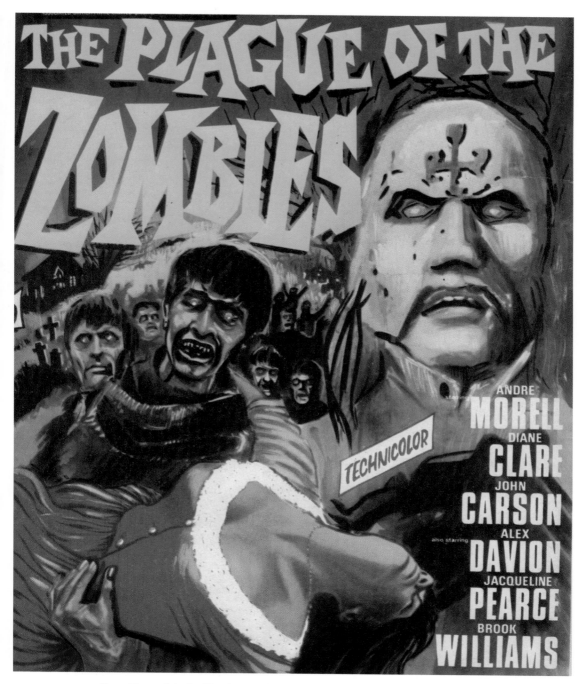

Above: *Plague of the Zombies*. *Opposite*: A double-bill poster for 1961's crude but effective
The Dead One and lacklustre 1959 effort *The Monster of Piedras Blancas* (above);
1957's low-budget sunken-treasure saga *Zombies of Mora Tau* (below).

Above: Original UK sleeve for *The Evil Dead*. *Opposite*: Reissue poster art for *The Beyond* (top left);
UK video sleeve for *Zombie Creeping Flesh* (top right); double-bill ad for *I Drink Your Blood* and
I Eat Your Skin (bottom left); German poster art for *Dawn of the Dead* (bottom right).

Starring
RICHARD JOHNSON
TISA FARROW
IAN McCULLOCH

...en the earth spits out the Dead... they will return to tear the flesh of the living...

ZOMBIE FLESH EATERS
x

RUNNING TIME 89 MINUTES , COLOUR
SEE WARNING ON REVERSE

VIPCO

British video sleeve for *Zombie Flesh Eaters*.

The acting is terrible – though the cast are certainly not helped by the fact that none of them have anything more than poorly conceived characters to work with. Romero's contempt for humanity seems to have reached the stage where he is no longer interested in even giving his protagonists any personality. When they die, no one cares because the director considered it unnecessary to imbue them with any humanity.

Even the finest actors would struggle with dialogue like, 'It used to be us against us. Now it's us against them, but they're us.' It's as if Romero is less interested in making a horror film than he is in bombarding the audience with a relentless monologue about what he considers to be wrong with the world.

Romero's attacks on 'running zombies' seem particularly bitter. A line of dialogue from *Diary of the Dead* – repeated by Romero in interviews with the BBC and others – dismisses the idea that zombies could possibly run 'because their ankles would break'. It's a ludicrous statement, because it attempts to impose some logic and some set of rules on to a fantasy construct.

We could just as easily question how zombies can bite chunks out of people without breaking their jaws or knocking out their teeth; how they can tear open stomachs without breaking their fingers; eat food without a working digestive system; lunge at people when they are otherwise slow-moving; or suddenly develop a sense of reasoning in their previously dead brains. But we don't because *zombies are not real* and the whole basis of a zombie film depends on the willingness of the viewer to suspend disbelief and accept the ridiculous idea that the dead can rise and that they will want to eat us.

Strangely, Romero seems to think he's doing something innovative with this film. Which might have been the case if we hadn't had *The Blair Witch Project*, or *The Last Broadcast*, or *Cannibal Holocaust*. But we have, and Romero's approach to the format is inferior to all three (as well as to *Cloverfield*, which was released shortly before *Diary…*).

In any case, the audiences seem to have made their choice. On an admittedly limited theatrical run, *Diary of the Dead* made less than a million dollars at the US box-office. International takings and DVD sales will certainly push the low-budget film into profit, but it's hardly a ringing endorsement of the director from his public.

Nevertheless, as this book nears completion, Romero has announced *Diary of the Dead 2* – a move that it's hard to see as anything other than desperation from a director who seems set on a path that only serves to undermine his reputation.

6. 'When There is No More Room in Hell, the Dead Shall Walk the Earth'

Europe's Zombie Holocausts

Night of the Living Dead heralded a new generation of horror cinema in the US, but in Europe it had a less immediate impact. Not that the genre wasn't changing – the success of Dario Argento's *giallo* thriller *The Bird with the Crystal Plumage* at the end of the 1960s, alongside a loosening of censorship restrictions, saw the continental horror film – not to mention its British cousin – start to slowly shake off the gothic cobwebs of Hammer and their imitators.

Nevertheless, zombies remained strictly second-division figures until the end of the Seventies, when they would suddenly hit the forefront of Euro horror's final golden age.

Throughout the first part of the decade, the living dead made few appearances, and these rarely acknowledged the revolutionary development of the sub-genre in the US. In Europe, zombies remained rather ineffectual figures, prone to vague menace, rather than overt cannibalistic threats.

While British horror was alive and well throughout the 1970s, zombies rarely featured – UK filmmakers of the period tended to favour the traditional gothic plots, or accounts of modern-day psycho-killers. There were only two zombie appearances in the decade, and neither of them featured flesh-hungry corpses.

Amicus Films had been making portmanteau movies since the mid-Sixties, when *Dr. Terror's House of Horrors* proved successful enough to pave the way for multiple follow-ups. The format was simple – find a handful of short stories and stitch them together with a flimsy linking device – usually the story protagonist telling a tale to the supporting company. These films generally worked because none of the stories were long enough to become dull, and allowed the movies to offer a broad mix of chills.

In 1972, Amicus made the first of two EC comics' adaptations – *Tales from the Crypt* (followed a year later with *The Vault of Horror*). Both were somewhat inconsistent – acceptable as horror movies, they somehow managed to strip the EC source material of its black humour and joyful tastelessness. Much of this can be put down to Amicus head and screenwriter Milton Subotsky, a man entirely unsuited to the task (Subotsky's fixation was to make horror films that were suitable for kids, eventually leading to the disastrous *The Monster Club* in 1980).

Tales from the Crypt featured a solitary zombie yarn – *Poetic Justice*. This overrated story starred Peter Cushing as Arthur Grimsdyke, a kindly old man who is driven to suicide by his wealthy neighbours, who see him as a blot on the local landscape. The final straw comes when Grimsdyke receives a series of hateful Valentine's cards – after reading the messages, he hangs himself. A year later, Grimsdyke crawls from the grave to rip out the heart of his tormentor.

The zombies attack during the brutal climax of *The Living Dead at the Manchester Morgue*.

Peter Cushing rises from the dead to take his revenge in *Tales from the Crypt*.

While the tone of the story is overly sentimental, the scenes of Grimsdyke crawling from his grave are genuinely creepy, and Cushing's corpse make-up is impressive – enough to make this one of the more memorable British horror pictures of the period.

The other British zombie film of the 1970s couldn't have been more different. *Psychomania* (1973) is part of a small sub-genre – the zombie biker film (others include *Chopper Chicks in Zombietown* and the early shot-on-video effort *Bikers vs. The Undead*). In spirit, *Psychomania* is closer to the New English Library pulp novels of Mick Norman, Peter Cave and others, who presented a very British version of the Hell's Angels in a series of short, punchy tales that were light on literary merit but heavy on sex, drugs, violence and action.

Sitting on the shelves alongside Guy N. Smith's sleazy horror tales and the *Skinhead* novels of Richard Allen, these books were devoured by an audience that had no interest in 'literature'. A few of these – Alex R. Stuart's *The Bike from Hell* for instance – touched on the supernatural, and it's easy to imagine *Psychomania* as such a novel. Like them, it's cheap, trashy, devoid of any literary merit – and thoroughly entertaining.

The film follows the adventures of a particularly lame and laughably polite British biker gang – The Living Dead – whose exploits consist mostly of making a nuisance of themselves

Scenes from *Psychomania*: Nicky Henson is temporarily laid to rest (above); the living dead set off for more mischief making (below).

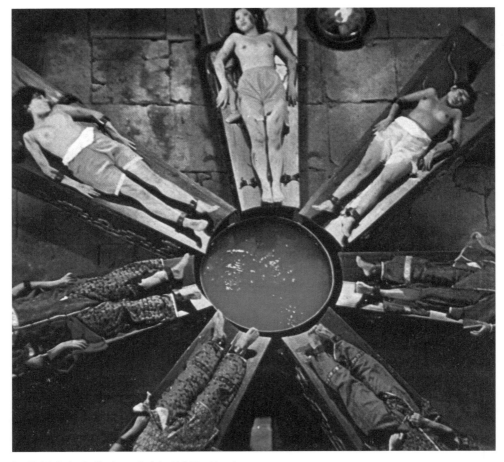

Sacrificial virgins in *The Legend of the 7 Golden Vampires*.

in shopping centres. Gang leader – the frightfully middle-class Nicky Henson (Tom Latham) – discovers that his mother (Beryl Reid) has the secret of eternal life. All he has to do is kill himself with the absolute belief that he'll return from the grave.

Henson tries it out and is successful, and it isn't long before the rest of the gang follow suit, freeing them to continue to wreak the mild havoc they were causing before (by modern standards, they probably wouldn't even qualify for an ASBO).

Psychomania co-starred an embarrassed-looking George Sanders – who killed himself shortly afterwards, which was somewhat ironic considering the film's pro-suicide subtext – and also featured Brit sleaze queen Ann Michelle. Dramatically, the film is awful – but entertaining nonetheless. The best element is the genuinely eerie opening titles, but fans of cheesy horror will find rich pickings here.

Zombies also made a pointless cameo in Hammer's 1974 genre bender *The Legend of the 7*

Demonic happenings in *Vengeance of the Zombies.*

Golden Vampires, which attempted to wed the company's gothic traditions to the kung-fu genre
for a mainstream Western audience. Hong Kong filmmakers were already making odd hybrid
horrors for the domestic market.

With a screamingly camp Count Dracula (grafted on to the story at the last minute), the
film never really gelled. This was possibly because director Roy Ward Baker and screenwriter
Don Houghton didn't really understand the martial-arts movie or the possibilities of oriental
horror. But some scenes – including the army of the living dead that accompany the Golden
Vampires – remain impressive, and the film has aged well. The US version, re-titled *The Seven
Brothers Meet Dracula,* and re-edited to the point of incoherence, is to be avoided.

1972's *Neither the Sea Nor the Sand* saw TV newsreader Gordon Honeycombe adapting his
own novel into a sluggish and depressing tale of love conquering death, as Michael Petrovich
returns from the grave to continue his affair with Susan Hampshire. Ineffective as a horror

movie, the film has its moments, but they are few and far between.

Less dour was Antony Balch's demented *Horror Hospital* (1973), which had mad doctor Michael Gough experimenting on hapless 'health farm' guests, turning them into mindless zombies. Balch had worked with William Burroughs in the 1960s and as a distributor was one of the first people to champion arthouse and grindhouse movies. His two feature films (the other being *Secrets of Sex* a.k.a. *Bizarre*) reflect this, offering a heady mix of sex, horror, trash cinema aesthetics and experimental filmmaking. Both are recommended.

While Britain and the rest of Europe carried on making films about Dracula, Frankenstein, ghosts and deranged killers during the early Seventies, Spanish filmmakers gave the Euro-zombie a new lease of life. Some of their films were pretty poor, but a few pointed the way for Euro horror in general – and the zombie film in particular.

In 1972, Paul Naschy turned his attention to the living dead in *Vengeance of the Zombies*. A torpid tale of Indian voodoo directed by Leon Klimovsky, the movie sees Naschy cast as a fakir who zombifies the daughters of former colonialists.

Later that same year he was back in José Luis Merino's dreadful *Beyond the Living Dead* (a.k.a. *The Hanging Woman/Return of the Zombies*), where he plays necrophiliac support to a mad scientist who is reviving the dead. Neither added much to the sub-genre, and, while some of Naschy's films transcend their limitations to become weirdly compulsive, these two efforts are simply bad.

Spanish director Jesus Franco had already spent a decade making all manner of bizarre horror, sex and action movies across Europe (and under a variety of pseudonyms) when he made *Virgin Among the Living Dead* (1971). Shot in the middle of a busy studio schedule of surreal gothic potboilers made for pan-European producers, the film is one of his more visually arresting pieces. Originally titled *Christina, Princess de L'Eroticisme*, the film is short on plot but long on style and, if you don't mind simply wallowing in atmosphere, it has plenty to offer.

The movie revolves around the eponymous heroine's visit to her uncle's château, where all manner of strange things occur, often involving nudity and briefly featuring some ineffectual zombies. Not much else happens – but it all looks very weird, and somehow holds the attention.

Viewers should avoid the US TV edit that appeared on video in the mid-Eighties – crudely hacked to remove any sex and violence, it makes even less sense than the original version, and the clumsy butchery effectively destroys the evocative atmosphere.

More interesting – and certainly more popular – were the 'Blind Dead' films made by director Amando de Ossorio during the first half of the decade. This quartet of movies re-established the zombie as a figure of fear across Europe, and offered a new twist on the sub-genre.

The four films are a loose series – other than the central premise, there are no notable connections between them, and in reality all follow pretty much the same story.

Based loosely on the legends of the Knights Templar – a 13th-century crusading army – De Ossorio's films have the long-dead soldiers returning from the grave, having swapped Christianity for the occult during the Crusades. This is usually shown in a pre-credit opening sequence where the Knights sacrifice a young virgin to Satan. Executed for their crimes, they were hung from trees where birds pecked out their eyes – hence their lack of vision when they rise as mummified, bloodthirsty corpses. Not that this handicap slows them down – instead, they use their other senses to locate new victims.

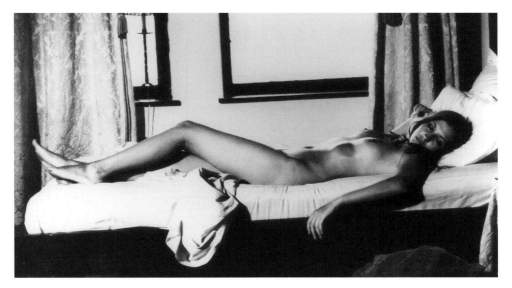

Jesus Franco's haunting *Virgin Among the Living Dead*.

The first film in the series, 1971's *Tombs of the Blind Dead*, sets the scene nicely. A young couple meet up with an old friend while travelling across Europe, but after an argument (caused by the girl's jealousy about her boyfriend being attracted to their companion, and guilt over a previous lesbian affair) the girl jumps train only to find herself in a ruined cemetery. Unfortunately for her, it's where the Templars are buried, and they rise up to brutally murder her.

Her boyfriend and the other girl investigate her disappearance, only to find themselves up against the Blind Dead, in a slow-moving but efficient movie that is heavy on atmosphere and – in certain prints – gore and nudity.

The Blind Dead were back in 1973, with *Return of the Evil Dead*, where the residents of a small village discover that the sightless zombies have been resurrected, and are picking victims off during local festivities. The local mayor attempts to cover up the truth, but eventually pools resources with the survivors to battle the revived Templars. The film lacked some of the verve of its predecessor, but was nevertheless a decent shocker.

1973's *Horror of the Zombies* saw the Blind Dead taking to the sea, as a bevy of bikini babes on a photo-shoot stumble upon a ghostly galleon. On board are the Knights Templar, and more mayhem ensues. This is probably the weakest of the lot, with too much padding and not enough action, while the seaboard setting serves to be creatively constricting rather than imbuing the film with a sense of claustrophobic dread.

Night of the Seagulls (1974) was a return to form. In this film, the inhabitants of a small fishing village placate the Blind Dead by sacrificing young girls for seven nights every seven years. A doctor and his wife, newly arrived in the village, find the locals cold and hostile, and set out to find out the truth behind their *froideur*. This is an atmospheric and eerie effort, and ended the series on something of a high note.

As a series, the Blind Dead films are generally impressive, with excellent music and some superb visuals – the shots of the Templars riding along on their equally undead horses are particularly striking (and their absence in *Horror of the Zombies* is one reason why that film is less engaging).

Interestingly, De Ossorio always maintained that his creations were Mummies, not zombies (and told *Fandom's Film Gallery* that their movements were down to 'a displacement in the relationship [between] time/space'.)

The Templars made a brief appearance in John Gilling's 1974 film *The Devil's Cross*, but have been unseen since. A revival seems long overdue.

The most significant Spanish movie of the 1970s was also the one closest to Romero's template. In fact, *The Living Dead at Manchester Morgue* was a direct imitation of *Night of the Living Dead*, but transcended its derivative roots to deliver some visceral shocks – and offer some social commentary of its own.

Released under a plethora of mostly terrible English-language titles *(Don't Open the Window, Breakfast at the Manchester Morgue, Let Sleeping Corpses Lie)*, Jorge Grau's film is, in its own way, every bit as groundbreaking as Romero's original.

This Spanish/Italian co-production was shot not in Manchester (which is used for a suitably bleak opening montage but nothing more) but in the Lake District. Grau's alien look at the British countryside gives the locations a sinister edge, as his tale of the dead being revived by sound waves designed to kill insects unfolds.

The biggest threat in *The Living Dead at Manchester Morgue* isn't, in fact, the cannibalistic ghouls who rise from the grave, but rather the boorish police sergeant McCormick (Arthur Kennedy), who refuses to believe antique dealers George (Ray Lovelock) and Edna (Cristina Galbó) when they try to explain that Edna's brother-in-law has been killed by a madman (in fact, a recently deceased local, Guthrie the Looney). Instead, he suspects the couple are responsible, a theory apparently enhanced by Lovelock's long hair and fashionable clothes.

Later, when zombies slaughter a police officer, McCormick holds the two 'Satanists' responsible. While George and Edna try to stop the undead uprising, McCormick tracks them down and shoots George in the head. 'I wish the dead could come back to life, you bastard,' he declares, 'because then I could kill you again.'

Grau's film is a success on virtually every level. Well paced, the excellent cinematography and assured direction give the film a gloss that few other Euro-zombie films have matched, while the grim atmosphere is impressive. The opening scenes of a pollution-filled, overcrowded Manchester seem to suggest that civilisation is already doomed.

The uncompromising view of the Manchester police force will strike a chord with anyone who remembers that city's notorious Chief Constable James Anderton (a lay preacher who conducted a personal *fatwa* against pornography and once accused AIDS victims of 'swirling in a cesspit of their own making').

On a more immediate level, the film certainly delivers sufficient gore to satisfy even the most bloodthirsty palate. The graphic nature of the violence was pretty extreme in 1973, and

The Knights Templar attack in *Night of the Seagulls* (above) and *Horror of the Zombies* (below).

A selection of images from *Night of the Seagulls*, originally featured on the UK video sleeve.

still has an impact today. Grau also created some of the best zombies ever to grace the screen, and iconic images from this film fired many a childish imagination when published in books by Alan Frank during the 1970s.

Although a popular success, *The Living Dead at Manchester Morgue* didn't open the zombie floodgates. But in 1978, a film with Italian connections would spawn a host of imitations. The Dario Argento cut of *Dawn of the Dead* opened in Europe before its US release, and immediately became a smash-hit. In the wake of its success, a slew of zombie output began to emerge from Italy, led by Lucio Fulci's *Zombie Flesh Eaters*.

Fulci was a journeyman director who had moved from assignment to assignment since the 1960s, working on a variety of genres. He did everything from sex comedies to Westerns to *giallo*, only rarely showing a glimmer of talent.

Like many jobbing directors in Italy, he was generally as good as the screenplays he worked with – and, while his *giallo* films (*Don't Torture a Duckling*, *Lizard in a Woman's Skin*, *Murder to the Tune of Seven Black Notes*) all had their moments, there was nothing in his work to suggest a particular affinity for the horror genre. Yet within a few years, Fulci would be inextricably linked with horror, and would subsequently milk the connection for the remainder of his life.

Global promotion for Amando de Ossorio's 'Blind Dead' films.
Above left: Redemption Films' video sleeve. *Above right*: French poster. *Below*: US ad material.

Edna's undead brother-in-law gets to grips with her in *The Living Dead at the Manchester Morgue.*

Zombie Flesh Eaters was made as a direct result of *Dawn of the Dead's* huge success in Italy, where Dario Argento's edit of the film was released as *Zombi.* Lax Italian copyright laws allowed producers to make films that not only copied the story from box-office hits, but also actually tried to pass themselves off as sequels. So it was with Fulci's film, released as *Zombi 2* in 1979. To confuse matters further, while Romero's film was released in the UK as *Zombies,* Fulci's film would appear in America as *Zombie.*

Fulci's film became a surprise hit. In the UK, it appeared in cinemas (minus around four minutes of gore) as *Zombie Flesh Eaters* a few weeks before Romero's film, and proved to be the bigger box-office draw. This success was possibly by virtue of *Flesh Eaters* having a more sensationalist title, a decent poster and a snappy, Romeroesque tag line: 'When the earth spits out the dead… They will return to tear the flesh of the living.'

In the US, the film followed Romero's lead and was released unrated – again, the film was an unexpected hit and its appearance on the cover of *Fangoria* magazine also marked the move of that publication away from broad fantasy and into full-blooded splatter horror.

The film is fairly basic in structure: when a yacht is found drifting off the New York coast, police investigate, only to be attacked by a particularly large and gruesome zombie. Investigative reporter Peter West (Ian McCulloch – best known for his portrayal of Greg Preston in the post-apocalyptic BBC series *Survivors*) teams up with the daughter of the yacht's owner, Anne Bowles (American actress Tisa Farrow), to uncover what has happened.

A gruesome zombie from *The Living Dead at the Manchester Morgue*.

Their investigation leads them to the island of Matul, chartering a yacht with Brian (Al Cliver) and Susan (Auretta Gay). On arriving, they meet Doctor Menard (Richard Johnson), who explains that the island is overrun with the living dead. As he searches for a cure, the zombies attack the hospital, and West and Bowles only just manage to escape. As they return home, New York radio reports that the infection has spread to the US, and the film ends with zombies crossing the Brooklyn Bridge – the film cleverly setting itself up as a prequel to *Dawn of the Dead*.

Zombie Flesh Eaters was roundly dismissed as unpleasantly violent trash at the time of release, particularly by established horror/fantasy critics. *Cinefan*'s Randall Larson dismissed it as an 'awful gross-out gore-fest', adding, 'it's films like this that give the horror genre its bad name'. But the movie's reputation – like that of Fulci – has grown steadily over the years.

In truth, it's no masterpiece; it has crude production values, is badly dubbed (in all versions – like many Italian exploitation films at the time, the multinational cast delivered their lines in a variety of different languages, and the sound was added later), some disinterested performances (international names Johnson, McCulloch and Farrow were all regulars in the Italian exploitation cinema at the time, but only Johnson looks like he's trying) and several gaping plot holes.

But the film has an undeniable *something*. The atmosphere is potent – you can almost smell the decay as the rotting zombies shuffle down deserted streets. Flies buzz constantly, the cast are drenched in sweat and the ubiquity of the dead and dying in the cramped hospital gives the film a visceral and claustrophobic feel that is hugely effective.

Fulci's zombies – created by Gianetto De Rossi – are far more believable than Tom Savini's ineffective designs for Romero. These zombies *look* like the walking dead, and Fulci shoots them perfectly. De Rossi's gore scenes are equally impressive – the graphic violence saw several minutes cut by UK censors and the uncut video release was banned under the Video Recordings Act.

However, the most famous moment in *Zombie Flesh Eaters* – while certainly an audacious slice of bad taste – also pointed to a weakness that would increasingly hamper Fulci's work. The eyeball scene – where Doctor Menard's wife emerges from the shower only to be attacked by a zombie, who grabs her by the hair and *slowly* pulls her towards a splintered door, eventually piercing her eye on a wooden spike – drags the action out, and requires the victim to hold still as the torturous shot continues. This could have been done just as effectively in half the time.

Fulci's later work would feature even more needlessly extended set-pieces (most notably the endless spider attack in *The Beyond*), and these moments make it hard to argue with critics who accuse the films of being little more than horror porn – dragging the most visceral scenes out for the vicarious delectation of the audience.

Gore aside, the movie still has plenty going for it. The soundtrack – be it Fabio Frizzi's Goblinesque synth score or the near-constant sound of drums on Matul – enhances the atmosphere considerably, while the entirely gratuitous scene where an underwater zombie battles a shark (following an equally unnecessary topless scene for Gay) might not add much to the plot, but is undeniably memorable.

Zombie Flesh Eaters is the one Fulci zombie film that still holds up today. Sadly, the same cannot be said for his follow-ups, which – ironically – all had much more ambition, though scarcely more originality than *Zombie Flesh Eaters*. All three are highly derivative of Dario Argento's *Suspiria* and *Inferno*, and they each suffer from major problems with pacing and structure.

Although there is much to admire in these films – their visual style, the Lovecraftian atmosphere – none of them are particularly entertaining when viewed today. How much of this is the fault of Fulci and how much the responsibility of writer Dardano Sacchetti remains a bone of contention – both parties have laid claim to being the creative force of the team and both have their supporters and detractors.

The first film in Fulci's loose, post-*Flesh Eaters* trilogy was 1980's *City of the Living Dead*. Set in the small town of Dunwich, the film follows a series of bizarre events that are set in motion by the suicide of a priest. His death opens the gates of Hell, and soon people in the town are becoming possessed by evil, while the dead are rising from the grave. Caught in the middle of this are reporter Peter (Christopher George), psychic Mary (Catriona MacColl), psychiatrist Gerry (Carlo de Mejo) and his patient Sandra (Janet Agren).

Dardano Sacchetti's screenplay is short on clarity, stringing together a series of unrelated, unexplained set-pieces that are only tangentially relevant to the central plot. Despite this, there are some impressive (if nonsensical) moments – George trying to free MacColl after she is buried alive by ripping open her coffin with a pickaxe, barely missing her face in the process, and the ambiguous closing scene.

Once again, Fulci again needlessly overextends too many of his gory scenes. The power-drill killing of Bob (John Morgen, a.k.a. Giovanni Lombardo Radice) and the entrails vomiting would be impressive if they weren't so slow (in the latter case, giving more screen time than is necessary to some poor prosthetics). Viewed today, scenes like this bring the film to a grinding halt.

1981's *The Beyond* is the film that Fulci's admirers tend to claim is his masterpiece. It's certainly the most visually impressive of his movies, and as an exercise in blood-drenched surrealism is fairly successful. Unfortunately, it's also the slowest of the trilogy, and includes one of the weakest sequences in horror-cinema history.

Catriona MacColl returns, this time as Liza, a woman who has just inherited an old hotel in New Orleans. Unfortunately, it has been built over a gateway to Hell – the 'Beyond' – and, as she renovates it, strange things start to happen. Workmen have accidents, people start to die and a

Iconic UK poster art for *Zombie Flesh Eaters*.

Starring
**RICHARD JOHNSON
TISA FARROW
IAN McCULLOCH**

When the earth
spits ou
the Dead...

they will return
to tear the
flesh of
the Living...

ZOMBIE
FLESH
EATERS

x

RUNNING TIME 89 MINUTES , COLOUR
SEE WARNING ON REVERSE

◉VIPCO◉

blind girl, Emily (Sarah Keller), warns her to leave. Along with local doctor John McCabe (David Warbeck), Liza starts to investigate the mystery, but, with the gate to Hell open, the dead are rising from the grave.

There's no denying that *The Beyond* looks incredible, and has some startling set-pieces – the pre-credit sequence where a painter is beaten to death, opening up the gateway, is a moody sepia-tone appetiser (although some prints have this scene in colour). Similarly, the climactic zombie attack is spectacular, never more than in the scene where the front half of a little girl's head is blown away – leaving the back unscathed. The bleak ending is also moodily impressive.

Again, Fulci overextends some scenes. The violent sequences often take an age to complete, and little of interest takes place in between. The death of Emily is copied from a similar scene in *Suspiria*, and his trademark eye trauma is again ineffective.

German poster for Lucio Fulci's cult classic *The Beyond*.

The worst moment in *The Beyond* comes when the wholly bogus spiders move in for the kill. The scene is interminable; pathetic fake arachnids amble slowly towards their victim and subsequently eat him at an equally leisurely pace. It's often the point where people who didn't grow up with the film throw in the towel.

House by the Cemetery (also 1981) once again starred MacColl, this time as Lucy Boyle, who moves to a large house with her husband Norman (Paolo Malco) and son Bob (Giovanni Frezza), only to find that a series of spooky, *Amityville*-style events begin to occur. Bob starts hanging around with the ghost of a little girl, a bat attacks Lucy, a wall drips blood and ghostly noises can be heard.

All this malefic activity can be ascribed to former owner Doctor Freudstein, whose zombified corpse is hiding out in the basement, where he continues with his vague experiments in immortality – all of which inevitably involve murder and mutilation.

More conventionally plotted than the previous two films, *House by the Cemetery* works better than either *The Beyond* or *City of the Living Dead*. It has fewer slow-moving moments and actually makes some sense. Ironically, many of the people who might enjoy this film for the well-presented haunted-house elements will probably be put off by the gore, which is as

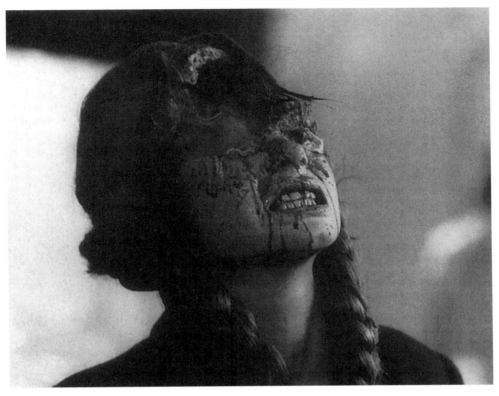

The Beyond pulled no punches, as this spectacularly gory shot shows.

graphic as ever. The ghost-child sub-plot is a little maudlin, though, and the children don't exactly help the film. The casting of Frezza – who is guaranteed to annoy the hell out of every viewer – would seem puzzling to those people who haven't seen many Italian horror movies, where strange-looking kids seem to be the norm (see also: *Nights of Terror*).

After *House by the Cemetery*, Fulci's career faltered. His gothic *Black Cat* (1981) and *Manhattan Baby* (which many feel should be bracketed with the trilogy, but is often ignored because there's no Catriona MacColl or zombies) were poorly received, while *The New York Ripper* (1982) was a trashy return to *giallo* (with a nasty streak).

Dogged by ill health, Fulci made a series of disposable films across several genres (usually ripping off hit films like *Mad Max 2* and *Conan the Barbarian*) before he returned to the zombie genre in 1988. Sadly, *Zombi 3* was hardly a triumphant comeback.

Announced as a sequel to *Zombie Flesh Eaters* (and at one time planned as a 3-D project), *Zombi 3* is dismal on all levels. It has a plot lifted from Bruno Mattei's *Zombie Creeping Flesh* (not to mention *Return of the Living Dead*) and Mattei stepped in to complete the film when Fulci dropped out due to illness. Fellow hack Claudio Fragasso was also involved with the script.

As you might expect, the end results are not good. Terrible dialogue delivered by dreadful

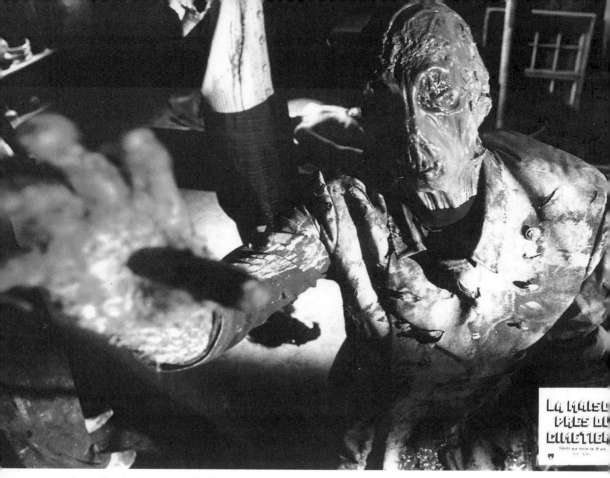

Doctor Freudstein attacks in *The House by the Cemetery*.

actors, clumsy direction (given the quality of Fulci's work at this time, it's hard to blame Mattei for it all), and an all-pervading air of cheapness make this movie a depressing experience all round.

The success of *Zombie Flesh Eaters* inspired other Italian producers to climb on the living-dead bandwagon in a frenzy of plagiarist cannibalism that any zombie would envy. As you might expect from films that are imitations of a rip-off, none of these movies scaled the heights of Fulci's film. Directed by journeymen who had none of the inspiration that had briefly seized Fulci, the spate of zombie films that appeared in 1980–81 all have their moments, and are certainly harmless timewasters – but none has any real value.

The incestuous, cannibalistic nature of the Italian zombie film is probably summed up in *Zombie Holocaust*. Made in 1980, the film – originally titled *Queen of the Cannibals* – shares both producer (Fabrizio De Angelis) and star (Ian McCulloch) with *Zombie Flesh Eaters*, and approximates much the same plot. Also on hand are some cannibals (then just as much in *vogue* with Italians as zombies).

Gory imagery in a Japanese ad for *City of the Living Dead*.

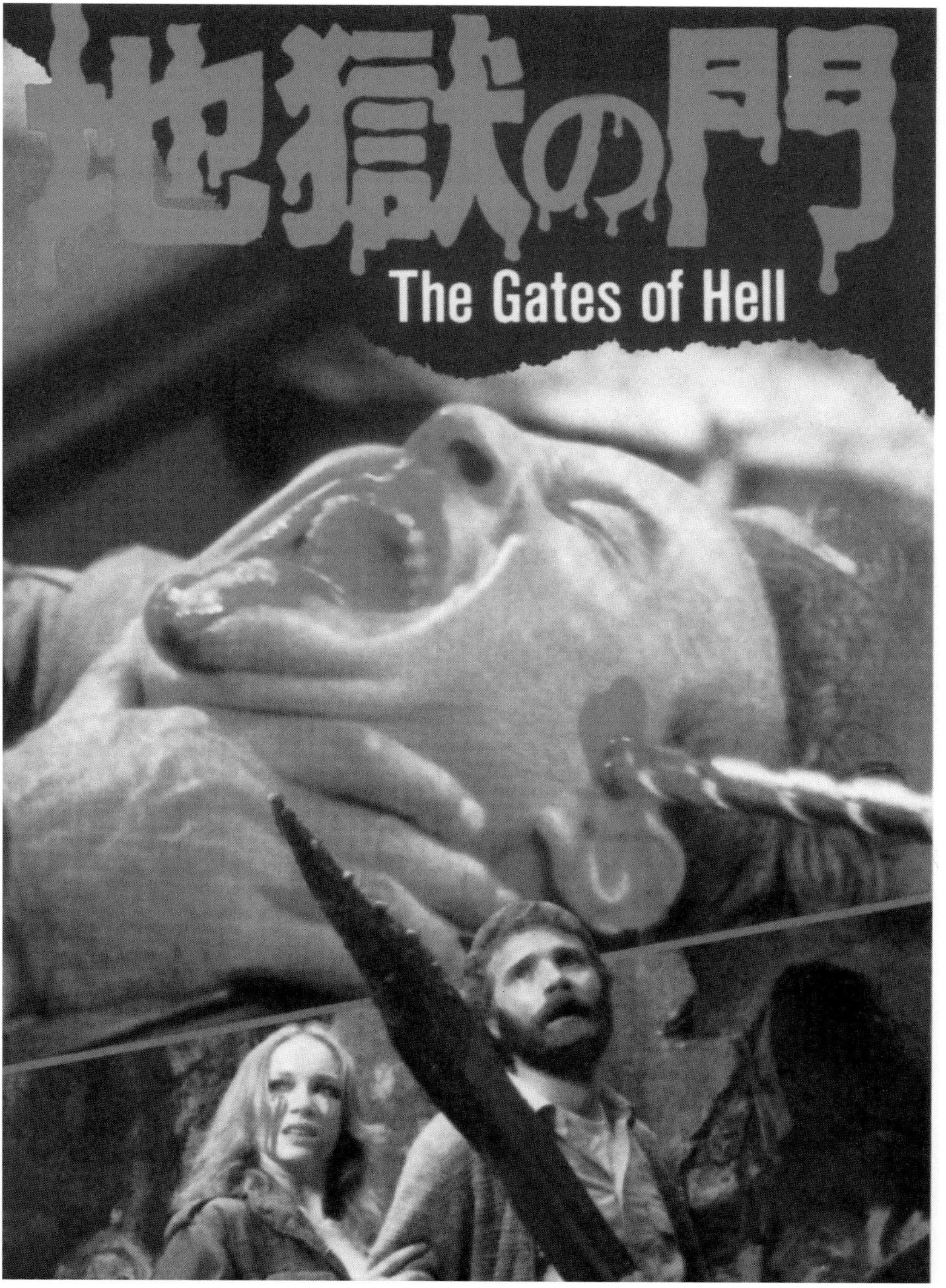
地獄の門
The Gates of Hell

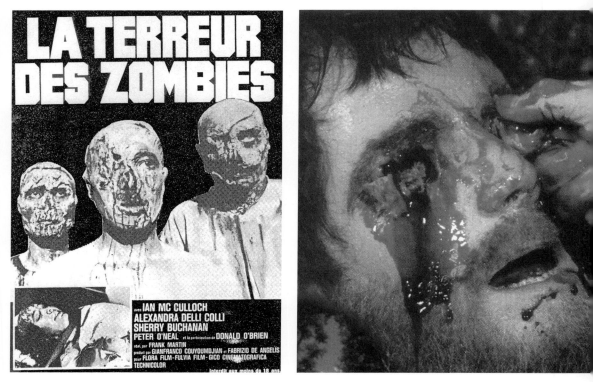

French ad art (left) and gory action from *Zombie Holocaust*.

The title is clearly inspired by the success of *Cannibal Holocaust* a year earlier and the film borrows elements from both genres (notably a cannibal tribe initiation ceremony for Alexandra Delli Colli, which was a copy of a scene featuring Ursula Andress in *Mountain of the Cannibal God* and which would later be referenced with a tribal-painted Margit Evelyn Newton in *Zombie Creeping Flesh*).

The plot sees McCulloch leading a band of explorers who head to a remote island after a spate of corpse mutilations carried out in a New York hospital are linked to a tribe in the area. On the island, they are attacked by cannibals before meeting Doctor Obrero (Donald O'Brien), who has been carrying out bizarre medical experiments on the natives, bringing the dead back to life.

While not exactly a masterpiece, *Zombie Holocaust* is fairly lively, and the mix of cannibals, zombies and mad doctors just about works – at least, the film never becomes dull, and gorehounds will be more than happy with the amount of graphic violence. Director Marino Girolami (under the name 'Frank Martin') does an efficient but uninspired job, while the cast, as is often the case, range from the dull to the demented.

In America, the film was bought by Aquarius Releasing, who proceeded to re-edit it, using footage from unfinished movie *Tales That Will Tear Your Heart Out*. A new soundtrack was added, and the film renamed *Dr. Butcher, Medical Deviate*.

The decayed dead from *Zombie Holocaust*.

A relentless publicity campaign involving a 'butchermobile' cruising the streets of New York managed to drum up more business than the film probably deserved. Sadly, this version seems to no longer be available.

The UK title of Fulci's breakthrough film was presumably the inspiration for the British release title *Zombie Creeping Flesh* (known elsewhere in the world as *Hell of the Living Dead*, or *Virus*, and originally titled *Inferno dei morti viventi*) and, like the new name, the film was a clumsy approximation of *Zombie Flesh Eaters*.

To be fair, the plot does attempt a small amount of originality before simply rehashing what has gone before. This time, the dead have been brought back to life after an accident at a chemical plant in Papua New Guinea (where scientists have been working on a way to solve third world hunger – by making the population eat each other). A female journalist and her TV news crew arrive to investigate the aftermath, only to run into flesh-hungry zombies. They are rescued by an inept SWAT unit who seem to be hot-foot from *Dawn of the Dead*, and the rest of the film follows the usual plot – survivors holing up in an abandoned house, fighting off the zombies while the infection spreads across the world.

Zombie Creeping Flesh is good for a few (unintended) chuckles, and certainly delivers on the gore, but director Bruno Mattei (under the pseudonym 'Vincent Dawn') has no sense of

Two clumsy efforts from Bruno Mattei. UK poster art for *Zombie Creeping Flesh* (left) and promo art for *Zombie 3* (right), started by Lucio Fulci, finished by Mattei and enjoyed by no one.

pacing or drama, and the film is largely unengaging. Goblin's *Dawn of the Dead* score is shamelessly reused here, along with plenty of stock jungle footage, all of which only serves to highlight the lack of originality.

Without doubt, the worst of the Italian zombie films from this period was *Nights of Terror* (a.k.a. *Zombie Horror/Zombie 3/Burial Ground*). This ham-fisted effort from director Andrea Bianchi opens with the dead being revived by a professor studying Etruscan rites, only for them to promptly eat him. Soon afterwards, a band of holidaymakers turn up at his villa for a weekend getaway. Amongst them are Italian sleaze stalwart Maria Angela Giordano and her son, played by Peter Bark.

Bark is, without question, the oddest-looking person ever seen on screen, and to this day people will debate whether he is a weird-looking child or – more likely – a dwarf. Either way, his character is as strange as his appearance, and the scene where he attempts to fondle

Two scenes from *Nights of Terror* – tool-wielding zombies attack (above),
and (below) one of Italian exploitation's most outrageous moments.

his own mother would be enough to make Oedipus queasy.

Not much happens in *Nights of Terror* until the end, when the zombies – who use weapons and are impressively decayed – finally break into the villa and wreak havoc. The survivors flee to another house, but are soon turned to zombie fodder. But all else fades into insignificance compared to the final moments, where Bark – now a zombie – confronts his mother, who promptly offers him her breast to suckle on. Her zombie son immediately sinks his teeth in and tears the breast off, in what has to be one of the most audaciously tasteless moments ever put on film.

Poor taste aside, *Nights of Terror* has little going for it. Bianchi is a terrible director and the film's pacing is leaden. While extremely gory, the death scenes are dragged out to Fulci-like lengths, and the cast – or at least their characters – are unsympathetic to the point of irritation.

The tawdry nature of the whole project can perhaps be summed up by the opening onscreen quote from the 'Profecy [sic] of the Black Spider', which reads: 'The earth shall tremble… graves will open… they shall come among the living as messengers of death and there shall be the nigths [sic] of terror.' With such attention to detail, what hope could there be for the film?

Nights of Terror was pretty much the last gasp of the zombie boom in Italy. Exploitation filmmakers moved on to other subjects and the dead were left to rest in their graves. By the second half of the decade, the Italian trash-movie industry was running out of steam. The glory days were over, and any films that were emerging were usually little more than pale imitations, destined to vanish into straight-to-video obscurity.

1988's *Zombie 4: After Death* was a typical example of these half-baked potboilers. Despite the failure of *Zombi 3* the same year, the writer of that film, Claudio Fragasso, directed this pointless effort, which saw explorers unleashing a zombie plague on a tropical island. In fairness, the film is better than *Zombi 3*, though it would be something of a challenge to make anything worse. And, with bargain-basement production values ensuring that the film looks terrible, it has little going for it. The presence in the cast of gay porn star Jeff Stryker is briefly amusing, but his acting is so wooden that he quickly overstays his welcome.

The same year saw *Killing Birds* (also released as *Zombie 5* – that's three bad non-sequels in twelve months). This bizarre *melange* has a bunch of college kids being attacked by zombies in the swamp, while also encountering a blind Vietnam vet who pops up for no good reason – his eyes having been pecked out by vengeful birds.

It makes little sense, and director Claudio Lattanzi (who was replaced mid-shoot by producer Aristide Massaccesi, a.k.a. Joe D'Amato) fails to inject any sense of horror or tension into proceedings. Former *Man from U.N.C.L.E.* star Robert Vaughn makes a brief, embarrassed appearance.

1994 saw the release of *Dellamorte Dellamore* (a.k.a. *Cemetery Man*) from director Michele Soavi, a filmmaker once hailed as the next great Italian horror maestro, but who had never really lived up to his potential.

Adapted from a graphic novel by Tiziano Sclavi, the film starred Rupert Everett as Francesco Dellamorte, a cemetery worker who routinely has to dispatch the 'returners' who come back from the dead a week after being buried. His zombie-killing life is one of routine and tedium until he falls in love with a recently widowed woman – whose dead husband then returns and catches them making love. She is bitten, and Dellamorte has to kill her, sending him spiralling into insanity.

Dellamorte Dellamore has a lot going for it – it's beautifully shot, and the sardonic humour is pleasingly effective. The film's cynical edge – Dellamorte seems less alive than the 'returners' – also works well. But it seems overly long, even though the running time only clocks in at 105 minutes, and the action sequences are incongruously dull.

While certainly worth seeing, *Dellamorte Dellamore* is more of a heroic failure than an unqualified triumph, and it didn't achieve the commercial success that many predicted. However, many of the themes of banality and avoidance that occupy the early part of the film would emerge in the postmillennial zombie film.

Eerie imagery in Jean Rollin's *The Grapes of Death*.

Outside Italy, it was – perhaps surprisingly – the French who attempted to seize the Euro-zombie mantle during the 1980s. Sadly, few of these French zombie films are of any value.

Jean Rollin rose to prominence at the beginning of the 1970s with a series of beautiful, slow and incoherent vampire movies that mixed lightweight eroticism with atmospheric horror. Although his work rarely had any impact outside France, he steadily built a reputation as an original voice in the sub-genre. But, like many other exploitation filmmakers in France, he found himself shooting hardcore by the mid-1970s, as the domestic market for anything but porn virtually collapsed. Subsequent government censorship killed off this porno boom, and by the end of the decade, he was back making horror movies. However, the stylish nature of his initial films was a thing of the past.

In 1978, Rollin made *Les Raisins de la Mort* (also known as *Pesticide* and internationally as *The Grapes of Death*). Somewhat inspired by *The Living Dead at Manchester Morgue* (and originally planned as a disaster movie before being reinvented as a zombie feature), the film sees villagers turned into zombies after wine is tainted with pesticide. Marie Georges Pascal plays the unfortunate young traveller who runs the gauntlet of the walking dead (who retain some intelligence and employ weaponry).

Rollin ladles on the gore, but his continued use of the slow pacing that made his vampire films so intriguing works against him. Although the director moves from incident to incident fairly quickly, his action scenes are unimpressive and, though it looks good, the movie fails to engage the viewer. That said, the film does have its admirers who perceive elements of style and quality that most viewers will be at a loss to appreciate.

Conversely, *Zombie Lake* has few fans. This sluggish story of Nazi zombies returning from

the dead to seek revenge after being killed by the resistance during the Second World War has little to recommend it.

Rollin directs at a snail's pace, and the only saving grace is the sheer volume of entirely gratuitous nudity, which served to make the film enticing for viewers too nervous to buy or rent soft-porn, but which hardly enhances the horror. Some prints don't even have this – alternative clothed scenes were shot for less liberal markets, and it was this version that was first unleashed on aghast British video viewers in the early Eighties, denying them even anything in the way of prurient thrills to relieve the boredom.

Rollin's Nazi zombies have poorly applied green make-up and do very little. The movie is hardly enlivened by a sub-plot in which a little girl encounters her undead father, who then becomes a 'heroic' zombie (the undead equivalent perhaps of the clichéd 'heroic Nazi' from so many exploitation films).

It might be unfair to hold Rollin responsible for many of these flaws. Originally planned as a Jesus Franco movie, the maverick director failed to show up to the set, and producers Eurocine drafted Rollin in as a last-minute replacement. He had no time to even read the script, let alone make any changes. The director subsequently disowned the resulting mess.

Franco did turn up for another Eurocine Nazi zombie film, 1982's *Oasis of the Zombies*, but failed to make any qualitative difference to this dull effort. This time, the zombie hordes are out in the desert, where they attack a bunch of treasure hunters searching for that ever-elusive Nazi gold. Lacking even gratuitous nudity to liven things up, the film is instantly forgettable, and certainly one of Franco's worst.

Rollin took another stab at the sub-genre in 1982, and this time he got everything right. *The Living Dead Girl* recaptured the poetic beauty of his earlier vampire films, whilst delivering some intensely gory horror scenes.

A typically dull Euro Nazi Zombie effort,
this time from Jesus Franco (above) and (below) Redemption's
video sleeve of Jean Rollin's downbeat classic.

Sex and violence combine in *The Living Dead Girl*.

A toxic-waste spill near a château brings Catherine (Francoise Blanchard) back from the dead with an appetite for human flesh. She snacks on some passing tourists, before her friend Helene (Marina Pierro) discovers her. Helene helps Catherine to find victims, while at the same time trying to bring her back into a state of self-awareness. But, as she does so, Catherine becomes dismayed at her condition, and insists on being put out of her misery. Helene refuses to kill her, setting the scene for the final tragic – and impressively low-key – finale which, despite its subtlety, is packed with death, angst and emotional impact.

The Living Dead Girl moves slowly, but is never less than engrossing, thanks primarily to the two leading women. While Rollin piles on the gore and nudity, the heart of the film is a haunting treatise on madness, love and obsession. Brian Yuzna would later use the theme of a zombie who is repulsed by her needs more effectively in *Return of the Living Dead 3*, but Rollin's film has an undeniable atmosphere that marks it as one of his finest works.

European exploitation cinema has always mixed sex and violence. Not necessarily in the same movies, but the gore and titillation often went hand in hand. Many of the biggest names in Euro-trash cinema happily crossed genres, making horror movies and soft and hardcore porn. So it's unsurprising that there are a handful of zombie sex films.

1987's *Revenge of the Living Dead* (a.k.a. *Revenge of the Living Dead Girls*) is a heady Gallic mix of soft-porn, hard gore and incompetence. After a town's milk supply is contaminated with toxic chemicals, three girls die, only to rise from the dead as bloodthirsty, sex-hungry

Zombies go hardcore in Joe D'Amato's *Erotic Nights of the Living Dead* (left) and *Porno Holocaust* (right).

zombies. That's pretty much it for plot. The remainder of the film is a series of graphic scenes with the undead girls (who have rotting faces and hands but perfect bodies) having sexual encounters that usually end in extreme violence.

The film revels in bad taste – there are graphic scenes of genital mutilation, a pregnant woman's stomach bursts open, and the mix of horror and eroticism will make many viewers uneasy. The unsatisfying ending (missing from some versions) explains events in a way that makes a nonsense of everything that has gone before. The acting is terrible and, although porn director Pierre B. Reinhard keeps things going at a fair pace, the film looks ugly. Viewers looking for a gross-out experience might well find this fits the bill, but many will simply be repulsed.

Joe D'Amato had directed the *Black Emanuelle* films during the 1970s and also helmed several horror movies such as *Death Smiles on a Murderer* and *Beyond The Darkness*, so it was almost inevitable that he'd mix the two genres. D'Amato's *Emanuelle* movies became increasingly dark and violent, and two of them – *Emanuelle In America* and *Emanuelle and the Last Cannibals* – took the series into horror territory (*Emanuelle In America* has some of the most disturbing imagery ever captured on celluloid, featuring distressingly realistic – but thankfully staged – 'snuff' footage).

By the end of the decade, he was dabbling with hardcore porn, and so it's perhaps unsurprising that his two 1980 zombie movies combine explicit sex and graphic gore.

Neither film is much good but, of the two, *Erotic Nights of the Living Dead* is the better, having at least the semblance of a plot. D'Amato regular George Eastman stars as a sailor who takes a businessman and his girlfriend to a remote island, where they meet Laura Gemser and are besieged by zombies.

Not much happens to fill out a running time of close to two hours. There are gory moments, and a handful of hardcore sex scenes (in the rarely seen uncut version; most prints have these severely truncated, and there also exists an edit that plays as a straight horror movie with no sex) but precious little plot to speak of.

The fact that neither Gemser nor Eastman were prepared to 'do' hardcore gives the film a bizarre quality, as it leaps from real sex to simulated lovemaking, but the movie is a pretty feeble effort. D'Amato was not quite the porn *auteur* he seemed to think he was (as anyone who sat through his late-1990s hardcore output could attest), and his horror movies were rarely more than tedious, so it's no surprise that his experiments in genre splicing would fail.

Still, the film is a classic when compared to *Porno Holocaust*. The best – in fact, only decent – thing about this movie is the audacious title. The rest is a mix of poor direction, grim porn and feeble horror. The film shares much the same cast as *Erotic Nights...* (and, again, Eastman avoids the explicit stuff, as do several other cast members).

The story revolves around a well-endowed zombie who (eventually) rampages across a Caribbean island, killing and raping. The horror is kept to the minimum, and D'Amato's sex scenes are shot in an ugly, ham-fisted way, rendering them entirely unerotic. Neither sexy nor scary, the film ends up as a squalid, seedy, often boring and somewhat tasteless mess.

D'Amato is often credited with *Erotic Orgasm* (1982), though the film was officially directed by Mario Siciliano – the confusion arising from the similarity in style and cast between this and D'Amato's porn work. Pretty much dispensing with horror altogether, the film has zombie sex slaves resurrected by a witch, resulting in wall-to-wall hardcore sex. It's a feeble effort that surely proves that sex and zombies just don't mix – though filmmakers would continue to try to blend the two.

The glory days of the European zombie film – in fact, the European exploitation film in general – are long gone. Euro-zombies these days are confined to the dismal shot-on-video work of clumsy (mostly German) filmmakers like Olaf Ittenbach (*Legion of the Dead*), Patrick Hollman (*Urban Scumbags vs. Countryside Zombies*) and Andreas Schnaas (*Zombie 90: Extreme Pestilence*).

It's unlikely that the current revival of interest in the living dead will be reflected in European cinema. A pity, as the best Euro-zombies not only expanded the horizons of the form, but also offered a deliriously unique take on their subject matter that was unlike anything coming out of America.

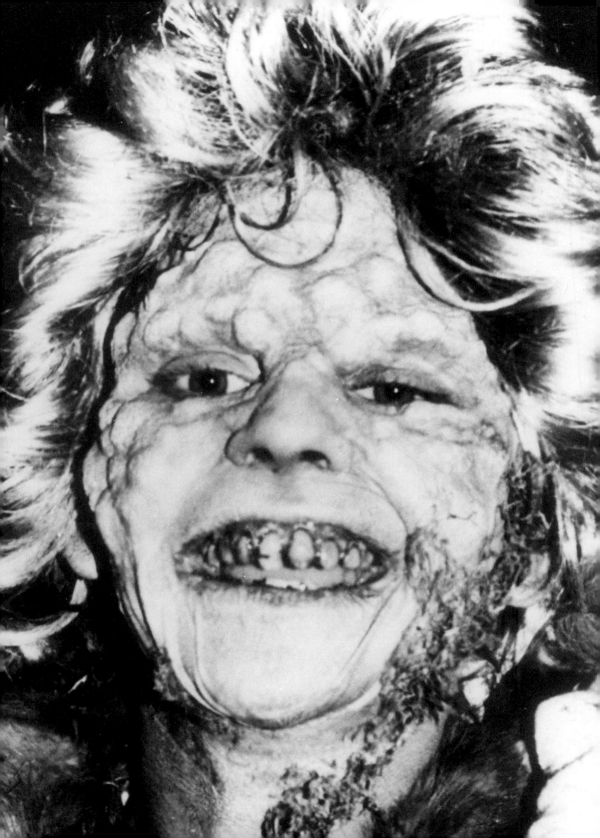

7. 'Brraaaiinns!'

The American Zombie Resurrection
and the Global Gorehound Cottage Industry

In the wake of *Night of the Living Dead's* success, Romero's film inspired several imitations, the first of which was the 1971 production *Children Shouldn't Play with Dead Things*.

The film was the direct result of aspiring filmmakers Bob Clark and Alan Ormsby noticing how successful Romero's low-budget movie had been. They realised that a horror movie could be made for very little money and still be a success and that, in many ways, the lack of studio gloss is what made horror films like *Night of the Living Dead* so effective.

At the time, Ormsby was an artist turned actor and make-up effects enthusiast who had shot a few home movies, while Clark was a playwright and filmmaker who had made a couple of very obscure feature films (*The Emperor's New Clothes* in 1966 and *She-Man* in 1967).

The duo met at the University of Miami where they began writing, directing and acting in each other's plays. A few years after graduation (with Ormsby developing into a serious playwright who saw several works produced), their paths crossed again. Revealing that he had raised a tiny budget to shoot a horror film, Clark invited Ormsby to help him complete the screenplay and take the lead role. Something of a polymath, Ormsby would also provide the make-up effects for the decaying zombies.

While *Night of the Living Dead* was presented via a straight-faced, almost documentary-style production, Clark and Ormsby's screenplay for *Children Shouldn't Play with Dead Things* aimed for as many laughs as screams. Ormsby sent himself up as the egocentric leader of an acting troupe who accidentally revives the dead after playing some remarkably tasteless pranks involving a corpse called Orville (including a gay, necrophile wedding).

Despite this – and the subsequent, genuinely scary zombie attack scenes – the MPAA in America gave the film a PG rating, clearly paying little attention to the criticism of the equally lenient certificate granted to Romero's film three years before.

Shot on 35mm for less than $100,000, the film looked cheap but was reasonably effective and, helped by the wonderful title and a tongue-in-cheek trailer, it became a moderate success at drive-ins and fleapits around the world.

On its initial release, the movie was given an extra promotional push by means of utilising the old exploitation standby gimmick – the 'free insurance policy'. However, as this policy only offered that 'your funeral expenses will be paid in full' if you were unfortunate enough to be 'attacked by a ghoul cannibal' during the showing, it's unlikely that the distributors had much cause to pay out.

While some critics and fans hailed the film as a low-budget masterpiece, others found that the mix of comedy and horror simply doesn't work. In particular, Ormsby's wildly over-the-top performance as the arrogant and foolishly dressed director has a polarising effect on viewers.

Zombies go mainstream – *Return of the Living Dead II*.

YOU'RE INVITED TO ORVILLE'S "COMING-OUT" PARTY...

It'll Be A Scream... YOURS!!

CHILDREN SHOULDN'T PLAY WITH DEAD THINGS!

A BENJAMIN CLARK FILM **PG**

RELEASED THRU GENENI FILM DISTRIBUTING CO COLOR

However, it is the lack of pacing and action that finally undermines the film, which has neither the characterisation nor the story structure to sustain over an hour of not very much happening.

Nevertheless, *Children Shouldn't Play with Dead Things* became something of a cult movie, particularly in the UK during the early days of video, when it was a much sought-after title amongst fans who had previously only been able to read about the film.

Clark and Ormsby returned to the living dead in 1974 with *Dead of Night* (a.k.a. *Deathdream*), though the film couldn't have been more different from its predecessor. In place of the black humour came a bleak retelling of *The Monkey's Paw*, informed by the war in Vietnam.

When her son is killed fighting the Viet Cong, a distraught mother (Lynn Carlin) wishes him home. That night, Andy turns up at the family residence, and his relieved relatives assume that the notification of his death was a terrible mistake. But Andy is no longer the boy he was. He's withdrawn, sullen and solitary, refusing to see his friends and prone to acts of violence. Eventually, it becomes clear that he is, in fact, dead.

Dead of Night is a potent allegory for the traumas of Vietnam. Andy's change of personality might be down to his zombie status, but his behaviour is not that far removed from the post-traumatic symptoms exhibited by many combat veterans. Clark and Ormsby are saying that war dehumanises — in this case, literally.

Bob Clark and Alan Ormsby kick-started their careers with this low-budget *Night of the Living Dead* spoof.

A subtle, understated film, *Dead of Night* includes a suitably grim finale, with Andy visiting the cemetery, where he digs his own grave – this is one zombie who is only too aware of his condition, and hates it. It's an unusual climax to a horror film, but one that fits perfectly with the thoughtfully sobering saga that has preceded it.

Of course, not all American zombie films in the 1970s were as intelligent as *Dead of Night*. There was plenty of schlock, exploitation and trash – some of it great, some of it awful and much of it distinctly average.

1974's *Sugar Hill* was the first blaxploitation zombie film, in the tradition of such movies as *Blacula*, *Blackenstein* and *Dr. Black & Mr Hyde*. In this instance, the blaxploitation motif at least has the historical associations of voodoo to underpin its basic premise, and this is a decent – if unremarkable – effort.

Zombies meet blaxploitation in the surprisingly decent *Sugar Hill*.

When Sugar's fiancé is murdered by gangland thugs who want his business, she goes back to her voodoo roots and calls on Baron Samedi to help her seek revenge. Up pop a bunch of zombies to kill off the bad guys in a variety of inventive ways.

Marki Bey is arresting as the titular character, transforming from victim to merciless killer with ease, and, with the likes of TV and horror veteran Robert Quarry in the supporting cast, *Sugar Hill* is one of the better black horror films of the 1970s. Curiously for the genre, it keeps its thrills strictly within PG parameters. For Paul Maslansky – better known as the producer of horror classics like *Death Line* and *Revenge of the Blood Beast*, and later responsible for the *Police Academy* series – this was to be his only shot at directing.

From Canada came the obscure *The Corpse Eaters*, made in 1973 by Drive-In theatre owner Lawrence Zazelenchuk on a budget of just $36,000. Directed by Klaus Vetter (after original director Donald Passmore was fired after just four days for reasons that remain undisclosed), the film was held up for a year awaiting money for processing, but eventually played in Zazelenchuk's 69 Drive-In before vanishing into obscurity.

The plot concerns a bunch of thrill-seekers who visit a local graveyard to have sex and summon up the devil. What they get are zombies, who attack them, follow them to the local hospital and invade a funeral home.

LET'S PLAY HIDE AND GO KILL. . .!

HARRY NOVAK presents

THE CHILD

The creepy Harry Novak production, also known as *Zombie Child*.

Despite the gore, nudity and brief running time (the film clocks in at under an hour), *The Corpse Eaters* still manages to be a struggle to sit through, thanks to the pitiful production values, shoddy performances and poor story. Sadly, films like this would become the norm for the genre throughout the 1990s.

In *Garden of the Dead* (1974), a group of chain-gang convicts opt to escape from grim reality by getting high on formaldehyde fumes. When they are killed during an escape attempt, they wind up buried in formaldehyde-filled graves (only in the movies), and are soon up and about again, wreaking bloody but boring vengeance on the prison guards.

Zombies came to the small screen in the 1974 television movie *The Dead Don't Die*, directed by Curtis Harrington and adapted from a novella by *Psycho* screenwriter Robert Bloch. Like most TV productions of the time, it was hampered by a low budget and the content restrictions of US networks, but nevertheless managed to be one of the more effective made-for-television movies.

Set in the 1930s, it stars former Hollywood heartthrob George Hamilton as Don Drake – a man trying to clear his brother's name after he had been sentenced to death for murder. Drake soon finds his own life is in danger because he is close to discovering the plans of Varrick (Ray Milland), a so-called 'Zombie Master'.

While not as good as the story it is based on, *The Dead Don't Die* is still an entertaining tale – though it's now a difficult movie to track down.

The Child (a.k.a. *Zombie Child*) was produced in 1977 by exploitation legend Harry Novak's Crown International, and is a low-key but effective shocker about a young girl (Rosalie Cole) who has the power to raise the dead. At first, the ambulant undead simply provide her with playmates, but she quickly realises that she can use them against anyone who crosses her – including her guardian Laurel Barnett. Director Robert Voskanian does a solid job of building tension and the climactic zombie attacks are surprisingly scary, with suitably gruesome ghouls seeking to chow down on their quarry.

Nazi zombies made an early appearance in 1977's *Shock Waves*, where a group of shipwreck survivors (including TV character actress Brooke Adams) find themselves trapped on a mysterious island, where they encounter a former SS officer (Peter Cushing in a rare non-British film appearance). Cushing is the only survivor of an earlier wreck involving a Second World War U-Boat that was populated by super-soldiers – undead warriors who can survive on land or undersea. Soon, the Death Corps are on the march, attacking the stranded yachting party.

With genuinely eerie underwater scenes and some of the creepiest zombies ever seen on film (the make-up department doing a good job of making the zombies appear not only decayed but also water damaged with pale, wrinkled skin), *Shock Waves* is a surprisingly good horror movie. Cushing lends a certain *gravitas* to proceedings, as does John Carradine, making

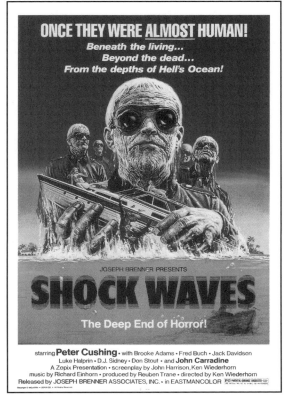

The first – and best – Nazi zombie film, 1977's *Shock Waves*.

another of his myriad cameos. Director Ken Wiederhorn does a good job with limited resources – and the end results are far superior to his next zombie movie, *Return of the Living Dead II*.

Exploitation director Fred Olen Ray began his long career in low-budget trash with *The Alien Dead* in 1980. After a meteor strikes a houseboat, the residents become zombies who feed on the alligators in the swamp before moving on to humans. It's pretty bad, with production values viewers would later become familiar with from the slew of amateur video productions during the 1990s – which this was very much a precursor to – and lacks even the sense of camp humour that made Olen Ray's later work palatable.

Heavy Metal (1981) was an ambitious adult animated film, based on the comic book of the same name that adapted French fantasy magazine *Métal Hurlant* for the US market. Containing six stories – some based on comic strips, others original works – the movie blended science fiction, action, fantasy, sex and horror in a variety of styles, the result of different animation crews working on each story. Inevitably, the resulting film is uneven, but never less than fascinating, and has developed quite a cult following.

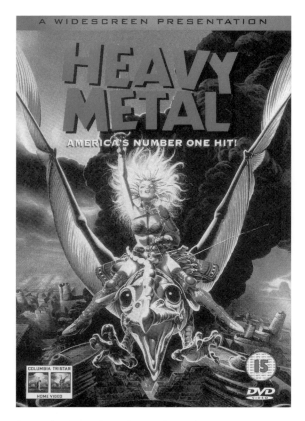

A WIDESCREEN PRESENTATION

HEAVY METAL

AMERICA'S NUMBER ONE HIT!

COLUMBIA TRISTAR
HOME VIDEO

Animated anthology *Heavy Metal* added zombie soldiers to its mix of sex and violence.

One story, 'B-17', has a Second World War bomber that has been badly damaged during a battle and is now limping home. When the plane is hit by the Loc-Nar – a green orb that acts as the film's omnipotent linking device – its dead airmen are revived as cannibalistic zombies. The surviving pilot manages to hold them off, only to land on an island populated largely by the walking dead. Written by Dan O'Bannon, the sequence is amongst the best in the film, with dark, creepy animation that was unlike anything seen before.

The Nazi zombies were back in 1981, with Joel M. Reed's *Night of the Zombies*. Unfortunately, this film makes even the weakest European efforts in the sub-genre seem accomplished. The plot has CIA investigator Jamie Gillis looking into reports that German soldiers from the Second World War are still alive. It turns out that an experimental gas ('Gamma 693') has turned them – and American soldiers – into zombies who need a regular fix of both the gas and human flesh to stay 'alive'.

With rock-bottom production values and a nonsensical plot (sometimes the zombies seem mindless, other times they actually have conversations), this film is one of the most pitiful in the genre. Reed's previous film, the notorious *Bloodsucking Freaks*, may have been highly offensive, but it at least had some verve. This is simply flaccid. *Night of the Zombies* was subsequently released under a plethora of alternate titles – *The Chilling, Night of the Zombies 2, Gamma* – so beware.

1981 production *Raw Force* is unquestionably one of the strangest zombie films ever made, and no one could accuse writer/director Edward D. Murphy of not delivering the goods. Here is a film that mixes genres with gleeful abandon, roping in zombies, cannibal monks, white slavers, martial arts, tits'n'ass comedy and more, and ensuring that, no matter how trashy the film is, it never becomes dull.

The tale begins on Warriors Island, where evil monks can hardly contain their excitement as they buy white slaves from a local crime lord (who looks like a chubby Hitler). A cruise ship is planning a visit to the island, and the villainous slaver is determined to stop it. On board the ship are a group of martial-arts experts and plenty of girls who can't keep their clothes on (including Camille Keaton of *I Spit on Your Grave* fame and scream queen Jewel Shepard). Despite the efforts of the slaver, they make landfall, whereupon they are attacked by hordes of blue-faced zombies.

A real mess of a story, *Raw Force* is nonetheless classic exploitation cinema, with entirely gratuitous nudity, sloppy gore, camp kung-fu battles and trash movie icon Cameron Mitchell. It's hardly a quality film, but it is a lot of fun. The promised sequel (the film ends with 'to be continued') has sadly yet to appear.

1981's biggest budget zombie film was *Dead & Buried*. Written by Dan O'Bannon, fresh from the success of *Alien*, and directed by *Death Line*'s Gary Sherman, the film had plenty going for it, but the production was a troubled one.

Dead & Buried started out as a black comedy, but, when the original production company was sold, the new owners wanted to remove much of the humour. Then a second sale took place, this time to people who insisted on an even more serious, gore-filled horror movie. Unfortunately, the distributors preferred the earlier versions, and an excess of editing ensued, resulting in a compromised version that seemed to satisfy no one.

But these issues aside, *Dead & Buried* remains a fascinating film, with plenty of twists and turns. The action takes place in

More Nazi zombies in Joel Reed's dismal *Night of the Zombies* (above); martial arts, sexploitation, cannibal monks and zombies combine in the astonishing *Raw Force* (below).

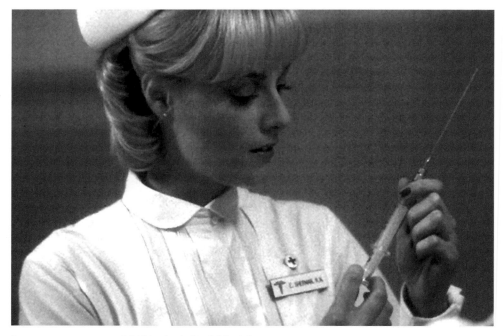

A nurse prepares a very painful injection in *Dead & Buried*.

the small town of Potter's Bluff, where a series of mysterious and gruesome murders are taking place, as mobs of locals attack visitors. Sheriff Dan Gillis (James Farentino) is unable to work out what is going on, but slowly begins to realise that town mortician Dobbs (Jack Albertson) is somehow involved. It transpires that Dobbs is reviving the dead – and that most of the locals are zombies.

Dead & Buried looks incredible – Sherman's decision to remove the colour red from the film (except in the gory bits, of course) pays off, as the film has a pale, otherworldly feel to it, and Sherman's direction is assured. The movie failed to find an audience on its original release (though Chelsea Quinn Yarbro's novelisation took on a life of its own, and proved a big hit in the UK), but is now something of a cult favourite.

Without doubt, the seminal zombie film of the 1980s was Sam Raimi's breathless *The Evil Dead* (1981). This low-budget shocker has become every bit as influential as *Night of the Living Dead* before it, particularly in the UK – where it became a massive hit, thanks to a simultaneous video and cinema release and sharp marketing from Palace Video.

The Evil Dead scores few points for plot originality – five students head into the woods for a weekend away in a run-down old cabin. Once there, they find an old tape recording of a professor reciting a demonic ritual. This unleashes the forces of evil, which set about possessing

The classic original promo art for Palace Video's release of *The Evil Dead*.

The possessed dead taunt Ash in *The Evil Dead*.

the students one by one. Soon, only Ash (Bruce Campbell) is left, facing an all-out assault by his former friends, who can only be stopped by 'the act of bodily dismemberment'.

Raimi skilfully mixes shocks with laughs in this remarkably gory film, playing up the absurdity of the situation. Campbell makes a suitably hapless hero, constantly under attack by the giggling dead, and he perfectly conveys the terror and paranoia of the character. The visuals are amazing; the camera swoops, glides and rushes though the woods while several surreal moments – Campbell putting his hand through a mirror – add to the overall sense of unhinged insanity.

Of course, the meagre budget shows. Several cast members left the project before it was completed (replaced by what Raimi called 'fake Shemps' – a Three Stooges reference), while Hal Delrich's (initially played by Richard DeManincor) hair changes length from scene to scene. But these flaws hardly register, thanks to Raimi's relentless approach.

At the time of release, *The Evil Dead* caused plenty of controversy. Issued in the UK with several cuts, the film nevertheless became a target during the 'Video Nasty' moral panic, and was hauled through the UK courts over sixty times – almost always being acquitted of obscenity charges.

Two promotional images – neither of which appears in the film – for *The Evil Dead*.

In the US, it struggled to find a distributor, and was eventually released unrated – in 1994, the MPAA rated it NC-17. It wasn't just the gore that upset critics – the early scene where Ash's sister (Ellen Sandweiss) is raped by demonic trees was widely condemned for its graphic nature. But the critics missed the point. All the blood and gore in *The Evil Dead* is so wildly excessive as to become comical (and notably, it was the less gory, but more realistic scenes of violence that the British censors cut) – it's closer to *Monty Python* than George Romero.

Despite the censorship hassles, *The Evil Dead* became a worldwide hit. In the UK, it was the top-selling video of 1983. Such success meant a sequel was inevitable.

Evil Dead II was financed by legendary producer Dino De Laurentiis, and, although the budget was low by most standards ($3.6 million), it was considerably more than the original film. However, Raimi was assigned to deliver an R-rated movie. He tried (and failed) to do this by toning down the gore – blood still gushes but, in this film, it's rarely bright red, instead being dark red, black or even green – the idea being that 'slime's no crime'.

The film starts with a mini-remake of the first film (the original footage not being available for legal reasons) before continuing from the moment *The Evil Dead* ended. *II* continues at a

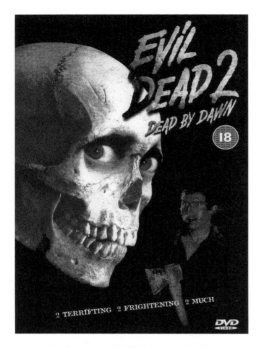

EVIL DEAD 2
DEAD BY DAWN
18

2 TERRIFYING 2 FRIGHTENING 2 MUCH

DVD

breakneck pace throughout. Bruce Campbell carries much of the movie alone, and Ash transforms from a hapless fool into a strange new breed of action hero (this despite a missing hand, having been forced to amputate his possessed limb and replace it with a chainsaw), complete with the requisite sardonic one-liners.

Although technically superior to the first film, *Evil Dead II* has less impact. Its animatronic demons, the lack of gore and an over-reliance on knowing irony tend to make this a less than satisfactory experience, at least for those who had grown up with the first film.

There are, however, a few people – usually those who saw *Evil Dead II* before the original and have a *penchant* for late-Eighties horror – who express a preference for the second film, being less enamoured with the low-budget, visceral approach of the original.

Evil Dead II works particularly well during the final moments, where Ash is swept into a time vortex and ends up in the past, caught in a war between humans and the dead. This *denouement* suggested great things for any third film in the series. However, it would be six years before the franchise was extended, and it would prove to be *very* different to its predecessors.

Army of Darkness starts where *Evil Dead II* finishes, with Ash in a medieval era, and follows his adventures as he convinces the knights who have captured him that he is on their side against the zomboid hordes ('Deadites'). Ash joins the knights in battle, while trying to find the *Necronomicon* – which is the key to returning him home.

Evil Dead II was a slicker, more mainstream and less visceral retread of the first film.

While it's a decent film in its own right, *Army of Darkness* is hardly a horror movie. Instead, it's more of an action-adventure flick, closer in spirit to Ray Harryhausen or the later *Lord of the Rings* movies than the original *Evil Dead*. Co-financers Universal insisted on a PG-13 rating. The film eventually wound up R-rated, causing Raimi to cut back from even the minimal blood-letting found in *Evil Dead II*. His original ending – with Ash finding himself in a post-apocalyptic future – was also rejected, and a new, happier ending shot instead.

One Dark Night (a.k.a. *Entity Force*) was released in 1983, and, despite some positive press coverage, rapidly sank into obscurity. A pity, as this old-fashioned movie has a lot going for it.

When Julie Wells (Meg Tilly) spends the night in an old mausoleum as part of a sorority initiation, her 'friends' plan to scare her with fake ghosts. But unfortunately for them, mass-murdering occultist Raymar has been buried there, and isn't quite dead. Using his psychic powers, he resurrects the dead to terrorise the girls.

Director Tom McLoughlin creates a decently creepy atmosphere and the finale is certainly spectacular (though clearly influenced by *The Evil Dead*) as the corpses sparkle with electricity and crumble away.

More wild effects in *Army of Darkness*.

NIGHT OF THE COMET

It was the last thing on earth they ever expected. 15

The teen movie meets the undead in cult favourite *Night of the Comet*.

Hard Rock Zombies was the first – but not the last – movie to mix zombies with heavy metal – though the 'hard rock' here is strictly of the insipid mid-1980s variety, so only hair metal heads are likely to find anything worthwhile here. Krishna Shah's film has a murdered rock band rising from the dead, alongside Adolf Hitler. Neither funny nor scary, this is to be avoided.

1984's *Night of the Comet* was a prime example of Eighties mainstream horror – slick, self-referential, with an awful overblown rock soundtrack, big hair and bad clothes – and unlikely to offend or challenge anyone. It's a typical PG-13 teen horror movie, with little gore, no sex and lightweight bad language. Bear all that in mind, and the film is pretty entertaining.

When a passing comet wipes out most of the human race, teenage sisters Regina (Catherine Mary Stewart) and Samantha (Kelli Maroney) are left to fend for themselves in a world where the only other survivors appear to be mutated zombies. While hiding out in the local radio station, the girls run into fellow survivor Hector (Robert Beltran) and then make contact with a group of scientists (including cult favourite Mary Woronov) who are working on a cure for the infection. The only problem is, the cure involves draining the survivors of their blood.

There's little in the film to enthrall the hardened zombie fan – in fact, the zombies only make a few brief and generally ineffectual appearances, and seem to have most of their faculties intact. But the film works well as a post-apocalyptic romp and the two female leads are appealingly fun. It's hardly the seminal 1980s horror classic that some fans have suggested but, taken on its own merits, is surprisingly cohesive, and despite being *very* much of its era, has stood the test of time a lot better than many contemporaries.

Interestingly, while the scenes set in a huge department store reflect *Dawn of the Dead* (with characters even referencing the fact that such places are shrines to consumerism), those in the science compound can be read as a precursor to the following year's *Day of the Dead* – and the idea of hiding out in a radio station would crop up again in the 2008 *Day...* remake.

The dead rise in *Return of the Living Dead II.*

1985 saw the release of an alternative sequel to *Night of the Living Dead,* which itself would generate its own franchise.

In the mid-1970s, a legal dispute between George Romero and *NOTLD* screenwriter John Russo ended with an agreement that Russo could use the 'Living Dead' name on future projects, while Romero would simply use 'Dead' for his. As Romero began work on *Dawn of the Dead,* Russo quickly churned out a terrible novel entitled *Return of the Living Dead,* which rehashed *NOTLD* to no great effect. After *Dawn of the Dead* was a hit, the film rights to *Return of the Living Dead* were sold to producer Tom Fox in 1979.

Russo had initially planned to write and even direct *Return...,* but that idea was quickly quashed – a relief to anyone who had seen his films *Midnight* and *One by One.* The project knocked around Hollywood for a few years before Tobe Hooper agreed to direct the film from a screenplay by Dan O'Bannon. Originally planned to be shot in 3-D (during the format's brief revival in 1982), both the third dimension and Hooper were dropped, with O'Bannon promoted to director.

Although Romero and his producer Richard Rubenstein expressed disquiet about the project and made vague murmurings about legal proceedings, telling *Fangoria,* 'Our... concerns are that

no one does anything to imply that something comes from George when it doesn't… we're concerned about anything that might reflect wrongly on George's reputation.' *Return of the Living Dead* could hardly be more different from *Dawn of the Dead*.

The film opens with James Karen and Thom Matthews playing two medical-supply warehousemen, discussing *NOTLD* – a neat way of tying the film to the original while setting it up as a separate entity. Karen explains that the events shown in the film 'really' happened, and occurred when a gas called Trioxin was released into the atmosphere, reanimating the dead.

A few of the bodies that piled up during this outbreak are being held in barrels at a morgue, but, when one leaks, the gas escapes and the dead once again start to revive. Meanwhile, a group of teens are partying in the cemetery and soon find themselves under attack from the newly reborn cadavers.

Return of the Living Dead deliberately plays with the rules set out in Romero's films. When they first encounter the zombies, funeral-home workers Clu Gulager, James Karen and Thom Matthews agree that a bullet or blow to the head will kill them, only to find that it has no effect. The zombies move quickly, and retain the power of speech, allowing them to articulate their sole desire – 'Brains!' (In another departure from Romero's template, these ghouls only eat the brains of their victims.)

These changes to zombie lore were significant: ask the average person about zombies now, and they'll tell you that the living dead hunger for brains – a direct result of this film.

A slick comedy horror, *Return of the Living Dead* split genre fans – many loved it, while others were annoyed with the use of 'splatshtick' humour that had become increasingly prevalent within zombie movies (then, as now, hardcore horror fans decried the commercialisation of the genre; ironically many of the films, like this one, which were condemned at the time are now seen as classics by fans who hate the new breed of visceral horror such as *Saw* and *Hostel*). But the general public loved the film, making it a huge hit at the same time that they were staying away from *Day of the Dead*.

Original poster art for *Return of the Living Dead* (opposite) and (above) an unusual German variant.

Brian Yuzna's excellent *Return of the Living Dead III*. The famous body-piercing zombie played by Melinda Clarke (left); even removing the head didn't kill the zombies in this film.

Certainly, it's no masterpiece, but *Return of the Living Dead* is tremendous fun. It moves at a fast pace and has a genuinely anarchic, rock'n'roll vibe (with a soundtrack to match from bands including the Cramps, the Damned, hardcore combo T.S.O.L. and former 13th Floor Elevator, Roky Erickson). The gore is plentiful, the humour mostly successful and the moments of bad taste pack a punch. The film launched the horror career of Linnea Quigley (who has a memorable striptease scene), and – sadly – paved the way for a deluge of dumb horror movies that failed to match the quality of this one.

One such picture was *Return of the Living Dead Part II*, written and directed by Ken Wiederhorn, who had earlier impressed with *Shock Waves*. This 1988 sequel rehashes the first film with considerably less success – James Karen and Thom Matthews are wheeled out again, despite being zombified in the first film (they play different characters here).

A third instalment appeared in 1993, though it couldn't have been more different. In the 1990s, producers realised that there was a ready-made market for horror franchises – a movie was seemingly guaranteed an audience if it had a familiar name. It didn't matter very much if the actual film bore any connection to its predecessors.

So, when *Society* director Brian Yuzna was handed the next *Return of the Living Dead* film, he was under no obligation to make anything relevant to what had gone before. So

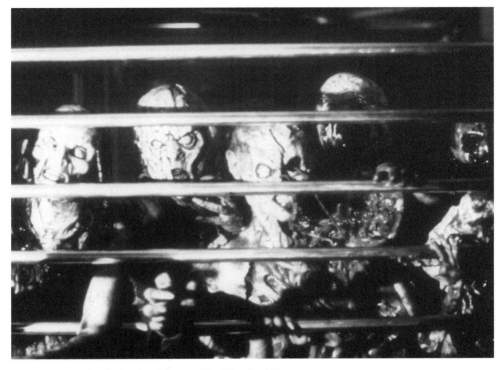

Captive zombies – but for how long? *Return of the Living Dead III.*

he didn't. Dropping the humour, Yuzna crafted a serious, bloody and oddly touching zombie love story.

Rebellious Curt (J. Trevor Edmond) and his girlfriend Julie (Mindy Clarke) sneak into an army base where his father, a colonel, works, expecting to uncover animal experimentation. There, they stumble upon Trioxin experiments aimed at raising the dead for use as super-soldiers.

Later, after a row with his father, Curt leaves home with Julie, but, when she is killed in a motorcycle crash, he sneaks back on to the base and uses Trioxin to revive her. But, while all initially seems well, Julie is not the same. She has a need for human flesh, and resorts to self-harming to numb her cravings. When they interrupt a robbery, the pair becomes the target of a Latino gang, but by the time Julie succumbs to her urges, the local hoods are the least of their problems.

Return of the Living Dead III is without a doubt the best zombie film of the 1990s. Its ill-fated lovers make an agreeable pair of leads, while the action scenes are pretty spectacular. But it's the idea that a thinking zombie would be horrified by her need to eat human flesh that makes this stand out. Mindy Clarke (who, as Melinda Clarke, subsequently enjoyed a lengthy run in the popular teen soap *The O.C.*) excellently conveys the horror and the pain of her condition, and her drastic attempts to deal with it are stunning.

John Russo's shameful *Children of the Living Dead*.

Yuzna drew graphic inspiration from the developing body-modification sub-culture, and Julie appears as the ultimate piercee – not only with nipple and lip rings, but also with chunks of metal and glass forced through her flesh in an effort to feel something other than hunger. As Yuzna observed, 'The dichotomy was set up that either love or pain would keep her from the hunger, from being just an animal and not having a soul. And to me that's real life because you see it all the time; people who aren't loved enough hurt themselves.'

Yuzna's film is a minor classic. With a suitably downbeat ending, it transcends its sequel-status limitations, and is in need of a critical reassessment. At the time, many people routinely dismissed it as another pointless franchise extension. Unfortunately, the film was not a financial success, and the series would remain dormant until 2005, when two more sequels were shot back to back.

Elsewhere, Russo hadn't finished milking *NOTLD* with *Return of the Living Dead*. In 2001, he produced *Children of the Living Dead*, a staggeringly bad sequel to his own 30th Anniversary rehash of the original film. With revived serial killer Abbott Hayes (*NOTLD*'s cemetery zombie, as previously seen in the 30th Anniversary version) on the rampage and for some reason kidnapping children (and then oddly not eating them).

Despite roping Tom Savini into the cast in an attempt to afford the picture some legitimacy, this feeble effort was never likely to be great, but, according to director Tor Ramsey, any chances it might have had were scuppered by Russo, who insisted on hiring his own crew and co-producer/writer Karen Lee Wolf – who vetoed any changes being made to her screenplay, and then threw Ramsey off the film during the edit, subsequently re-inserting all her dialogue.

Unsurprisingly, the resulting film is a mess. Ramsey wrote a lengthy letter to *IMDB* in response to negative viewer comments on the film, where he stated, 'I am writing to you to offer my sincerest apology for the ninety minutes of your life wasted watching the movie *Children of the Living Dead*.

'The Executive Producer's daughter Karen Lee Wolf wrote a script so horribly incompetent

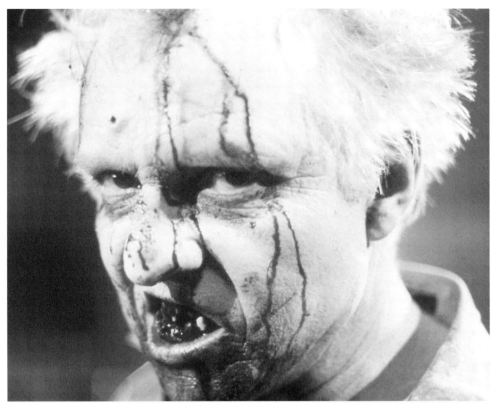

Stuart Gordon's gleefully gory take on H.P. Lovecraft's *Re-Animator*.

that nearly a dozen writers and directors had walked off the project due to her obsessiveness over no changes being made to her script… Russo insisted on shooting without an on-set art department, no Assistant Directors, no Script Supervisors, no Wardrobe department and no make-up department. Also no Production Manager. Basically we had a nine-man crew made up of friends of Russo.'

Russo wasn't the only *NOTLD* veteran trying to bleed the film dry. In 1988, Bill Hinzman decided that playing the lead ghoul in Romero's film qualified him to make his own zombie film. *Flesh Eater* (a.k.a. *Revenge of the Living Zombies, Zombie Nosh*) was written, produced and directed by Hinzman. He also cast himself as the lead zombie who rampaged around tearing women's tops off and ate a few people.

Dreadful on every level, with shoddy acting, clumsy direction and a lousy script all combining to produce an offering that's slower moving than its title character. This was an insult to the viewer, and makes you wonder if there were any depths that some former *NOTLD* cast and crew wouldn't plumb in order to exploit their past. As I write, Russo is at it again, with *Escape of the Living Dead* in production, starring Gunnar Hansen and Tony Todd.

Released shortly after *Return of the Living Dead, Re-Animator* proved to be another classic horror-comedy, and one that would prove influential. Based – loosely – on H.P. Lovecraft's inferior pulp serial *Herbert West – Re-Animator*, the film followed the experiments of medical student West (Jeffrey Combs), who has developed a serum to conquer brain death and bring the dead back to life.

West involves roommate Dan Cain (Bruce Abbott) in his work, which has decidedly mixed results – although the dead do indeed revive, they tend to come back as raving, super-strong maniacs. Before long, Dean Halsey (Robert Sampson) has been killed, revived and locked away as a madman, and West's tutor and rival Doctor Hill (David Gale) has been decapitated – the head and body then separately revived. However, Hill isn't about to allow a minor detail like death to stop him from stealing West's formula, or molesting Cain's girlfriend Megan (Barbara Crampton), leading to a final showdown between West and his creations.

Skilfully mixing black humour with extreme horror, co-writer and director Stuart Gordon crafted a highly effective horror movie. The violence was extreme enough to see the film released unrated in America. In the UK, censors insisted on several cuts – most notably to the gleefully tasteless scene where Doctor Hill's severed – but still quite horny – head is placed between the legs of the naked Megan. In fact, the film's joyful plunge into bad taste is one of its most endearing elements – little sense of restraint is evident in this movie.

Combs and Gale are excellent protagonists, and have some great verbal sparring matches (West: 'You'll never take credit for my discovery, who'd believe a talking head? Get a job in a sideshow'), and the production values are excellent for such a quickly shot, low-budget film.

Re-Animator spawned two sequels, both directed by the original film's producer Brian Yuzna. *Bride of Re-Animator* (retitled *Re-Animator 2*) was released in 1990, and presented a darker take on matters. West and Cain are back, this time trying to build a woman in order to resurrect Megan (who Cain failed to save in the first film, but whose heart has been preserved). West has also been tinkering with building some very weird creatures out of body parts (a hand with an eye, for example). Meanwhile, Doctor Hill's head is back – this time sporting bat wings.

Less effective than the original, *Bride of Re-Animator* still has plenty of worthwhile moments. The *Bride of Frankenstein* pastiche is a neat twist, and Yuzna directs well. The humour is still there, but this is a much bleaker film than the first, with a darkness and sense of tragedy that Yuzna later perfected in *Return of the Living Dead III.*

Thirteen years later, Yuzna again revived the concept for *Beyond Re-Animator.* The film opens with West being arrested – Cain having finally turned him in. It then leaps forward twelve years, where we find West established as an inmate in a brutal prison.

A new prison doctor, Howard Phillips (Jason Barry), arrives, and West is appointed his assistant. It soon turns out that West has been continuing his experiments. Inevitably, it all goes wrong – and soon half the prison population have become re-animated maniacs.

Although vastly inferior to the earlier films, *Beyond Re-Animator* is entertainingly trashy. Yuzna clearly hasn't got much of a budget to play with, but packs the film with so many moments of bad taste and ludicrous imagery (a severed penis not only stays alive, but actually battles a rat!) that you can't help but enjoy it.

Two entirely disposable zombie quickies from the 1980s.

Not all the low-budget zombie films of the time could compete with *Re-Animator* or *Return of the Living Dead III*. In fact, most seemed pretty awful at the time, and can scarcely be said to have improved with age.

Zombie Island Massacre (1984) was a terrible film with little zombie action to liven it up. The massacre indeed takes place on the eponymous-but-misleadingly-named island but it is carried out by drug dealers. *Zombie Nightmare* (1989) starred heavy metal sideshow act Jon Mikl Thor (whose brief period of fame was entirely to do with his ability to inflate and explode hot water bottles with his mouth during gigs, rather than his music) as a vengeful zombie resurrected by voodoo. It's pretty bad, with little to hold the interest beyond the novelty of Thor, who sadly doesn't repeat his stage show here.

Raiders of the Living Dead (1985) tried to cash in on Indiana Jones fever, but this bland tale of zombies in a former prison failed on pretty much every level. While 1989 movie *Dead Heat* had a bigger budget and vaguely name cast (Treat Williams, comedian Joe Piscopo and a cameo by Vincent Price), this zombie/cop buddy movie hybrid was equally unsuccessful.

Novelist S.P. Somtow's *The Laughing Dead* (1989) was an interesting but flawed attempt to mix zombies with Aztec lore. Mostly starring Somtow's writer buddies, the film has plenty of gore, and a bizarre scene where zombies play basketball with a severed head.

Nostalgic spoofs like *I Was a Zombie for the FBI* (1984), *I Was a Teenage Zombie* (1986) and

A poster that has been seen by far more people than the actual movie.

Night of the Creeps (1986) failed to hit the mark. The best of the three was *Night of the Creeps*, though Fred Dekker's tale of alien takeover was too uneven to really work. Dekker's next attempt at horror nostalgia – kids' film *Monster Squad* – fared little better.

Gore-Met Zombie Chef from Hell (1986) is a bargain-basement video production that fails to live up to the promise of its title (though the poster was good), while *Zombie High* (1987), *Redneck Zombies* (1987), *The Video Dead* (1987), *Neon Maniacs* (1986) and *Night Life* (1989) were all bland, entirely derivative and instantly forgettable.

The end of the 1980s saw a couple of military zombie films emerge. 1986's *The Supernaturals*, directed by Armand Mastroianni and starring *Star Trek*'s Nichelle Nichols, saw American Civil War zombies battling the modern-day army during a training exercise that goes badly wrong in a passable but unmemorable film. Elsewhere, Australian movie *Zombie Brigade* saw Vietnam Vets rising as vampires, after a war memorial is demolished by a property developer – only to find themselves battling zombies from the Second World War. It's every bit as contrived as it sounds.

The military also rose *en masse* from their graves in *Curse of the Cannibal Confederates* (1982) and *Ghost Brigade* (1992), neither of which added anything to the sub-genre (the makers of *Ghost Brigade* can't seem to decide if their monsters are zombies, vampires or ghosts, and so settle for some sort of nebulous hybrid).

Zombiethon (1986) was hardly a film – instead, director Ken Dixon (who had previously made the seminal trailer compilation movie *The Best of Sex and Violence*) cobbled together footage mainly drawn from a bunch of European zombie films and shot some weirdly surreal linking segments where cheap-yet-eerie-looking zombies chased women on the beach or into theatres. These throwaway segments have a dreamlike feel and almost (but not quite) pass as art.

As a zombie sampler, there was little faulting the film. Dixon selected all the 'best' bits (namely those featuring gore and nudity) from the likes of *Zombie Lake, Zombie Flesh Eaters, Oasis of the Zombies*, as well as non-zombie films like *The Invisible Dead* and *Fear*. Sticking out like a sore thumb are the clips from the sex- and violence-free *Astro Zombies*.

Another compilation was *Mad Ron's Prevues from Hell* (1987) in which ventriloquist Nick Pawlow and his zombie dummy Happy present a stellar selection of movie trailers. The linking footage has the promos being screened to a cinema full of zombies, who are occasionally given a few minutes to gnaw on each other and shuffle about. This is much to the irritation of most viewers, who would have preferred more trailers and less filler. Nevertheless, *Mad Ron's Prevues...* remains the best-loved compilation of its kind.

A zombie ventriloquist dummy wasn't the lowest conceptual ebb to which the sub-genre descended during this period. That probably came in *Linnea Quigley's Horror Workout*, released in 1989. Since *Return of the Living Dead*, the diminutive Quigley had carved out a

Civil war zombies in *The Supernaturals*.

niche as a scream queen in a series of low-budget, straight-to-video movies. Even so, it's uncertain just who this was aimed at, as Linnea and her friends strip down to their lingerie, flash a little skin and perform some exercises.

There are clips from her movies, a brief career interview and – most bizarrely – a poolside workout with Linnea and a bunch of embarrassed-looking zombies. It's a pretty awful example of how every last drop was squeezed from the 1980s scream-queen cult.

T&A were also the order of the day in 1987's *Night of the Living Babes* (starring Quigley's fellow scream queen Michelle Bauer), Hugh Gallagher's 1994 *Gore Whore*, *Hot Wax Zombies on Wheels* (1999) and 1998's nasty *Zombie Ninja Gangbangers*, which features the first – and hopefully last – zombie rapists.

Wes Craven tried to take the zombie movie back to its roots in 1987's *The Serpent and the Rainbow*, based on the book by Wade Davis. Bill Pullman plays a scientist sent to Haiti in order to discover the truth behind reports of a zombification drug. Once there, he becomes a target for the corrupt government and voodoo priests.

Craven's film is a slick, effective movie, though less a horror film than a study of how political leaders in Haiti like the infamous Baby Doc Duvalier (whose overthrow was

Yet more militaristic zombies in *Zombie Brigade*.

recounted within the narrative) have used the zombie phenomenon as a tool to retain power. As one might expect, Craven provides plenty of horror (which takes liberties with Davis' non-fiction tome) and the film is an unusually intelligent look at the traditional zombie.

Zombies mixed with aliens in Peter Jackson's 1987 sleeper hit *Bad Taste*. This low-budget New Zealand-made film certainly lived up to its name as the Astro Investigation Defence Service (or AIDS) battle invaders from space, who have resurrected the dead.

This highly rated movie is in fact pretty poor; crass humour and grossed-out gore effects might appeal to more juvenile viewers, but most discerning fans need a *little* more – a story for instance. There are moments amongst the crudity but, in reality, this film is not too far removed from the tackiness of straight-to-video flicks.

Jackson returned to the zombie theme again in 1992 with the aptly named *Braindead*. His budget was bigger, but his sense of humour remained puerile. After a mutant monkey bites his mother, Lionel (Timothy Balme) has to watch as she slowly deteriorates into a bloodthirsty zombie. Inevitably, she starts to eat visitors, and soon Lionel has a whole house full of zombies to keep in check. The final third of the film is a non-stop barrage of gore, as Lionel battles the hungry zombies, and is pretty spectacular – but also rather facile.

If *Bad Taste* lived up to its name, then *Braindead* comes close to doing likewise, and is saved

Peter Jackson's gore-filled crass comedy. Who would have expected him to go on to *The Lord of the Rings*?

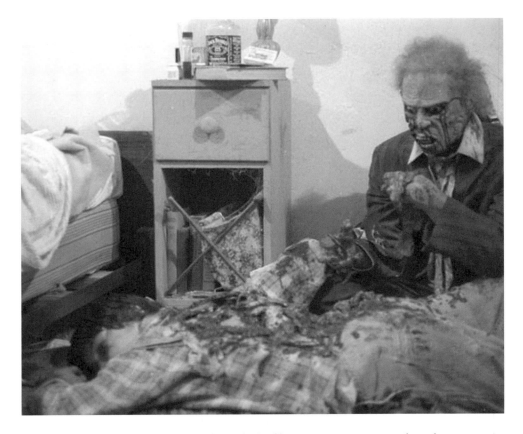

only by the odd moment of wit. In the end, the film is as vacuous as any cheap horror movie, and less subversive than most.

Remarkably, Jackson eventually went on to shoot the epic *The Lord of the Rings* trilogy – which features its own zombie demons – and just goes to show that you can't write anyone off.

Biker zombies returned for another spin in *Chopper Chicks in Zombietown*. As the title of this 1989 release suggests, the bikers this time are female, but sadly this is no *She Devils on Wheels*. Despite being a Troma release, this story of electronically controlled zombies has little of the gratuitous sex, violence and bad taste associated with the studio. A pity, as the film has little else going for it.

The shot-on-videotape *Nudist Colony of the Dead* (1991) is unquestionably one of the more eccentric zombie films – a musical comedy featuring barely naked nudists and cheesy-looking zombies. It takes a traditional horror plot and twists it: after prudish locals force the closure of their nudist camp, die-hard sun worshippers kill themselves. When, years later, a summer camp is set up on the location, the naked dead rise to take their revenge.

Nudist Colony of the Dead is not *quite* as bad as it's been made out to be and, for a short time, it's actually mildly amusing. But it does start to drag after a while, with poor songs and

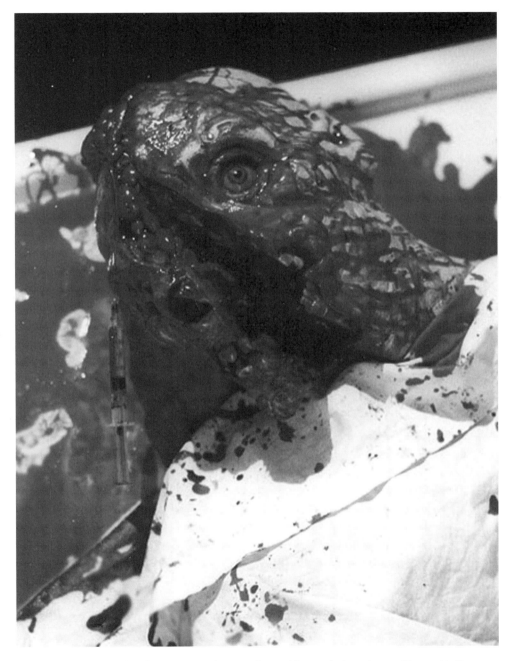

Left and above: *The Dead Next Door*, the movie that started a trend for zero-budget, shot-on-video zombie films.

terrible acting not helping proceedings. Oddly, given the premise, it's coy about nudity – most of the 'naked' zombies are carefully covered up. Certainly not worth looking for, and hardly worth watching even if you stumble upon it, *Nudist Colony of the Dead* is unlikely to ever gain a following – though bizarrely, it wouldn't be the last zombie musical.

The Dead Next Door (1988) is the father of all the shot-on-tape zombie films that followed, and deserves condemnation for that alone. But even if it had spawned no bastard offspring, the film would be a lamentable effort. Ironically, it wasn't shot on video, but rather Super 8 film.

Shamelessly aping Romero, the movie starts with a zombie outbreak and then moves forward five years. Zombie Squads roam the country trying to contain the zombies with little effect, while scientists – as ever – work on a cure for the phenomenon.

With shoddy effects, terrible acting and poor production values (even taking into account the shooting format and low budget, this is an amateurish effort), director J.R. Bookwalter has created little more than a home movie retread of Romero. But thanks to his tireless promotion, and some easily pleased fanzine writers, the film became a surprise success. The result was that just about every trailer-park resident with a camcorder and a few friends suddenly thought that they too could make a zombie film.

This mindset is perfectly demonstrated by the 1999 documentary *American Movie*, which followed the efforts of hapless director Mark Borchardt to shoot a zero-budget horror opus, *Coven*. Sadly, most of his contemporaries didn't have even the modicum of talent and imagination of Borchardt (who at least came up with an original idea, and ended up shooting a not entirely awful short). Instead, most were content to churn out rank Romero copies that add nothing to the genre. In fact, they were directly responsible for sending the zombie film – and the horror film in general – spiralling into the gutter.

It wasn't the mainstream horror movies that left so many hardcore fans disillusioned. Nor the PG-13 horror films that held back on the gore to make more money. Horror was being destroyed by the very people who professed to love it – the people who, after renting one of these awful, awful films, would not bother to do so again. With horror movies again proving popular, it's hard to recall just how marginalised the genre had become in the 1990s. But it was – and nothing more so than the zombie film, which was now almost entirely in the control of no-hopers churning out empty-headed crap.

Few are more awful than Todd Sheets' *Zombie Bloodbath* series, which is possibly right at the bottom of the barrel when it comes to zombie home movies. Featuring an unfashionably mulleted cast, these numbingly awful films have no value whatsoever. Instead, they simply rehash the bits of Romero's canon that the director presumably found most exciting – the gore and the shuffling zombies. The fact that Sheets has made so many of these films does suggest that somewhere, somehow, there is an audience for this stuff, which is a singularly depressing thought.

Not that Sheets was alone in his efforts to grind the genre into the dirt. Throughout the late Eighties and Nineties – and continuing to this day – a seemingly endless stream of talent-free amateurs picked up their camcorders and set off to make Romero imitations. A sampling of titles includes: *Legion of the Night, The Dreadful Dead, Zombie Cop, The Necro Files, The Dead Hate the Living, Zombiegeddon, The Stink of Flesh, Dead Meat, Biker Zombies from Detroit, Death Metal Zombies, Zombie Toxin* – the list is apparently endless.

The video market ranged from the sublime to the ridiculous. *Zombie Toxin* (left) was a retitled version of UK 'comedy' *Home Brew*; Scooter McCrae's *Shatter Dead* (right) showed what could be achieved on a low budget.

Worst of all are the works of Andreas Schnaas, who somehow manages to keep churning out his technically incompetent, pathetically offensive offerings. After starting his career in 1989 with the aptly named *Violent Shit*, he's churned out a bunch of entirely worthless video films since. His 1990 opus *Zombie 90: Extreme Pestilence* is a fair example of his work – utterly loathsome on every level, it tells the story of a military aircraft carrying biological weapons that crashes, the resulting spill causing the dead to return to life.

This is little more than an excuse to show badly staged scenes of sexual violence (breasts are hacked off, a woman has her vagina sliced open) and juvenile crassness (the virus turns out to be a new strain of AIDS). With production values that make even the cheapest shot-on-video productions look professional, this is a wholly disposable film. Other Schnaas films to avoid include *Demonium* (2001) and *Don't Wake the Dead* (2008).

Day of the Dead 2: Contagium is noteworthy only for the sheer nerve of the title. Entirely unrelated to Romero's film, the makers of this extraordinarily clumsy effort managed to get away with this outrageous rip-off because Romero no longer owned the rights to the original film. The title aside, there is nothing to differentiate this from the glut of amateur video productions that have blighted the zombie sub-genre. Bad acting, poor production values, slow pacing and an entirely unjustified sense of self-importance sink this feeble effort.

There were, of course, exceptions. A couple of shot-on-video movies showed that, with a little thought, it was possible to make an original or engaging zombie film.

Scooter McCrae's *Shatter Dead* (1994) was a dystopian look at life after a zombie outbreak, where the living dead equate to the homeless and the dispossessed. The dead here are not mindless cannibals – they retain their faculties, and are acutely aware of their condition. They simply exist among the living, unable to get work or pay bills. Heroine Stark Raven is trying to return home to her (dead) boyfriend while all around her zombies beg, campaign for their rights and cope with evangelists who want to destroy them.

Shatter Dead offers viewers an uncomfortable mix of graphic violence, equally graphic sex (in some versions, at least) and arthouse sensibilities grafted on to a zero-budget video production. It's grim, slow, unglamorous and unlike anything else you've ever seen. McCrae's willingness to indulge in unnecessary moments of splatter aside, it's quite brilliant

British 16mm film *I Zombie: A Chronicle of Pain* (1998) is even grimmer. It tells the story of Mark (Giles Aspen), who is bitten by a zombie early in the film. We follow his gradual decay as he dies and revives, locked in his tiny bedsit and only venturing out to prey on the homeless.

Director Andrew Parkinson set out to make the most depressing film ever made, and may well have succeeded. The film's unflinching look at the physical and mental deterioration of its 'hero' will alienate many, but, for those who can stick with it, this is a brutal but fascinating movie. Parkinson followed this up with *Dead Creatures* in 2001, extending his earlier take on the zombie apocalypse with an equally dour tale of female zombies luring male victims to their hideout.

McCrae and Parkinson signposted a new direction for the sub-genre – away from the cheap Romero rip-offs and back towards originality and critical respectability. Surely, all it would take to put the zombie back on top were a couple of hits.

8. Books of the Dead
The Zombie in Literature

It's only in recent years that the zombie has made any impact in the literary field. Previously the living dead were, for the most part, unseen – horror writers generally preferring to focus upon the classical archetypes of vampires, ghosts and werewolves. But, as with cinema, the zombie has slowly risen up to take its place at the forefront of horror prose fiction.

One of the difficulties in discussing early zombie literature is defining the precise nature of what constitutes a zombie. Many books and short stories certainly featured the living dead (or at least those who appeared to be zombies), but a number of these were the result of vampirism, experiments by mad scientists, alien invasion and hypnosis. This can also be said for cinema – but while zombie films use a visual code to identify themselves, the written zombie is a harder beast to pin down.

H.P. Lovecraft's *Herbert West: Reanimator* is a good example. While Stuart Gordon's visceral film interpretation of this story is clearly a zombie film – albeit one with Frankenstein connections – Lovecraft's original story is less clear. Originally written as a serial for *Home Brew* magazine, under the title *Gruesome Tales* in 1922, it has little of the style and atmosphere that readers associate with the author, and its episodic format detracts from the flow of the narrative, with the author forced to summarise chunks of earlier instalments for new readers.

Herbert West: Reanimator follows the experiments of the eponymous character as he battles to conquer death, with varying results. Miskatronic University's Dean Halsey is revived, but as a maniac, while later experiments seem no more successful, and West hits the road to avoid being tracked down by his failures. One episode sees him in the First World War (a theme that also would crop up in the movie *Bride of Re-Animator*), and, eventually, West 'disappears'.

While the story is an entertaining read, it doesn't really go anywhere until the final chapter, where West's victims – including a headless doctor who 'disguises' himself with a dummy head and carries his own reanimated head in a box – finally take their vengeance on the mad scientist. Such scenes serve to demonstrate that similar events in Stuart Gordon's film were not a cheap gag, but actually taken from Lovecraft.

Also notable is the depiction of zombies as crazed, bloodthirsty maniacs – something that the cinema wouldn't do for almost half a century. This represents degrees of gore and action that are most un-Lovecraftian.

Modern readers are more likely to find the racist content of chapter three, 'Six Shots by Moonlight', distasteful. Lovecraft describes a black boxer as 'a loathsome, gorilla-like thing'. Although all literature needs to be seen in the context of the standards of the time it was made, such unenlightened observations (and there are more) come as something of a shock.

Robert Bloch's novella *The Dead Don't Die!* also first appeared in pulp magazines – 1951's *Fantastic Adventures*. Filmed as a TV movie in 1974, Bloch's story is an intriguing mix of the horror and detective genres.

It tells the tale of a prison guard referred to only as 'Bob' and his charge Cobo Colluri, a circus strongman who is placed on death row after being wrongly convicted of murder. Just prior to his execution, Colluri gives Bob a letter to take to The Great Ahmed, a palmist, instructing him to give the guard his $8000 savings to help clear his name. But as he investigates, the prison guard is drawn into a world of murder, voodoo, blackmail, zombies and surreal hallucinations.

Finding himself on the run for murder, Bob also has to contend with his former friend Colluri returning from the dead, and the evil Varek, who is reviving the dead for his own purposes. Bloch's tale is a highly engaging horror story, with enough twists and turns to keep the reader more than satisfied.

Mention should be made of Richard Matheson's *I Am Legend*, which – although not technically a zombie novel – has had undoubted influence on the genre, being the inspiration behind George Romero's *Night of the Living Dead*. Filmed no less than three times (1964's *Last Man on Earth* being the most effective version), Matheson's apocalyptic tale is virtually a blueprint for the nihilistic zombie movies that would emerge at the end of the 1970s.

The first zombie novel to make a real impact was John Russo's 1974 novelisation of *Night of the Living Dead*. Although it was unusual for a film to be novelised so long after production, Russo adds little fresh material, instead opting for a fairly straight retelling of the story, with no additional effort made to develop the characters for the printed page. Still, the book was a huge hit on the back of the film's ongoing popularity, and so Russo came up with a sequel.

Russo and George Romero had previously reached an agreement that allowed both parties to produce their own sequels to *Night of the Living Dead* and so, as *Dawn of the Dead* was shooting, Russo wrote *Return of the Living Dead*. This sequel took place some time after the events in *NOTLD*, at which point the undead outbreak is largely contained. The deceased have spikes driven into their skulls to prevent them returning, and things seem under control. Not for long, though, as the infection re-emerges and spreads through a small town.

Russo's novel is fairly poor. Badly plotted, unengaging and with generally unsympathetic characters, it's a bog-standard example of throwaway pulp fiction, sadly lacking in the verve that makes the best trash genre writing of the Sixties and Seventies so appealing.

It's little wonder that the story was jettisoned for the movie version (though Russo's dreadful additions to the 'special edition' of *Night of the Living Dead* and his own atrocious *Children of the Living Dead* both draw from this novel). Notably, the word 'zombie' doesn't appear in the book – the living dead are referred to as 'ghouls', reflecting the original description used in *NOTLD*.

Russo has subsequently eschewed zombies in his novel writing, though he has regularly revisited the living dead in movies and, more recently, comic books.

Not to be outdone, George Romero (in collaboration with Susanna Sparrow) novelised *Dawn of the Dead* in the same year. Like Russo's novelisation, the book adds little to the original film, but is nonetheless an effective horror novel in its own right. Romero's florid dialogue seems less forced and obtrusive than Russo's and both the tension and the action sequences translate well from screenplay to novel.

Romero and Sparrow had previously adapted his film *Martin*, but there have been no novelisations of Romero's later zombie films – a pity, as the format offered Romero the opportunity to deliver his original vision for *Day of the Dead* to the public. Fans of more recent zombie franchises can enjoy a series of novels based on the *Resident Evil* series (both the games and the films) – none are exactly great literature, but they just about pass muster as movie tie-ins.

RETURN OF THE LIVING DEAD

John Russo

1978 UK edition of John Russo's sequel to *Night of the Living Dead.* The subsequent film has no connection with the novel.

Peter Tremayne's old-school zombie story (left) ignored Romero-style gut munching; (right) a collection of zombie tales appeared in this anthology.

British author Peter Tremayne (real name Peter Berresford Ellis) was a fairly prolific horror/fantasy author during the late 1970s, churning out a series of entertainingly disposable novels. These were often inspired by literary figures or movies, including several popular Dracula novels, *The Vengeance of She* (not related to the Hammer movie of the same name), *The Curse of Loch Ness, The Ants* and several others. In 1981, he tackled zombies, though his story would oddly disregard the dynamics of the undead's contemporaneous cinematic depictions. The titular figure in *Zombie!* was not in the least cannibalistic, as Tremayne took the genre back to its Caribbean roots.

Zombie! tells the story of June and Steve Lambert, a couple from London who are invited to a small Caribbean island to claim June's inheritance after her grandmother dies. Unfortunately, the island of St. Miguelon is not the welcoming tropical paradise they'd hoped for, with sullen locals, warnings of danger and strange voodoo happenings.

Tremayne's book moves at a steady pace and, though not his best work, is still an entertaining read. A black heroine – and an atypical one at that – is unusual for the time and the genre, and Tremayne gets more out of his plot than it probably deserves. Zombie fans might feel somewhat cheated, though, as the book not only lacks any flesh-eating ghouls, but also actually fails to deliver any real zombie action until the final moments – and then only briefly.

THE
ZOMBIE
SURVIVAL GUIDE

COMPLETE PROTECTION
FROM THE LIVING DEAD

MAX BROOKS

Zombie Survival Guide was at the forefront of the explosion in zombie literature in recent years.

It would be another decade before the zombie really made inroads into the world of horror literature, in the form of the influential 1990 short-story collection *Book of the Dead*. Edited by John Skipp and Craig Spector – then at the forefront of the 'splatterpunk' movement – the book and its 1992 sequel featured modern zombie tales from some of the biggest names in the horror genre. This was no delicate compendium of geriatric terror tales that treated excess with disdain, but rather a graphic, Romero-influenced collection of shockers from the likes of Stephen King, Ramsey Campbell, Richard Laymon and Poppy Z. Brite.

This potent collection of stories was a major success, and led to various imitations. One such was Stephen Jones' 1993 *Mammoth Book of Zombies*, which mixed modern and vintage tales (the former generally by the same authors who turn up in all of Jones' collections) in a collection that succeeds as much by quantity as quality. The good material is very good, the rest considerably less so.

The zombie novel has come of age since the turn of the century. The last few years have seen a sudden explosion in zombie-themed literature.

Max Brooks' *World War Z* is one such slice of post-modern, post-millennial prose. In 2003, Brooks had written the humorous *Zombie Survival Guide*, a spoof survivalist manual that outlines how to deal with a zombie attack. A surprise hit, several websites, writers and home moviemakers have copied the book.

2006 novel *World War Z* was the follow-up, a more conventional tale written in the style of an historical account of a zombie outbreak (written ten years after it began), recounted by survivors. With its global scale, the book is epic in scope and provides far more details about the cause and effects of the zombie virus than any movie.

In Brooks' world, the zombification results from a highly contagious pathogen that is spread via bodily fluids. Zombies have just one urge – to eat human flesh. They can survive for years before decomposing and, in colder climates, the dead would freeze during winter before thawing out and continuing their rampage.

Brian Keene's 2003 novel *The Rising* gave us intelligent flesh-eating zombies, this time the result of demonic possession (a rare religious explanation for a zombie outbreak). Hero Jim Thumond travels across America in search of his son and is joined by a rag-tag band of survivors, battling both zombies and humans along the way. The story is a well-paced adventure, but will doubtless disappoint some zombie fans with its digressive demonic subtext. Keene followed *The Rising* with a sequel, *City of the Dead* (2005).

As with video, zombie fiction has unleashed its fair share of lesser works. Bryan Smith's *Deathbringer* features a Reaper (who collects the souls of the dead) rebelling against God and unleashing a zombie plague in Dandridge, Tennessee, in a book that proves that trashy horror fiction is not dead.

Nathan Tucker's *Eve of the Dead* is little more than a Romero rip-off – its one-dimensional characters even hide out in a superstore (or shopping mall if you wish) and several aspects of *Dawn of the Dead* are shamelessly rehashed.

Rhiannon Frater's *As the World Dies* trilogy offers a feminine perspective, with a battered housewife and a lesbian attorney getting together to flee the apocalypse, but otherwise brings little new to the sub-genre.

Such disposable efforts notwithstanding, the genre has thrown up a handful of genuinely interesting works.

J.L. Bourne's *Day by Day Armageddon* is more interesting than the clumsy title might suggest, weaving a Romero-esque tale of urban survival as the dead rise across the globe. The narrator (and, indeed, the author) is a US Naval officer, giving the story a unique military perspective, and the novel is left open-ended, which may frustrate some readers.

Bourne's publishers, Permuted Press, also published Jason S. Hornby's *Every Sigh, the End*. Set in 1999, it features the ultimate Millennium Bug. As Y2K approaches, paranoid slacker Ross Orringer realises that everyone *is* out to get him, and, when a reality-TV crew complete with a pack of hungry zombies turn up, things go from bad to worse. Surreal, twisted and very bitter, Hornby's book is worth seeking out.

Also from Permuted comes Z.A. Recht's *Morningstar Strain* series, beginning with *Plague of the Dead* in 2006 and continuing with *Thunder and Ashes* two years later. Recht's stories are more conventional – a mysterious plague is bringing its victims back from the dead and the military have to try to contain the outbreak. The story covers little fresh ground, but it's action-packed fun nonetheless.

Possibly the most successful zombie franchise of recent years – in creative terms – has to be David Moody's *Autumn* series. British author Moody self-published *Autumn* online in 2002 (you can download the e-book for free) and is a one-man operation, not just writing novels but designing and publishing them too.

Thus far, Moody's series consists of four instalments that track the disintegration of society after most of humanity is wiped out by a mysterious plague that also revives the dead. As the saga progresses, the living dead slowly evolve from lumbering, mindless creatures to become self-aware and sentient.

The first *Autumn* novel works well as a stand-alone story, but it was with *Autumn: The City* that Moody's epic tale really took off. Starting with the first days of the infection – where ninety-nine percent of the world's population has been killed instantly by an unknown plague – the

David Moody's bleak *Autumn* series was high on misery and despair.

book follows the lives of a handful of survivors, immune to the infection, as they slowly connect with one another. Initially, it's simply a case of coping with the sudden death of everyone – but then some of the bodies start to revive.

At first, the revived are little more than empty, shuffling husks who seem unaware of anything going on around them, but slowly, they become more aggressive and threatening. Moody's zombies are not cannibalistic – instead, they are a threat through sheer weight of numbers, and – over time – develop an enmity towards the living that sees anyone unfortunate enough to be caught by them torn to pieces.

Autumn: Purification completes the story arc as the increasingly desperate survivors try to avoid the increasing numbers of 'bodies' (Moody avoids the word 'zombie'), hoping to hold out until the walking dead finally decay. The story includes such engaging devices as a bunker full of soldiers who cannot venture outside without protective clothing – as breathing in the plague-ridden air will kill them instantly.

Autumn is unquestionably a bleak, disturbing read, but no less interesting for that. The series may well represent some sort of pinnacle for the zombie novel in terms of uncompromising horror. There's no sensationalism here – just a relentless sense of hopelessness as the small number of survivors struggle to cope.

Moody's great innovation – and it's not such an original concept, but is depicted in ways that no film or book has previously done – is the idea that any sound (and, in a dead world, even the quietest sound will carry) instantly attracts the dead in their thousands. The author's descriptions of buildings besieged by an endless army of the dead are genuinely unnerving.

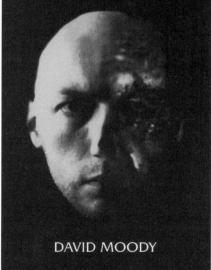

A fourth book, *Autumn: The Human Condition*, is a series companion that provides backstories for some established characters as well as introducing a number of new faces. It's a fascinating addition to the story – though readers should avoid diving in before they have read the rest of the series, as many of the stories won't make sense otherwise.

Moody is not the only writer to make use of the internet to promote his work. As mainstream publishers show less interest in edgy horror, so authors have begun to promote and present their work online.

David Wellington's impressive *Monster Island* began life as a blogged serial before being adapted for print, and was followed with the sequels *Monster Nation* and *Monster Planet*. Nathan Piekos' *Dead Ends* is a sporadic web-based series, while Joe Knetter's *Zombie Bukkake* is a self-published gross-out novel that mixes porn, gore and bad taste in equal measure.

Len Barnhart's *Reign of the Dead* series – three books so far – traces a zombie apocalypse across the United States in an impressive collection of stories, while William Zedalis' *Zombie Me: Patchwork and Pieces* is another ongoing blog, this time from the zombie's point of view.

Of course, the very nature of self-publishing and online literature makes it hard to track down everything that is out there. It's quite possible that the best zombie novels in the world are out in cyberspace somewhere, just waiting to be discovered.

The web, with its artistic freedoms, has allowed several voices to expand the zombie mythology – not all successfully, admittedly (there is as much bad zombie-themed writing online as there is for any other topic or genre), but, at best, the bloggers and web serialists – unhampered by word counts, commercial considerations or editorial constraints – are giving new life to the living dead in a multitude of ways.

Two more evocatively packaged entries in the *Autumn* series.

9. PlayStations of the Dead
Rise of the Virtual Zombies

It seems that each successive generation must endure a moral panic tied to some form of new entertainment medium. In the 1950s, it was the horror comic. In the 1980s, 'Video Nasties' were blamed for all manner of society's ills. And in the first decade of the 21st century, it has been the computer game.

Whether it's online, on PC or on console systems, the video game is currently the *bête noire* of the tabloids, opportunistic politicians and easily panicked parents. Matters are not helped by the ongoing ignorance of critics, who seem to blindly assume that games are aimed at kids – this despite BBFC age ratings and the fact that the average gamer is now twenty-eight-years-old.

While violent, sophisticated games like *Grand Theft Auto* and *Manhunt* have been the subject of much controversy, horror-themed games have had much less press attention. This is despite one of the biggest game franchises of all time being a gory, Romero-influenced zombie epic. But *Resident Evil* was far from the first game to feature the living dead.

Back in 1984, when the domestic video game was a pretty primitive creature, *The Evil Dead* joined a select number of horror films (*Halloween* and *The Texas Chain Saw Massacre* were the others) to be adapted for games consoles – in this case the Commodore 64 and ZX Spectrum.

As you might expect, the game had little in common with the movie other than the premise. Ash (the player) must try to stop the dead from entering the cabin by closing windows and doors, whilst dealing with the Deadites who are already inside. Produced by Palace Software, the game offers little in the way of entertainment, even by the standards of the day, with pitiful graphics and a distinct lack of action.

Despite this, *The Evil Dead* would continue to appear in computer games, with an equally forgettable Atari 2600 compatible *Evil Dead 2* spin-off released around 1987. Standards improved slightly with the 2000 release of *Evil Dead: Hail to the King*. Set eight years after *Army of Darkness*, the game sees Ash and fellow S-Mart employee Jenny return to the original cabin in the woods, where, once again, the Deadites are attacking.

Plot wise, *Hail to the King* is a mix of *Evil Dead* dynamics and original ideas (the bleak ending is excellent), and enhanced by well-realised graphics, the game at last came close to matching the mad ferocity of the movies.

Producers Heavy Iron Studios followed up with *Evil Dead: A Fistful of Boomstick* in 2003 for PlayStation 2 and Xbox. Set twelve years after *Hail to the King*, it opens with Ash sitting in a bar watching TV. His choice of viewing is a show called *Mysteries of the Occult*, on which a colleague of Doctor Professor Knowby (the scientist whose work started the whole *Evil Dead* phenomenon) plays the original tape that summons the dead. Ash tries and fails to stop it, and soon, the Deadites are unleashed in Dearborn, Michigan (and, presumably, elsewhere – though the game doesn't make this clear). It's up to Ash (i.e. the player) to stop them.

With a solid plot, good gameplay, decent graphics and Bruce Campbell providing dialogue, *A Fistful of Boomstick* is a better-than-average entry into *Evil Dead* lore.

The most recent addition to the franchise is *Evil Dead: Regeneration*, released in 2005 on

PlayStation 2, Xbox and PC formats. Unrelated to the previous games, it opens with Ash institutionalised. His doctor has taken possession of the *Necronomicon Ex-Mortis* – the *Book of the Dead* – and, in a doomed attempt to use it as a means of gaining power, unleashes the dead. Only Ash can stop the hordes of Deadites and the mad doctor.

Campbell again provides vocal contributions (alongside Ted Raimi from *Evil Dead 2*) and, with impressive graphics and smooth gameplay, *Regeneration* is a worthwhile addition to the series.

1984 saw another early example of the zombie video game, in the form of Sandy White's *Zombie Zombie* for the ZX Spectrum. In this, the player runs around (or flies a helicopter) to defeat the zombies – a feat achieved by causing the undead to fall off buildings. Better than Spectrum's *Evil Dead*, this proto-zombie effort is nonetheless pretty feeble stuff. The fact that designer White's inclusion of a disclaimer stating that the game doesn't reflect an interest in the occult is indicative of the manufacturers targeting a very young demographic.

1985's *Ghosts 'N' Goblins* is a fairly juvenile platform game where the player battles zombies and demons to rescue a princess. A 1988 sequel, *Ghouls 'N' Ghosts*, offered more of the same. Fairly popular with kids, the games are less than challenging and only offer the most basic thrills.

In 1986, Ubisoft's debut game *Zombi* may have lifted its name from Lucio Fulci, but took the work of George Romero as its inspiration. This multi-platform game featured the undead infesting a shopping mall from which the four protagonists have to escape. The game was improved upon for a 1990 revamp, though neither version holds up today, with poor graphics and basic gameplay limiting its appeal.

Beast Busters was an incongruously named 1989 game from Japan for the Commodore Amiga and Atari ST. A Romero-inspired shoot-'em-up, it allows the player to choose from three characters that have to escape a flesh-eating zombie-infected city. The graphics and gameplay are considerably improved from earlier zombie efforts, but remain crude by modern standards.

In 1990, Japanese NES game *Zombie Nation* offered a strange mixture of traditional (flesh-hungry) zombies and Japanese eccentricity, with the player controlling a severed Samurai head that defeats enemies by firing beams from its eyes, or by vomiting on them. Aside from this slightly mad concept, the graphics are poor and the shoot-'em-up gameplay basic.

1992 saw the release of *Alone in the Dark*, a popular and influential game that mixed violent action with strategy and puzzle solving. It has the player wander through a haunted house battling monsters (including the living dead) while trying to solve a mystery.

Such releases represented the electronic equivalent of strategy board games like *Dungeons and Dragons* that were popular in the late 1970s and early Eighties. This being a genre which, in turn, has spawned several zombie-related games – including an official *Dawn of the Dead* tie-in, but which became increasingly redundant as computer gaming increased in popularity and complexity. With 3-D graphics – unusual at the time – and a mix of styles, *Alone in the Dark* was a huge hit, and inspired a run of less impressive sequels (1994's *Pt 2* was zombie-less, while the living dead were back in 1995's *Alone In The Dark 3*, which features zombie cowboys). A 2001 revival of the franchise dropped the zombies, as did the 2005 movie and fifth instalment of the game that saw release in 2008.

1993 game *Zombies Ate My Neighbors* (a.k.a. *Zombies*) features a pair of teenage heroes who have to save their neighbours from a variety of monsters – not only zombies, but also vampires, demons and werewolves. It's supposed to be humorous, though, as with most games, the comedy value tends to fall flat once the play starts. The game spawned an unsuccessful sequel, *Ghoul Patrol*, a year later.

1994's *Corpse Killer* was part of a short-lived craze for using live-action video in games that emerged as CD-ROMs and other CD-based platforms became more widely available. Gamers soon realised that these games offered less interactivity and gameplay (not to mention acting and production values generally only found in the worst movies), and the market soon dried up.

The game is played from the perspective of a US Marine who is dropped on to a tropical island in order to eliminate a rogue scientist who is planning to unleash his zombie army. After being bitten in the opening scenes, the player has to battle zombies while trying to find enough ammunition and medication to remain alive.

Lacking in action and largely bloodless, *Corpse Killer* came and went without making much of an impact. The cast – other than John Cassini and *Texas Chainsaw Massacre 2's* Bill Mosley – are mercifully unknown.

The zombie game came of age in 1996, with the release of the first *Resident Evil*. This series has gone on to achieve levels of commercial success that most moviemakers would envy – not only a slew of sequels and spin-offs, but feature films, novels, comic books, toys and beyond. No zombie movie has ever been able to match its popularity, which has shifted over thirty-four million units to date.

Known in Japan as *Biohazard*, the game effectively spawned the 'survival horror' format (it was far from the first to use the style, but certainly popularised the ground rules), where the player has to battle through a series of undead opponents to reach their goal. Heavily influenced by Romero (who would shoot a commercial for the game, only aired on Japanese TV), it took computer horror to new levels.

In *Resident Evil*, the player controls one of the Alpha Team troopers who are charged with investigating both cannibalistic murders in Racoon City and the disappearance of a previous team that had been sent to investigate these slayings. The troop enters a seemingly deserted mansion, only to find it populated with zombies. Further investigation reveals that the mansion is owned by the mysterious Umbrella Corporation, who have been experimenting with an illegal bio-agent known as the T-Virus.

The player has to negotiate their way through the mansion, fighting zombies, collecting weapons and solving puzzles. The Japanese version contains considerably more blood than the US and European releases (a handful of versions are the uncut edition). The 'Director's Cut' released in 1997 contains more content but not the missing gore. The 2002 GameCube version is considerably different from the original game, with improved graphics, sound, gameplay and a rewritten script.

With its winning mix of action, horror, interactivity and high-quality production values, *Resident Evil* was an instant hit. *Resident Evil 2* followed in 1998, with the gameplay taken out into Racoon City after the zombie infection has spread.

Resident Evil 2 was more of the same, with the innovation of having two individual scenarios for the playable characters, which then feed into each other – actions taken by one character impacting upon the second. This time, it was the Japanese version that was less violent (and also less difficult), being aimed at a younger audience.

Resident Evil set a new standard for horror gaming.

The original *Resident Evil* story is concluded in *Resident Evil 3: Nemesis*, released in 1999. A prequel to *Resident Evil 2*, it takes place two days before the events of that game and concludes after it. This time, the player only has one character option – Jill Valentine, S.T.A.R.S trooper – who battles through the zombie-infested Racoon City and eventually faces off with Nemesis, a mutated bio-weapon. It was this game that inspired the plot for the second *Resident Evil* movie.

After this, the *Resident Evil* video game story becomes more complicated, and smacks increasingly of cynical profiteering. Producers Capcom reached a deal to make titles exclusively for the Nintendo GameCube, which resulted in a revamped version of the first game, *Resident Evil Zero*, and a further sequel, *Resident Evil 4*.

Zero was a prequel to the original game, taking place in the mountains outside Racoon City, where commandos from S.T.A.R.S investigate grisly murders. The game's unique feature was the ability to control two characters at once, but otherwise it was business as usual. 2005's *Resident Evil 4* takes place a few years after *3*, with the Umbrella Corporation having been crippled by previous events. For the first time, the series eschews zombies in favour of other threats, making the game more unique but somehow less interesting.

In 2000, a spin-off series aimed at light-gun users appeared. *Resident Evil: Survivor, Resident Evil: Survivor 2 – Code Veronica* (2001) and *Resident Evil: Dead Aim* (2003) are all pretty forgettable arcade games that do little for the franchise other than to dilute it.

This state of affairs was scarcely improved by the 2002 Game Boy instalment *Resident Evil: Gaiden*, a more juvenile side-project. 2004 saw the launch of *Resident Evil: Outbreak*, which re-hashed the original story as an online multiplayer game. It was followed a year later by *Resident Evil: Outbreak File #2*.

Since 2005, new *Resident Evil* releases have been restricted to portable devices (other than fresh ports to platforms such as the Wii), with mobile phone games *Resident Evil: The Missions, Resident Evil Confidential Reports* and *Resident Evil: Genesis*, as well as the Nintendo DS only *Resident Evil: Deadly Silence*. Whether the bottom of the barrel has been scraped bare remains to be seen.

The other popular zombie franchise also began in 1996. *House of the Dead* differed from *Resident Evil* in that it began life as an arcade game, where players in amusement arcades, pubs and clubs would use a light-gun to blast away at the zombies who attack on a big screen. The graphics were crude, the gameplay basic and the plot nothing to get excited about, but the basic interactivity of standing with the gun shooting the living dead proved popular.

House of the Dead 2 appeared in 1998, *House of the Dead III* followed four years later, with *House of the Dead 4* arriving in 2005. All followed the same basic formula – with refinements such as better graphics and bigger guns – and all were eventually ported to domestic platforms.

Offshoot titles from the *House of the Dead* series include beat-'em-up game *Zombie Revenge* (which drops the light-gun in favour of hand-to-hand combat) and some weirder spin-offs: *Pinball of the Dead* is fairly self-explanatory, and makes a degree of sense, but educational games *The Typing of the Dead* (which has two volumes) and *English of the Dead* are simply bizarre.

CarnEvil appeared in 1998, though not for home use. This arcade game featured zombies populating a haunted carnival that the player blasts away at using a light-gun. As with most arcade games, it's fairly simple stuff – after all, who in a club or bar wants to spend ages working through puzzles and complex rules when you can simply point and shoot?

1998's *Akuji the Heartless*, despite the Japanese-sounding title, features a voodoo priest (voiced by *Shaft's* Richard Roundtree) who has been cursed to

The Resident Evil series has spanned platforms and spawned several spin-offs, sequels and revamps.

173

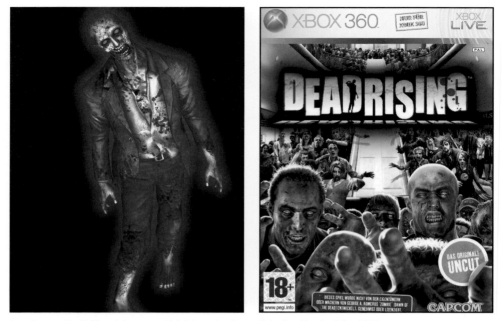

A rotting zombie (left) and the cover (right) from the *Dawn of the Dead*-inspired *Dead Rising*.

wander through Hell. Akuji (the player) has to gather souls to have any hope of redemption. Although not strictly zombie-based, the dead and voodoo ritual play a major role in this game.

The controversial road rage games *Carmaggedon* (1997) and *Carmaggedon 2* (1998) also featured zombies, though only in censored versions. In these editions, the player must run down zombies on the street; in the uncensored versions, the victims are regular pedestrians.

Voodoo also played a role in 1999's *Shadow Man* (based on a comic-book series), which featured moaning zombie-like creatures that the player had to defeat. The game's central character was a former voodoo slave who now ventures to the Deadside to save the world from 'the Five' – dead serial killers attempting to unleash an army of horror into the world.

With excellent graphics and gameplay that mixes action and mystery, *Shadow Man* resembles games like *Tomb Raider* in style, but is arguably more stylish. A hit on release, the game spawned a sequel, *Shadow Man 2: 2econd Coming* (2002).

1999 action game *Abomination* featured zombies in its story of post-apocalyptic survival, where most of the population of the United States have been wiped out by a mysterious plague. However, despite the zombie theme, the gameplay centres on a cult trying to resurrect Lovecraftian 'Old Gods'.

2003 saw the release of *Judge Dredd: Dredd vs. Death* in which the *2000AD* anti-hero battled his undead nemesis and the other Dark Judges (Mortis, Fire and Fear) who have unleashed a zombie plague in Mega City One. A tie-in novelisation was also published in 2003.

The Japanese series *The Onee Chanbara* began in 2004, with seven episodes/upgrades appearing to date. Released in Europe as *Zombie Zone*, *Zombie Zone 2* and *Zombie Hunters*, the

Fighting back against the zombies in *Left 4 Dead*.

games feature Aya, a bikini-clad heroine who wears a cowboy hat and wields a samurai sword as she gorily slices through undead armies.

The game is visceral stuff – Aya's sword becomes increasingly drenched in blood, which eventually slows her down unless she cleans it off, while the cumulative body count increases the character's 'blood lust', which also serves to inhibit the character.

The series is due to make its US debut in 2009 as *Bikini Zombie Slayers*, and a live-action movie is due for release in Japan in 2008.

George Romero finally gave his official blessing to a game in 2005 when *Land of the Dead: Road to Fiddler's Green* was issued to coincide with the movie. Movie-based games are rarely the top of the range, and this was no different, being a basic first-person shooter. It sets itself up as a prequel to the movie, as a farmer makes his way across country to Fiddler's Green, where Kaufman hires him to clear the zombies and thus make the building inhabitable.

Another Romero-themed project, *City of the Dead*, was announced in 2004 for a 2006 release. Reportedly reaching new levels in gore, the game was loosely based around *Day of the Dead*. However, the producers encountered financial difficulties, and the game remains unreleased.

2005 saw the release of *Stubbs the Zombie in Rebel Without a Pulse*. This humorous game tells the story of Stubbs, a travelling salesman who is killed in 1933 after impregnating the daughter of a farmer. His son grows up to be a powerful industrialist who founds the city of Punchbowl in 1959. Unfortunately, a vengeful Stubbs has risen from the dead to make the city his own.

With decent gameplay, some effective humour and a soundtrack of Fifties cover versions by indie bands like the Flaming Lips and Death Cab for Cutie, *Stubbs the Zombie* is an entertaining – and, for once, original – addition to the zombie gaming catalogue.

2005 saw zombies come to the PlayStation Portable in *Infected*, where the player has to battle through New York after a virus has transformed most of the population into the living dead. The player has to survive while seeking out a cure for the infection.

2006's *Dead Rising* was one of the most impressive zombie-themed games since *Resident Evil* – though its derivative nature would cause publishers Capcom a few problems.

Played from the perspective of photojournalist Frank West, who finds himself trapped in a shopping mall overrun with zombies. He has to search for weapons, rescue survivors and avoid attacks (not just from the dead) while trying to discover the cause of the outbreak. Mostly, he has to blast zombies in a satisfyingly gory fashion.

Dead Rising is spectacular stuff, with engaging gameplay and excellent graphics that helped the game shift more than a million units in its first five months on sale. The violent nature of the game saw it banned in Germany, and the plot caused a lawsuit from Richard Rubenstein's MKR Group, who own the rights to *Dawn of the Dead*.

MKR alleged that both the film and the game featured 'thoughtful social commentary on the "mall culture" zeitgeist' as well as 'a sizeable portion of sensationalistic violence', and that the shopping mall setting was clearly a copy of that found in *Dawn…* Capcom responded by stating, 'humans battling zombies in a shopping mall is a wholly unprotectible idea'. Currently, the case has yet to be resolved.

In 2007, zombies came to the Nintendo DS system with *Touch the Dead* (a.k.a. *Dead 'N' Furious*), a basic effort where the player blasts away at zombies on a disused military base. The touchscreen play is unusual, but the game itself is average stuff.

Zombies have also turned up as supporting or peripheral characters in games like *Castlevania* (1986–2007), the *Monkey Island* series (1991–2000), *Doom* (1993–2004), *Metal Slug* (1996–2006), *Quake* (1996), *Blood* (1997), *Thief: The Dark Project* (1998), *Hunter: The Reckoning* (2002) and numerous others.

Generally, the walking dead tend to be utilised as one of several threats to be eliminated (usually with big guns). Strategy game *Warcraft III* offers an entire undead-themed level.

While rarely the prime focus of gamers or developers, zombies have had a long and impressive life in the gaming world, and there is no sign of that stopping. As this book goes to press, *Dead Island* – where the player battles the living dead on a secluded island – and *Left 4 Dead*, which offers a choice of role play between that of survivor or zombie, and *Teenage Zombies: Invasion of the Alien Brain Thingys* (for the Nintendo DS) are all scheduled for release.

As zombies progressed from rough-hewn groups of pixels to the photo-realistic monsters seen in modern games, they have proven to be an unstoppable force in the gaming world, and, as such games become ever more complex, it seems that the best is almost certainly yet be to come.

10. The Living Dead Return... Again
Zombies Invade the Box-Office

During the 1990s, it seemed that the zombie film was again in terminal decline. Reduced to a seemingly endless collection of amateurish, clumsy gore-for-gore's-sake video atrocities made by increasingly incompetent fans. The idea of zombies returning to the mainstream seemed laughable. But with the onset of the new century, the living dead have returned to the silver screen with a vengeance.

The first signs of something interesting happening in the sub-genre came from Japan. By the latter half of the 1990s, discerning horror fans had come to rely on movies from South East Asia to deliver the innovative shocks that were missing from Western genre movies, and a substantial market had begun to grow for such films, both in the West and in their home territories.

Hong Kong had already brought us the entertaining *Bio Zombie* in 1998 – a Romero spoof/tribute/copy where bootleg DVD traders battle zombies in a shopping mall. Now it was Japan's turn to reinvent the zombie film.

Versus, made in 2000, is an exercise in style superseding substance. Weakly plotted, the film is dazzling to look at, and unlike any zombie film that had come before.

A pair of escaped convicts meet a group of gangsters and a kidnapped woman in The Forest of Resurrection – the 444th portal to 'the other side'. During an argument, one of the gangsters is shot and killed, only to return to life a few moments later. Soon, all the dead bodies in the forest – many of them buried there by the gangsters – start returning to life. Ultimately, there is a showdown between good and evil in the shape of the gangster's leader and the surviving convict, both of whom are reincarnations of ancient adversaries.

Versus mixes gore, martial arts, slick *yakuza* action and the supernatural into a visual and visceral whirlwind that rarely makes much sense, yet doesn't need to – it works through sensory overload. The ending is left open to facilitate a sequel.

Japanese movies like the action packed *Versus* brought new life to the zombie genre.

Also shot in 2000, *Wild Zero* may well be the most deranged zombie film ever made. A vehicle for Japanese garage punk band Guitar Wolf, the picture ostensibly tells the story of would-be rocker Ace, who encounters love, redemption and zombies on his way to a Guitar Wolf gig.

Unfortunately, the story jumps from plot point to plot point so frequently that the movie is almost impossible to follow, particularly during the first fifty minutes. With sub-plots involving alien invasions, meteors, sleazy promoters, yakuzas and gunrunners – not all of which go anywhere – the film is, structurally, something of a mess. Despite this confusion, it has such verve and abandon about it that the viewer hardly cares.

With transsexuals, super-powered rock stars, flaming exhaust pipes, Day-Glo wigs and hot pants (the latter two items both sported by the same male character), *Wild Zero* is – as the name suggests – pretty wild.

On the downside, the editing is pretty sloppy, and there are a few scenes which director Tetsuro Takeuchi could have tightened up – some moments during the final third of the film run overly long. Overall, this is a hugely entertaining, deliberately trashy exercise in excess. The zombie scenes are suitably gory, with more exploding heads that you'll see in any other movie. Complete with a blasting Jap-punk soundtrack, this unique movie seems to capture something of the punk rock spirit – loud, exhilarating and trashy, it's the most unique zombie film made to date.

2001's *Stacy* – sometimes referred to as *Attack of the Schoolgirl Zombies* – is another excellent and innovative take on the sub-genre. In the early 21st century, girls aged between fifteen and seventeen suddenly start dying, then inexplicably returning to life as cannibalistic zombies.

Rock band Guitar Wolf battled zombies in the demented *Wild Zero*.

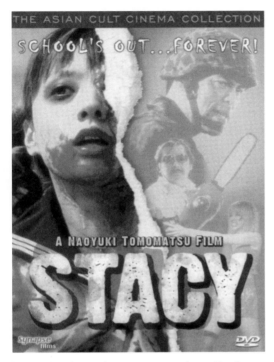

THE ASIAN CULT CINEMA COLLECTION

SCHOOL'S OUT...FOREVER!

A NAOYUKI TOMOMATSU FILM

STACY

Synapse films   DVD

Schoolgirl zombies in the gory, yet strangely touching *Stacy*.

They become known as 'Stacys' and loved ones are encouraged to 're-kill' them. To make things worse, in the weeks before death, the girls experience Near Death Happiness – a euphoric state that allows them to accept their coming fate but which makes the pain of what is about to happen all the more difficult for their friends and families.

This unusual film follows a dual narrative. In the first story, a student joins the 'Romero Re-Kill Squad' – a quasi-military group who dispose of rogue Stacys and clean up the remains – in the hope of saving his girlfriend Momo, who has become one of the undead. In the second, a teenage girl who is about to die befriends a puppeteer, and an unlikely romance blossoms, even though he knows he will have to 're-kill' her. Also thrown into the mix are a band of teenage Stacy killers who pattern themselves on Drew Barrymore.

Stacy is a compulsively strange film that runs a diverse gamut that includes cheesy comedy, extreme graphic gore, and emotionally affecting scenes that explore the nature of love. It's love that the Stacys want – and eating people is an act of love for them. Somehow, the whole thing gels nicely and the ending offers hope of a future where zombies and humans can not only reconcile, but also create a new hybrid – the next step in evolution.

The film unashamedly displays its influences – as well as the 'Romero Re-Kill Squad', we see ads for the 'Blue Campbell Right Hand 2' – a chainsaw clearly patterned after the one used by Bruce Campbell in *Evil Dead II*. There are further verbal and visual references to Romero's zombie series dotted throughout. Despite this, *Stacy* manages to be wholly original in both style and concept, and is quite unforgettable.

While these Japanese films had little impact in the West, in 2002, a film with strong Japanese connections would become a smash-hit, reviving and reinventing the zombie genre for a new generation. Fundamentalist zombie fans invariably hated it, but *Resident Evil* was in fact just the kick in the ass that the sub-genre had needed to put it back on the mainstream agenda.

Based on the hugely successful video-game series, the film was never going to please the more elitist horror fans. This negative dynamic was exacerbated once George Romero was kicked off the project and replaced with Paul W.S. Anderson, who had previously helmed the movie adaptation of another arcade classic, *Mortal Kombat*. Predictably, the letters pages of

The *Resident Evil* movie brought a whole new audience to the zombie film, and dragged the genre fully into the mainstream.

Fangoria and internet forums buzzed with angry horror fans who were condemning *Resident Evil*, even before a frame was shot.

The story was that Romero's film had been too gory, too intense, and just not mainstream enough. Yet any gory screenplay can be toned down during rewrites, filming or editing. The truth – that Romero's screenplay may just have not been good enough for producers Capcom – was clearly too much for the faithful to contemplate.

Anderson seemed like a good choice for the film. Unlike Romero – who had openly expressed his disdain for such games – Anderson was a gamer himself, and a big fan of *Resident Evil* in particular. Clearly, Anderson was far more likely than Romero to deliver a film that the game's fans would enjoy and, like it or not, that's who this film was aimed at.

When finally released in 2002, *Resident Evil* received a predictable mauling from mainstream and genre critics alike, but this didn't matter – the film became the most commercially successful zombie film to date. Evidently, its target audience were more than happy with it, and didn't give a damn about what a bunch of elitist hacks thought.

In reality, the film is far from great, but does have its moments and, as a slice of action-horror, is more than satisfactory. It opens with Alice (Milla Jovovich) waking up in an empty mansion,

Milla Jovovich in *Resident Evil: Extinction.*

unaware as to how she got there. As her memory returns, she recalls that she was part of a secretive organisation called the Umbrella Corporation, researching bio-weaponry in The Hive – an underground laboratory where an outbreak has turned the scientists into ravenous zombies. As she explores the now seemingly deserted mansion, she is joined by a military unit, who need to contain the outbreak and secure the lab before it self-destructs, battling the zombies, a controlling computer and mutant monsters – as well as their own inner demons – as they go.

Resident Evil unfolds very much like a video game – the cast move through various levels, are given clues and have to solve puzzles to reach their destination. To criticise the film for this seems totally idiotic – what did anyone expect? The gore is, of course, fairly minimal (and rendered less extreme through CGI), but the action comes thick and fast, and Jovovich makes a feisty heroine.

It may be fairly vacuous, but *Resident Evil's* pace and visual style makes up for that. It's notable that the same genre writers who sneered at this tend to adore Lucio Fulci's equally empty-headed zombie movies from the 1980s, which don't even have the virtue of having flashy, rapid-fire entertainment to compensate for their lack of substance.

In fact, the reaction to films like *Resident Evil* from many genre writers seems to be a depressing generational echo of the days when writers like Denis Gifford and Alan Frank would write gushingly about the Universal and Hammer films they'd grown up with, while dismissing (or ignoring) the new generation of cutting-edge productions. Like ageing hippies complaining about punk rock, they had become the very thing they had once rebelled against.

2004's *Resident Evil: Apocalypse* picks up from the ending of the first film, with the zombies

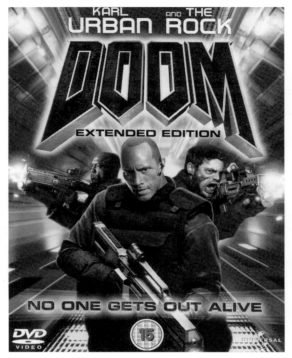

More game-based zombie-movie action.

having escaped The Hive and now on the loose in Racoon City, where they have rapidly spread. Alice and her fellow survivors are once again plunged into battle. Luckily, she's been bio-enhanced, giving her super powers, which she needs to help rescue a small band of the uninfected and escape the city.

However, they are in a race against time, as the Umbrella Corporation is planning to destroy Racoon City, wiping their failed experiment off the map. And, as if that wasn't enough, they are also hunted by Nemesis, a huge mutant super-soldier.

This time around, Anderson wrote and produced, but handed the directorial reins over to Alexander Witt, a well-known cameraman making his debut. Witt keeps the action flowing and – like the first film – produces a tightly paced, video-game-style experience.

Apocalypse is low on characterisation, high on action and entertainingly disposable. Milla Jovovich is every inch the action superhero, and manages to be both sexy and savage. At times, the editing is a little too frenetic – a problem with many action movies in the CGI age – and becomes a confusing blur, but on the whole, like its predecessor, the movie is entertainingly empty-headed fun.

Once again, the critics sneered. Once again, the public ignored them, and the success of this sequel guaranteed another entry in the series.

2007's *Resident Evil: Extinction* was helmed by *Highlander* director Russell Mulcahy, and takes place some years after *Apocalypse*. By now, the zombies are overrunning the world, and any survivors lead a perilous, nomadic existence. Alice has struck out on her own, but runs into a band of humans who need her help, and she joins them as they head for Las Vegas in search of supplies, hoping to finally make it to safety in Alaska. Meanwhile, the Umbrella Corporation's Doctor Isaacs (Iain Glen) is working on a way of controlling the zombies, and part of his plan involves Alice.

With less full-throttle action and a little more plot than *Apocalypse*, *Extinction* represents a solid addition to the series. Alice now has even more powers – with no explanation – and the gore level is up from the earlier films but, otherwise, it's business as usual. Fans lapped it up (though some gamers were disgruntled that, by now, the films had moved away from the original game scenario).

Like *Resident Evil*, 2005's *Doom* was also based on a shoot-'em-up video game. It too was hated by critics and also found itself mauled by gamers who were justifiably upset that it failed to transfer many of the game's ideas to the screen. However, judged for what it is – an escapist action movie that is more inspired by than based on the original game – the film is passable enough.

A group of soldiers are sent to investigate a research facility on Mars, where something has evidently gone awry – all communication has ceased and the facility is apparently in a state of quarantine. When the militia arrive, they find that mysterious forces have somehow been unleashed – a variety of huge monsters are attacking people, and the dead are reviving.

Doom is largely throwaway stuff – its characters are all little more than outlines – although the plot device that sees the heroic Sarge (played by pro-wrestler The Rock) become more and

BASED ON THE BEST SELLING SEGA VIDEO GAME

HOUSE OF THE DEAD

"THE MATRIX MEETS DAWN OF THE DEAD"

Much maligned game adaptation *House of the Dead*.

more psychotic is interesting. On the whole, *Doom*'s plot is under-developed – there are few coherent explanations as to what is going on, director Andrej Bartkowiak being apparently more interested in packing his movie choc-full of flashy images and CGI shocks.

The original game concept – that Hell has been unleashed – is discarded in favour of a less religiously contentious genetics plot, which doesn't help the film at all, and the horror element of the game is by and large replaced with widescreen-friendly action scenes.

Yet *Doom* has its moments – the climactic scenes where the film duplicates the point-of-view perspective of the original game is fun. Taken on its own merits, the movie is an entertaining, undemanding romp with smatterings of gore, clichéd characters (we're treated to a corny introduction to all the soldiers as their rather obvious nicknames are announced by the computer) and big monsters. All of which will satisfy viewers who are not overly concerned about engaging their brains.

Viewed without any expectations, *Doom* is inoffensive fun, but little more. The zombies add nothing to the story – they're just another level of shock thrown into the plot because they'd appeared in the original game. They may, however, go down in history as the most ineffectual members of the living dead since the 1940s, as they do absolutely nothing threatening.

The least worthwhile video-game adaptation of this period was *House of the Dead*, shot in 2003 by the infamous Uwe Boll – often described as 'the worst horror director in the world' by genre fans, thanks largely to a series of dire video-game adaptations such as *Bloodrayne* and *Postal.*

For his part, Boll is more certain of his abilities, and has been known to challenge his critics and rivals – including Quentin Tarantino and Roger Avery – to boxing matches, several of which occurred in September 2006 (Boll won them all; Tarantino and Avery didn't rise to the challenge, though, and his opponents were instead hapless internet critics). More recently, he has issued a video stating that directors Michael Bay and Eli Roth are 'fucking retards' and once again issuing a boxing challenge. Clearly, he's an entertaining character. Sadly, his films are not so much fun.

Given that *House of the Dead* was a Sega arcade game that consisted of nothing more than aiming a laser pistol at the screen and shooting zombies, it's unsurprising that the film has little in common with its source material. Instead, it tells the story of a bunch of teens who travel to a mysterious island for a rave, only to find it deserted. Eventually, they stumble upon a few friends, who explain that the party was invaded by decayed zombies, who set about slaughtering everyone there. As the zombies attack again, the group hold them off with an arsenal of weapons provided by a local smuggler, as they seek to discover what is behind the phenomenon.

While not quite as bad as it's made out to be (at the time of writing, it sits at number forty in *IMDB's* 'Bottom 100 Films of All Time'), *House of the Dead* is pretty dismal. Certainly, it's action-packed, but the key battle scene is interminable and hampered not only by the use of *Matrix*-style visual effects but also through the inclusion of footage from the original game (complete with on-screen text) that is inserted throughout the fight. There's no creative reason for this and it effectively sinks an already flawed movie.

Interestingly, no one involved in the film seemed particularly satisfied with the results or with Boll's work. Even before *House of the Dead* was released, producer Mark Altman was talking about how the next film in the projected franchise would be more like a horror film than an action movie – a strange comment, given that the first film was supposed to be a horror film.

In 2008, Boll finally seemed to accept the criticism with his bizarre *House of the Dead: Director's Cut* – a 'funny' version of the film that opens with the director being held hostage and forced to watch his own movie. The 'fun' continues with 'humorous' outtakes replacing some scenes and pop-up captions mocking the acting, the script and the 'bullet-time' effects. Sadly, it doesn't make the film any more entertaining than it was before.

Although there was little clamour for any sequel to *House of the Dead*, in 2005 one came along anyway. Surprisingly, the Michael Hurst-directed *House of the Dead 2* was a considerable improvement on its predecessor – which is, admittedly, not much of an achievement. But, despite being cheaply made for video release (having premiered on the Sci-Fi Channel), the movie manages to rattle along efficiently enough.

The opening scenes don't promise much – a bunch of frat boys invade a sorority house, taking photos of naked girls and spraying their lingerie with water pistols in a scene that has absolutely no bearing on any other part of the story. We then cut to mad doctor Sid Haig who is trying to discover the secret of raising the dead (a role he'd more or less reprise in *Night of the Living Dead 3-D*), only to fall victim to the subject of his experiments.

The rest of the exposition takes place during the opening titles, effectively dispensing with the plot and allowing the remainder of the film to be one long battle between soldiers, scientists and zombies. The scientists are trying to locate the source of the outbreak in the hope of developing a serum, while the army is determined to contain the whole sorry mess.

On a basic level, *House of the Dead 2* works – the zombie attacks come thick and fast, the gore quotient is high and the pace fairly relentless. It goes nowhere in terms of story development, but is a straight-faced shocker with decent performances from the cast, and has an enjoyably bleak ending. There are even a couple of innovations – the obvious but hitherto unexplored idea of the blood-borne zombie virus being spread by mosquito bite is an interesting one, as is the 'patient zero' theory – the idea that, if you find the original source of infection, you might be able to use their blood to create a vaccine against infection.

The first signs of post-*Resident Evil* revival in the zombie sub-genre came with a film that doesn't technically feature zombies at all. The British apocalypse tale *28 Days Later* was an international success

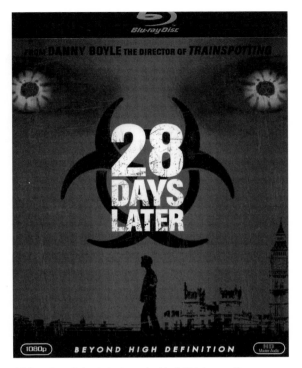

28 Days Later helped start a revival in British horror film production, and also introduced the idea of running zombies.

and spawned a slew of new, edgy movies that made the living dead scary once more.

Trainspotting director Danny Boyle's film opens with a botched raid by animal liberationists on a lab where chimps have been infected with a highly contagious virus called 'Rage'. The raid releases the chimps, which ungratefully infect their rescuers. Twenty-eight days later, the virus has spread across the country, turning people into maniacal, zombie-like (but not dead) killers.

In a hospital, Jim (Cillian Murphy) awakens from a coma to find the building – and most of London – deserted. After narrowly escaping the infected, he meets a few fellow survivors, and they leave the capital in search of safety. Instead, they end up at a military fortress near Manchester, where the power-crazed, sex-hungry and thuggish soldiers pose a far greater threat than the Rage-infected people outside the compound.

28 Days Later is, for the most part, a hugely successful reinvention of the genre. The scenes of a deserted London – famous landmarks normally teeming with people now empty – are genuinely eerie, and the infected, with their red eyes and relentless fury, are a frightening variant on the zombie template. In fact, the film is closer in spirit to Romero's *The Crazies* and David Cronenberg's *Rabid* than it is to *Dawn of the Dead*, but the impact of the fast, running 'zombies' can't be overstated. The shuffling dead would never seem so threatening again.

28 Weeks Later was the more ambitious sequel to *28 Days Later*.

However, it's the uninfected humans who are the real monsters here. In a more successful twist on Romero's *Day of the Dead* military subtext, the film shows the real danger comes not from the infected – who will soon die – but from Christopher Eccleston's band of militaristic survivors. Eccleston's group cling to power as the world crumbles around them, and have unsavoury designs on the two female survivors, Selena (Naomie Harris) and Hannah (Megan Burns). The inference being that, if these people are the future of humanity, then perhaps we would all be better off dead.

Shot on digital video – with speeded-up sequences to make the infected attacks appear even more frenetic – the film has an immediacy and pace that was new to the sub-genre. The original British ending is optimistic, suggesting an end to the infection; the US ending is somewhat darker. DVD viewers can see both.

The success of *28 Days Later* facilitated a 2007 sequel, *28 Weeks Later*, which develops the story along much broader, action-movie lines.

Opening during the original outbreak, Don (Robert Carlyle) narrowly escapes from the farmhouse he's been sheltering in when the infected attack. In his panic, he abandons his wife and leaves her at the mercy of the marauding maniacs. Six months hence, he is among a group of survivors being returned to London after the infection has been contained. The US army is in control of the city, and the survivors are kept in strict quarantine areas. But Don's children slip out to revisit their old home – where they find their mother, still alive.

When the military return her to the base, they discover that she has a natural immunity to the infection, and plan to use her to develop a vaccine. But when Don visits her to beg for forgiveness, she infects him – revealing herself to be a carrier – and he in turn spreads the contagion further. As a handful of survivors flee, they are in danger from both the infected and the military, who are determined to wipe out the disease, even if it means killing everyone.

Spanish director Juan Carlos Fresnadillo's film is far more grandiose than *28 Days Later* – there are car chases, huge explosions and epic action scenes. Yet it maintains the tension and sense of anxiety established in the first film. This time, the military threat is less personal – the army simply wants to stop the infection from spreading, and, if that means slaughtering the uninfected too, so be it. With a higher gore quotient (particularly during the opening sequence), *28 Weeks Later* is much more of a traditional horror movie than its predecessor, but no worse for that.

The announcement of 2004's *Dawn of the Dead* remake was greeted with howls of outrage from horror fans, many of whom equated it with remaking *Citizen Kane*. Internet petitions were launched against the film, bitter gorehounds wrote angrily on forums, and influential genre writers spread mendacious rumours that the film was being remade as a PG-13-rated teen comedy.

All this hue and cry seemed rather silly when the film finally appeared. The retooled *Dawn of the Dead* was a stunning movie, every bit as good as – and in parts superior to – the original film.

Rookie director Zack Snyder's movie opens with a bang – Ana (Sarah Polley) is a nurse who returns home after a hard shift to relax with her husband Luis (Justin Louis). But the following morning, a neighbour's child appears in their bedroom, and attacks Luis, who dies, and then revives as a ferocious, psychotic zombie. Ana manages to escape, only to discover that the neighbourhood is in chaos as the zombie outbreak rapidly spreads. She subsequently flees the city only to crash her car, forcing her to search for safety on foot.

Ana then meets a handful of fellow survivors – including cop Kenneth (Ving Rhames) and Michael (Jake Weber), and they take shelter in a shopping mall. More survivors arrive, and, for a while, they can pretend that life is normal. But the outside world is now full of the living dead, and reality can only be evaded for so long.

Dawn of the Dead features one of the best opening ten minutes in film history – a furiously paced set-up that leaves viewers breathless. It's the most unnerving depiction of instant social collapse ever captured, and leads to a powerful opening title sequence (backed by Johnny Cash's suitably apocalyptic 'The Man Comes Around').

The rest of the movie doesn't disappoint. Romero's story is expanded via a larger cast and greater thematic scope, and the addition of fellow survivor Andy – alone in the gun shop across from the mall – is a neat twist to the story. James Gunn's screenplay makes reference to Romero (as does Snyder, who features Tom Savini and original cast members in cameos), but the picture has enough originality to stand on its own merits.

The remake of *Dawn of the Dead* attracted much pre-production criticism, but the quality of the film made most critics swallow their words.

Dawn of the Dead combines good actors with rounded characters – something missing from Romero's original – and develops the story so that the viewer actually cares about what happens to them. There are no mere zombie-fodder ciphers in this film.

Although clearly inspired by *28 Days Later*, the running zombies are unquestionably scarier than slow, shuffling corpses that never seemed to pose much of a genuine threat (especially when it appeared possible to shove them aside with ease). These fast, strong, single-minded killing machines are a genuinely fearsome prospect, and the scenes where hordes of the living dead rush after the heroes are heart-stopping.

Of course, some critics complained that Snyder's *Dawn of the Dead* didn't match the social commentary of the original. Well, that's questionable; certainly, it doesn't ram an anti-consumerist manifesto down your throat, but the implications – that people shut out the grim realities of life by ignoring them – are subtly imparted. And in any case, such criticisms miss the point – are we supposed to believe that people actually watch Romero's films because of their social relevance, rather than for visceral horror kicks?

The relentless pace of *Dawn of the Dead* is rigorously maintained, it features plentiful gore (especially in the unrated director's cut), inspired music choices, excellent set-pieces, avoids lame attempts at humour, and wraps up in a grim *denouement* that continues through the closing credits. It's pretty much everything you need in a modern zombie film, and sits at the forefront of the recent revival in hardcore horror.

2004 also saw the re-emergence of a rare beast – the British zombie movie. More than that, a successful British horror-comedy. *Shaun of the Dead* was a sleeper-hit, combining humour, gore, action and romance in a witty tale of a young man's coming of age during a zombie apocalypse.

Shaun (comedian Simon Pegg) is a twenty-nine-year-old slacker whose life is going nowhere. Stuck in a dead-end job, his girlfriend Liz (Kate Ashfield) has left him because he refuses to go anywhere apart from his favourite pub, and his existence seems to consist of hanging around with equally unambitious mate Ed (Nick Frost). But, when the dead inexplicably start to return to life, he has to turn his life around – rescue his mum and Liz, and find somewhere safe to lie low until 'it all blows over'.

Shaun of the Dead is a witty take on the zombie movie. The idea that modern society is self-absorbed to the extent that most people wouldn't notice a zombie outbreak is well handled. Shaun visits a shop, walks past zombies (thinking they are homeless) and sits on a bus with the undead, oblivious to what is happening. Even when a zombie confronts him in his garden, his immediate reaction is to think she's simply a drunk.

But once the action starts, the film proves that it can more than hold its own. TV comedy director Edgar Wright skilfully handles the zombie battle set-pieces, and the scares are played admirably straight – with the odd scenes of extreme gore coming as a genuine shock.

The film has its faults – Nick Frost's character is a bit too annoying, and it's hard to imagine anyone being quite that dumb. However, on the whole, *Shaun of the Dead* is hugely enjoyable and, unlike the slew of video imitations, is the sort of loving tribute that even George Romero appreciated (Wright and Pegg subsequently landed cameos in *Land of the Dead*).

Cheaper, tackier and far less worthwhile, Australian low-budget horror-comedy *Undead* (2003) nevertheless managed to transcend the usual straight-to-video standards with plays at film festivals. International distributors tried valiantly to suggest that the film was in the vein

EVER FELT LIKE YOU WERE
SURROUNDED BY ZOMBIES?

SHAUN OF THE DEAD

A ROMANTIC COMEDY. WITH ZOMBIES.

www.romzom.com

Shaun of the Dead deftly mixed comedy and horror.

of *Bad Taste*. They had a point – *Undead* is equally crass and dumb.

The action begins as the dead are returned to life by a passing meteor shower, a handful of survivors hide out at the ubiquitous zombie-flick farmhouse and fight for their survival, discovering along the way that there may be more to this zombie outbreak than meets the eye.

Twin directors Michael and Peter Spierig throw a lot of blood, swearing, flashing cinematography and crude humour at the screen, but the effect is negligible – we've seen it all before, and done with more aplomb. The CGI effects – created on a laptop apparently – are predictably shoddy, the acting terrible and the comedy – well, you either appreciate Australian toilet humour or you don't.

Referencing *The Evil Dead*, George Romero and Peter Jackson, *Undead* is a forgettable mish-mash that hardly deserves to have been elevated from the ranks of the video home movie.

The *Return of the Living Dead* franchise was revived in 2005 with a pair of movies shot back-to-back in Eastern Europe. Although the two resulting films were very different, they had one thing in common – both were breathtakingly awful.

Return of the Living Dead: Necropolis stars an embarrassed-looking Peter Coyote, clearly slumming it as a member of a huge multinational that specialises in everything from breakfast cereals to weapons research. He travels to Chernobyl to locate the remaining Trioxin containers, which he then returns to the US.

When a teenager is injured in a dirt-bike accident, the boy is pronounced dead at the local

A hungry zombie from the Australian movie *Undead*.

hospital. In fact, he is covertly taken to Hyber-Tech headquarters, where he joins other test subjects, as the company attempts to create a zombie army. Discovering this, his friends (including a little fat kid who seems to have wandered in from *The Goonies*) break into the building to rescue him, but instead end up releasing the zombies.

Necropolis is staggeringly poor. Films featuring 'spunky' teens are rarely entertaining and, in this case, the cast are so annoying that you can't wait for them to die – which not enough of them do. The zombie attacks are reasonably bloody, but poorly staged and repetitive. Not only do the zombies seem merely content to bite a chunk out of their victims' heads, but they also all shuffle along moaning, 'Braaaiiinns' like an undead Greek chorus. This continues until the finale, when a freshly zombified teen is suddenly revealed to be capable of carrying on a cogent conversation.

Worse still is the complete absence of any originality. The super-soldier zombies are facsimiles of *Star Trek*'s Borg, while the Hyber-Tech Corporation is ripped off from *Resident Evil*. The zombies themselves seem pretty useless – a shot to the head kills them (unlike the original film) and a quick shove is usually enough to knock them flying.

Poor as it is, *Necropolis* is a masterpiece compared to *Return of the Living Dead: Rave to the Grave*, which is probably one of the worst movies ever made.

With the surviving cast of *Necropolis* returning (though Peter Coyote is quickly killed off), this dismal film attempts to be a knockabout comedy. The plot centres on a painfully unfunny pair of Interpol agents attempting to track down the missing Trioxin tanks. When Julian (John Keefe) discovers the canisters stashed in a hidden room at his uncle's house, he takes one to college for analysis (although you'd think the events of the previous film would have given him some clues – but this is apparently not so, as none of the characters here seem to remember past events).

When his friends discover that the chemical is similar to ecstasy, they start to manufacture it into pill form and sell it to the local drug dealer. Eventually, all hell breaks loose at a rave party (good to see the makers have their fingers on the pulse of pop culture – or would have if it were fifteen years earlier).

It's something of a challenge to comprehensively express just how awful *Rave to the Grave* is. The attempts at humour are pitifully inept, the direction is terrible, the acting awful and the concept idiotic. As with its predecessor, it makes no attempt to explain why half the cast speak with East European accents, and is so full of plot holes that you have to assume that no one involved in the production gave a damn. An insult to even the most zomboid intellect, *Rave to the Grave* is unforgivable.

Like *House of the Dead 2*, both films made their debut not at theatres or on DVD, but on the Sci-Fi Channel.

Also pretty poor was *Fido*, made in 2006 by Andrew Currie and starring Billy Connolly in the title role, a tame zombie who is treated (as the title suggests) like a pet dog. In a 1950s world where the living dead have been domesticated, Fido is the zombie pet of Timmy Robinson (K'Sun Ray) and the film follows their *Lassie*-style adventures. It's a one-joke movie that has a few moments (the pastiche on 1950s small-town conformity is reasonable, but has been done plenty of times before), but which ultimately wears thin rather quickly.

Low-budget animated film *City of Rott* (2006) tried to do something a little different. It tells the story of an elderly man who ventures out into the zombie-infested city in search of a new pair of slippers. Unfortunately, this is a crudely realised effort that tends to overstay its welcome, even at a scant seventy-eight minutes. Watching angry old Fred battling zombies with his walking frame is only amusing for so long, and the poor-quality Flash animation becomes migraine-inducing after a while – no matter how outrageously gory the action might be.

One-man band Frank Sudol (who directed, wrote, produced, edited, wrote the music and provided the voices) should be congratulated for getting any sort of release for this, though it might have been better as a ten-minute internet short.

Zombies went hardcore again in 2005, with a movie based on Edward Lee's short story and comic strip *Grub Girl*. Craven Moorehead's film stays close to Lee's story of the 'grub' (i.e. corpse) played by Brittney Skye, who is killed by radioactive fallout and then quite literally fucked back to life by a couple of morgue attendants, who are then slaughtered for their troubles. She then goes back to her career as a hooker – with the advantage that grubs don't have any diseases and can't feel pain, making her perfect for the more perverted clients. After offing her pimp with a spot of fellatio/castration and gut chomping (both achieved with amusingly cheap and cheesy not-so-special effects), she sets up her own brothel for dead girls and their admirers.

Clearly not a film that will win any awards for subtlety, *Grub Girl* is certainly one of the weirder adult video productions. The juxtaposition of gore (Skye is painted grey and covered in scars, and the more visceral scenes are unusual for this type of sexploitation movie, where blood and guts are usually considered as being contrary to titillation) and regular porn is a little incongruous, but somehow works, and Moorehead's direction is pretty solid. Produced by rock star Glenn Danzig's Verotik Publishing, the film has an industrial metal soundtrack, including an unreleased Danzig remix.

Self-evidently not for everyone, *Grub Girl* is nonetheless amusing stuff for the hard-to-offend, and Skye is effective as the sassy undead hooker. The film's success suggested a sequel, though none has yet emerged.

Nevertheless, there were more porno zombies and more heavy metal in Rob Rotten's *Porn of the Dead* (2007) – a title that was surely years overdue. This shot-on-video production starts out impressively – a decaying female zombie shuffles down a dusty road in a genuinely eerie moment, suggesting that the film will be a heady mix of sex and horror.

However, *Anal Swine* director Rotten fumbles the ball and, instead

Zombies as pets in *Fido*.

of making a bizarre crossover movie, he's content to shoot what is a straightforward – if somewhat grungy – porn flick. Only two scenes mix gore and sex – the opening, where a zombie blow job ends with a graphic fellatio/castration scene that is outrageously tasteless (but much more effective than the segment in *Grub Girl*), and the finale, which features a zombie disembowelling her partner after exploring a comprehensive gamut of sexual positions.

Porn of the Dead's production values are poor, the make-up mostly lousy (a zombie's cosmetics start to rub off during a sex scene) and the movie is a series of unconnected *vignettes*. You have to wonder what particular demographic this is aimed at. Regular porn fans are unlikely to be thrilled by the penis severing and entrail ripping, while gore fans will generally find the relentless porn (and the sex scenes are as lengthy as in any regular porn movie) too much.

Only the soundtrack from extreme metal bands like Deicide, Decapitated and Gorerotted stands out – it's not the sort of music you'd associate with porn, but it works extremely well. Overall, *Porn of the Dead* can be most charitably viewed as a wasted opportunity to mix horror and erotica.

A moment of extreme bad taste in the generally disappointing *Porn of the Dead*.

The film should not, by the way, be confused with British hardcore movie *Porn of the Dead* (2008) that – despite the title – has no zombies. *Zombie Nation* is another UK porn film from the same year that mixes the living dead with X-rated action, though this contains little in the way of horror.

Demonstrating that zombie porn is becoming a strangely established sub-genre, 2008 also saw Rodney Moore's *Night of the Giving Head*, where a virgin is conned by her slutty friends into drinking a glass of semen, only to become a 'sperm zombie'. She rapidly infects a surprisingly large cast of topless starlets who shuffle along, attacking helpless men in their search for 'cock' and 'cum'. While the production values are low, Moore's film is a mildly amusing spoof for the more open-minded zombie fan.

Zombies meet swingers in *The Stink of Flesh* (2005), a clumsy mix of gore and soft-porn from director Scott Phillips. Here, survivors of a zombie holocaust not only have to deal with the usual problems of a world filled with flesh-eating ghouls, but also have to accept that their pool of potential sexual partners has now been drastically reduced. While the film could have been subversively entertaining, the low-budget, poor acting and a cast who – to be blunt – should not be taking their clothes off rather let this down.

The living dead scuffed their cadaverous way around the unlikely location of Greece for *To Kako* (2005), released in English-speaking countries as *Evil*. Not generally known for its horror movies, Greece had nevertheless contributed a few examples to the genre during the 1970s and

Sex and death. 'Sperm zombies' in porno movie *Night of the Giving Head*.

Eighties, often at the hand of director Nico Mastorakis. But the Greek filmmakers had never entered the zombie milieu until *Evil*.

The movie opens in a cave, where three construction workers are infected with a mysterious illness. Later that night, the trio change into flesh-eating ghouls. Inevitably, this infection rapidly spreads, and soon the whole city is a zombie-ridden no-go zone, sending the handful of survivors in search of somewhere to hide.

Influenced by Romero, *28 Days Later* and just about every other cult zombie film you could think of, *Evil* is no masterpiece, but it does offer some entertainment value for less demanding viewers. With plentiful gore, cheap gags and sound – though unremarkable – production values, it's a decent debut from writer/director Yorgos Noussias.

British film *The Zombie Diaries* (2006) is primarily notable for using the *faux*-documentary format that George Romero would later adapt for *Diary of the Dead*. This was hardly groundbreaking – *The Blair Witch Project* had already popularised this conceit – and the film was let down by poor performances and production values. That said, it's considerably better than Romero's efforts in the same vein.

2007's *Hell's Ground* answers that most burning of questions: Would *The Texas Chain Saw Massacre* be improved if set in Pakistan and with zombies needlessly crowbarred into the storyline?

Unsurprisingly, the answer is 'no', but there is plenty of fun to be had in discovering this. The movie certainly piles on the horror clichés – five teens on their way to a rock concert get lost in the woods after taking a 'short cut' and find themselves besieged by a demented killer (this film's Leatherface is a mace-wielding maniac in a burka). Inexplicably, thirty minutes into the film, the hapless teens' van is attacked by a group of zombies, who cause a few minutes of havoc, bite one of the group and are then never seen again.

Lack of living-dead action aside, the British-produced film is cheerfully gory nonsense, and certainly offers a different view of Pakistani culture than Western audiences are used to seeing. There is a long tradition of both Indian and Pakistani horror movies, but, to date, few have been widely seen in the West.

Swingers battle zombies in *The Stink of Flesh*.

As the US zombie revival rolled along, a diverse selection of new movies emerged. Most notable was 2007's *Flight of the Living Dead* (also known as *Plane Dead*), an unashamedly trashy mix of 1970s disaster-movie clichés and modern zombie action that apparently owed much to the trashy Samuel L. Jackson vehicle *Snakes on a Plane* (2006) – though *Flight...* was already in pre-production when *Snakes...* was released.

Set on a transatlantic flight to Paris, *Flight of the Living Dead* eases slowly into the undead action, establishing the *dramatis personae* through a series of introductions to stereotypical airport-movie characters – there's even a nun aboard. In the hold is the cryogenically frozen body of a scientist who has been infected with a new virus.

Developed as a bio-weapon, it causes the organs of the body to temporarily shut down, with revival taking place shortly afterwards. It also induces a standard set of symptoms consistent with zombification – a loss of reason and the overwhelming need to eat human flesh. When turbulence causes the container to crack open, the infected doctor breaks loose, and before long almost everyone on board – including the pilots – are rampaging through the plane. The few survivors – an air marshall, a cop and his prisoner, and a single stewardess – have to fight off the zombies while trying to land the plane before the government has it shot down.

Once the action starts it is maintained relentlessly – having the zombies contained within such a confined arena is an inspired move that gives the film a marked sense of claustrophobia. It's all very silly of course – the number of gunshots and explosions on board the plane would certainly have a more devastating effect in real life. But that's fine, because no one seems to be taking *Flight of the Living Dead* too seriously.

Director Scott Thomas does a good job mixing humour with horror, and his fast-paced zombies are virtually impossible to stop – even destroying the brain only slows them down, given that all their organs regenerate. With the living dead still going strong at the film's conclusion, it seems that a sequel is likely once the DVD sales rack up.

The wittiest part of *Undead or Alive* (2007) is probably the title. This zombie western comedy (or 'zomedy') tells the story of a couple of cowboys who are on the run after robbing a corrupt sheriff. The buddies team up with an apache woman who wants revenge against the white man's army. The trio head for a military outpost (with plenty of breaks for poor-quality jokes along the way). However, Geronimo's curse has brought the dead back to life – and they're hungry.

With a cast headlined by *Saturday Night Live* (and a host of failed movies) star Chris Kattan, *Undead or Alive* is sadly neither funny nor scary; packed with pathetic-looking zombies and juvenile humour, it feels like a throwback to the 1980s.

Anyone excited by the idea of the living dead and the Wild West clashing should note that, despite the title and artwork implications, 2006 production *The Quick and the Undead* is not a zombie western, but

What's worse than snakes on a plane? How about zombies? The gleefully trashy *Flight of the Living Dead*.

rather a post-apocalyptic action movie from Australia about bounty hunters tracking down zombies after a viral outbreak.

Texas Chain Saw Massacre director Tobe Hooper had been connected with zombie projects on a few occasions – most notably *Return of the Living Dead* – and was briefly engaged to direct *Wicked Little Things* (released in the UK as *Zombies*), which has a group of zombie children – trapped in a mine in 1913 – who escape and terrorise a local family. The film was eventually helmed by J.S. Cardone (who made a minor impact in 1982 with the low-budget shocker *The Slayer*) and originally played the States as part of the touring '8 Films To Die For' Horrorfest.

Wicked Little Things is nothing special, but after a slow start manages to at least provide a few atmospheric moments, thanks primarily to the genuinely eerie children, whose emotionless white faces and dead eyes are pretty unnerving. But the picture would work better as a ghost story, which is effectively what it is – the flesh-eating scenes add nothing to the plot and seem grafted on to validate the zombie motif.

Hooper took his first proper stab at the sub-genre in 2005 with *Mortuary*. Unfortunately, the director had long since passed his creative peak, and the film is a fairly tame effort. The story begins with a family moving to a small town in California to take over a mortuary, only to find that the place is the subject of local gossip and superstition, with rumours that it is haunted. The stories turn out to be true, as a mysterious fungus on the walls causes the dead to return to life.

There's no real explanation for any of this, and Hooper directs in an efficient but uninspired way. The story is dull, the action infrequent and the scares minimal in this forgettable feature.

Hooper did a little better the following year with *Dance of the Dead*, part of the *Masters of Horror* series. Shot for American cable television, *Masters of Horror* presented exclusive mini-features from a stellar cast of directors including John Carpenter, Takashi Miike and John Landis, which were often better than some of their theatrical work.

Hooper's film wasn't one of the best episodes. Based on a Richard Matheson short story, this post-apocalyptic tale follows Peggy (Jessica Lowndes), punk biker Jak (Jonathan Tucker) and their friends as they visit The Doom Room, a nightspot where reanimated corpses are made to dance for the entertainment of the public.

A victim of the *Wicked Little Things*.

The film presents a solid allegory upon the dehumanisation of survivors and Robert Englund gives a lively performance, but *Dance of the Dead* is too slight to sustain interest. A much better instalment of this series was Joe Dante's *Homecoming*.

Perhaps best known for directing family fare such as *Gremlins* and *Innerspace*, Dante is not a director one associates with dark, serious cinema, but that's very much the terrain covered by *Homecoming*. There's satire, but it's angry, bitter and jaded.

Set in an alternate reality during the lead-up to the 2004 presidential election, Dante's 2005 film tells the story of Republican presidential aide David Murch (Jon Tenney), who appears on a television debate about the Iraq War and wishes that the dead soldiers could return as they would unequivocally demonstrate their support for the war.

Unfortunately for him, he gets his wish – in part. The military dead do indeed rise and demand their right to vote – but not for the President. The soldiers are only too aware that the war is immoral, illegal and the reason that they are dead in the first

The dead attack in Tobe Hooper's *Mortuary*.

place, and vote overwhelmingly against it. But, thanks to ballot manipulation, their votes are discounted, and the President re-elected. This upsets the dead, who come back in ever greater numbers – from all wars past – to overthrow the incumbent regime.

Dante's film makes no bones about where it stands. The right-wing characters are all cynical, hateful and corrupt – far less human than the zombies. Dante viciously spoofs far-right commentator Ann Coulter, George W. Bush and others, making them the real monsters of the story. *Homecoming* has the morality-play feel of the most memorable *Twilight Zone* episodes and an EC Comics sense of black humour. It's one of Dante's best works.

Troma made their name in the mid-Eighties with gory, camp horror comedies like *Toxic Avenger*, and in 2006 came up with their 'finest' work to date (which isn't saying much) – *Poultrygeist: Night of the Chicken Dead*. This gleefully trashy film tells the story of Arbie, a loser in love who takes a job at the newly opened American Chicken Bunker fast-food outlet. Unfortunately, the Bunker has been built on an Indian burial ground, and before long, mutated human-chicken hybrid zombies have been created via the consumption of possessed fried chicken.

Poking fun at lesbians, Muslims, vegetarians and just about every other PC sacred cow, *Poultrygeist* revels in its trashiness. There is plenty of gratuitous gore and nudity, deliberately

Dead soldiers return to make a political point in *Homecoming*.

bad dialogue and several songs. Crude, rude and tacky, *Poultrygeist* is also quite funny – unlike Troma's earlier works. Director Lloyd Kaufman appears in the film as the older version of Arbie, trying in vain to mentor his younger self.

The most eagerly awaited zombie film of 2007 was Robert Rodriguez's *Planet Terror*. Unfortunately, few people got to see it in the way it was originally intended.

Planet Terror started life as part of *Grindhouse*, an ambitious double-bill that also featured Quentin Tarantino's *Death Proof* and a series of spoof exploitation movie trailers by the likes of Rob Zombie, Eli Roth and Edgar Wright. Complete with film scratches and other visual damage, *Grindhouse* aimed to recreate the exploitation glory days of the 1970s, when run-down cinemas showed sex- and violence-packed double-bills on a regular basis.

Unfortunately, modern audiences found the experience too confusing. There were reports of people leaving the theatre after one movie, seemingly unable to cope with the concept of the double-bill, and, in general, people stayed away completely. Producers Miramax panicked, pulled the film and split the two movies up, releasing longer versions of each as stand-alone features.

In *Planet Terror*, a bio-weapon is accidentally released at a Texas military base, turning people into cannibal zombies. As the infection spreads, it's down to stripper Cherry Darling

(Rose McGowan) to save the dwindling band of survivors – aided by her newly acquired machine-gun leg.

Unlike Tarantino, who cleaned up his solo version of *Death Proof*, Rodriguez leaves the fake film damage and missing reels intact in this version, though he does reinstate about thirty minutes of deleted footage. The resulting film is slightly overlong, but still a fast-paced, tongue-in-cheek, gory pastiche of horror movies from the past. The original *Grindhouse* is still the version to see, but this is a passable alternative.

The 2008 remake of *Day of the Dead* was doomed from the start – at least as far as the horror obsessives were concerned. Showing that they had learned nothing from the *Dawn...* remake, irate Romero fans started another pointless internet petition against the movie (despite the fact that no studio would be likely to cease production on a movie on account of a petition put up by a handful of angry geeks).

Such prejudicial furore conveniently ignored the fact that Romero's original 1985 film is dreadful, and this re-imagining – which thankfully disregards more or less everything from the original – is not that bad. Of course, that's not to say it's any kind of classic – it has plenty of faults. But taken for what it is, the film is entertaining enough.

Day of the Dead kicks off in a small Colorado town, where a virus that initially seems to be a severe form of flu proves to be far more deadly – it kills the infected, and then revives them as zombies, who in

Bad taste, zombie chickens and musical numbers in Troma's *Poultrygeist* (above); Robert Rodriguez's tribute to Eighties Italian horror, *Planet Terror* (below).

Horror remakes keep on coming. Steve Miner's *Day of the Dead*.

turn infect others. Soldier Sarah Bowman (Mena Suvari) leads a handful of survivors in their battle against the dead.

At a brisk eighty-six minutes, *Day of the Dead* moves as quickly as the high-speed zombies it features. Criticism of the film for being a teen horror movie is unwarranted: there are only a couple of teenage characters and they are not that annoying. Unlike Nick Cannon's Salazar, whose macho theatrics and wooden acting ensure that most viewers will be looking forward to his demise almost from the moment he first appears. The gore quotient is satisfactorily strong and Steve Miner's direction is solid enough.

The downsides? Mena Suvari holds her own, but is somewhat unconvincing as a hard-nosed soldier, and the presence of Ving Rhames is unnecessarily confusing – he's not playing the same character as he did in the *Dawn...* remake, and his part here (as Captain Rhodes) is little more than a glorified cameo.

Will Smith comes to face-to-face with a feral mutant in the big-budget *I Am Legend*.

The idea of Bub (or Bud, as he is in this version) becoming a harmless zombie because in life he was a vegetarian is rather trite, and the zombies who climb walls and run along the ceiling are probably a step too far (especially as they are rendered in unconvincing CGI). Regardless of these flaws, *Day of the Dead* is an acceptable, high-octane retread of a lacklustre original.

For a genuinely unnecessary remake, viewers should look no further than *Night of the Living Dead 3-D*, released in 2007 without any of the vitriolic fanboy hysteria that had been aimed at the other Romero remakes. Which is odd, as not only is *NOTLD* the most sacred of the original *Dead* trilogy, but this revamp is shockingly poor.

Starting out as a faithful copy of the original film (which is shown briefly on a TV during the opening scenes and then pops up throughout the film), this version soon veers off into its own world, changing the original story – though not for the better.

After Barb (Brianna Brown) and her brother Johnny (Ken Ward) are attacked by zombies at the cemetery, he drives off leaving her alone and in danger. She manages to flee and is rescued by student Ben (Joshua DesRoces), who takes her to a remote farmhouse. The farm owner, Henry Cooper (Greg Travis), doesn't believe her story, and is reluctant to call the police because of the cannabis farm he has out back. But, when the zombies attack, they are forced into action.

Where this film deviates most from its source material is during the closing sequences. It transpires that the dead have been revived by mortician Gerald Tovar (the hammy Sid Haig), using experimental drugs that were kept in his storeroom. These subsequently combine with the embalming fluid to create a chemical reaction that induces a zombie state.

With wholly unpleasant characters played by generally poor actors, uninterested direction by Jeff Broadstreet and a revamped story that not only makes little sense but also fails to engage the viewer, this is disappointing fare. A smattering of gore and some gratuitous nudity are not enough to make this watchable, and the 3-D is pretty bad, going from poorly focused to barely noticeable. As this was never going to have a widespread theatrical release, more effort should have gone into making the 3-D effects more effective when viewed on video.

Night of the Living Dead 3-D is depressing stuff – a Romero remake that really is as bad as everyone feared the *Dawn...* and *Day...* revamps would be. Currently, it appears that

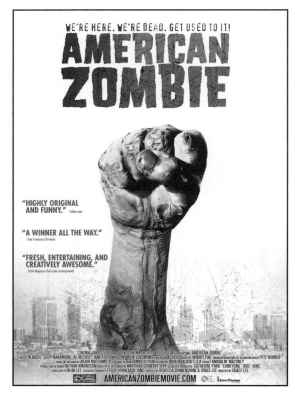

WE'RE HERE. WE'RE DEAD. GET USED TO IT!

AMERICAN ZOMBIE

"HIGHLY ORIGINAL
AND FUNNY." - Salon.com

"A WINNER ALL THE WAY."
- San Francisco Chronicle

"FRESH, ENTERTAINING, AND
CREATIVELY AWESOME."
- SLUG Magazine (Salt Lake Underground)

AMERICANZOMBIEMOVIE.COM

American Zombie saw the living dead standing up for their rights.

Broadstreet is set to carry on trashing the past by remaking the unique, and completely un-remakeable, *Spider Baby*.

2007 saw another remake, a big-budget, major studio retread of Richard Matheson's *I Am Legend*. This version was the first to use the novel's title, yet ironically made a nonsense of it by stripping the main character (here played by an unusually restrained Will Smith) of his moral ambiguity and reducing the 'vampires' (mostly seen as unconvincing CGI-created mutants) to fairly mindless monsters. The film also disregards more or less every other interesting element of Matheson's book (including the moment where anti-hero Neville's wife returns from the dead to confront him), and instead contents itself with being a glossy, loud and ultimately empty action movie that cribs from *28 Days Later*. As such, it's not without moments of entertainment, and certainly flies by painlessly enough – but it's a wasted opportunity.

Independent filmmaker Grace Lee's American Zombie (2007) is a spoof documentary about how the revived dead are 'living' in society. Here, the zombies are cogent, opinionated and even militant (when asked if there are flesh-eating zombies, one character retorts 'are there flesh-eating humans?'). The film's concept is similar to the online serial *Dead End Days* and aborted TV series *Babylon Fields*, where the living and the living dead have to somehow get along. Lee's 'mockumentary' format is interesting, and gives the film a certain edge. It's no masterpiece, but *American Zombie* shows that there is still scope to try new ideas within the sub-genre.

Zombie Strippers (2008) is a film that clearly has no interest in exploring the subtler nuances of the sub-genre. Instead, this is a gleefully trashy, and surprisingly entertaining effort that may be the best Troma film that Troma never made.

Set in a nightmarish near-future, where George W. Bush is into his fourth term as President and is starting wars all over the globe, the film opens with some straightforward (if moderately humorous) zombie action. Scientists are working on reviving the dead as super-soldiers, but inevitably things go wrong and the zombies break free. A soldier, bitten by a zombie, manages to escape and stumbles into a nearby strip club where he manages to infect the lead dancer.

11. Zombies Invade the Home
The Living Dead on TV and Online

Zombies have made numerous guest appearances on TV shows, but, unlike vampires, werewolves and other monsters, have never taken centre stage – though it seems that this may be about to change.

One of the earliest appearances of the living dead on TV – made-for-television movies aside – was in *Kolchak: The Night Stalker*, a short-lived 1974 supernatural detective series which was in many ways a precursor of *The X-Files*.

Kolchak was spun off the success of two TV movies, *The Night Stalker* and its sequel *The Night Strangler*, both of which set record viewing figures in America. The films pitted downtrodden newspaper reporter Carl Kolchak against supernatural foes, and the series followed much the same format. Unfortunately, there was little variety in each episode other than a 'monster-of-the-week' and the series was cancelled midway through its first season after a pay dispute with star Darren McGavin.

The second episode of the series was entitled 'The Zombie', and had Kolchak investigating the mysterious deaths of crime-syndicate members, who have been found with their spines snapped. His investigation leads him to Haitian voodoo practitioners, as he discovers that a murdered man is being revived to take revenge on his killers.

'The Zombie' is a fairly entertaining episode of an uneven series, but also suffers from the restrictions of 1970s network TV, with the horror being distinctly bland.

A decade and a half after *Kolchak*, the series helped inspire Chris Carter's *The X-Files*, which became a much more successful supernatural/paranormal detective series, running throughout the 1990s and spawning two feature films. Although generally seen as a show about alien abduction and governmental malpractice, the series did feature many out-and-out horror episodes. Although a couple of *X-Files* dealt with the living dead, they were not among the long-running series' most significant stories and the zombie elements were often largely incidental.

Season two saw 'Fresh Bones', with Fox Mulder (David Duchovny) and Dana Scully (Gillian Anderson) investigating Haitian voodoo, but the episode made little reference to zombies.

More interesting was 'Millennium', which featured Frank Black from the recently cancelled series of that name. Black assists the pair in investigating the disappearance of a corpse two days before the year 2000 begins – a necromancer has revived the body as one of the 'four horsemen' to usher in the apocalypse. The episode is not bad, but the series as a whole was past its best by this point.

In the 1970s and Eighties, good movies often became bad TV shows. By the end of the 1990s, the reverse was true. One such example was *Buffy the Vampire Slayer*, which began in 1997. Based on a pretty poor 1992 horror-comedy film, the series rapidly developed into a witty, edgy and increasingly dark show, with Buffy (Sarah Michelle Gellar) and her friends battling evil – and increasingly finding that 'evil' wasn't always so clear-cut.

Darren McGavin as Kolchak in *Night Stalker*.

Aside from the eponymous vampires, Buffy faced all manner of supernatural foes, including a smattering of zombies. In the second episode of season three, 'Dead Man's Party', Buffy is confronted with assorted zombies that have been revived by a mysterious Nigerian mask.

In season five's 'Forever', Buffy's sister Dawn attempts to bring back their recently deceased mother using magic. In a nod to *The Monkey's Paw*, we never get to see the revived corpse, as the spell is broken just as she knocks on the door.

Buffy spin-off series *Angel* also featured the living dead. Designed as a more adult version of *Buffy*, *Angel* starred David Boreanaz as the vampire with a soul, who has moved to Los Angeles where he runs an investigation agency and fights evil.

By season four, *Angel* had assumed a distinctly dark edge, and the eighth episode 'Habeas Corpses' was especially brutal, particularly for TV. After demonic monster The Beast attacks the offices of Wolfram & Hart (the satanic law firm which had been Angel's nemesis throughout the series), Angel's son Connor finds himself in peril. Angel rushes to his aid, but finds that the murdered staff in the building are returning as zombies – who are then dispatched with gory abandon. The zombie attacks are atmospheric and intense – certainly the closest any TV show has come to emulating a zombie-outbreak movie.

Not that *Angel* is all grim. There's still time for some humour, particularly in the fractious relationship between Connor and Angel:

Connor: What's a zombie?
Angel: It's an undead thing.
Connor: Like you?
Angel: No. Zombies are slow-moving, dimwitted things that crave human flesh.
Connor: Like you.

In Britain, the revived *Doctor Who* faced zombies in the third episode of the new series, 'The Unquiet Dead', in which The Doctor (Christopher Eccleston) and Rose (Billie Piper) – alongside Charles Dickens (Simon Callow) – faced corpses that had been reanimated by alien invaders. Ninety-one viewers – presumably too consumed by moral hubris to remember their own childhoods – complained to the BBC about the content of the show, claiming it to be 'too scary' for children.

In reality, it is one of the creepier episodes, but not exactly terrifying – writer Mark Gatiss having been told by producer Russell T. Davies to tone down his original 'bleak' screenplay.

It's not just in horror and fantasy shows that zombies have made their mark. Many humorous series have featured the living dead.

Naturally, Scooby Doo and his ever-curious chums ran into several 'zombies' in their time, although – in keeping with the style of the show – these all turned out to be criminals in disguise. The series (which began in 1967 and has been through various incarnations ever since) was revamped in 1998 for the feature-length *Scooby Doo on Zombie Island*, where – for the first time – the threats turned out to be genuinely supernatural. This popular movie (which mixed classic Scooby Doo with a few knowing post-modern elements to keep parents amused) led to a revival of interest in the hapless hound, who has gone on to appear in several more feature-length adventures.

The Simpsons has featured zombies on a couple of occasions, most notably in 'Tree House of Horror III'. This instalment of the annual Halloween episode featured 'Dial Z for Zombie', where Bart and Lisa manage to raise the dead ('They prefer to be called the living impaired,' explains Bart). The zombies hunger for brains – something which saves Homer when they tap on his head and then walk away disappointed.

South Park has also referenced zombies in several episodes, most notably 'Pinkeye', where the much-killed Kenny is revived as a zombie and starts to infect the other people of the town, and 'Night of the Living Homeless', where the destitute stand in for zombies (demanding 'change' rather than 'brains') in a parody of *Dawn of the Dead*.

Outside the world of animation, the episode of *Frasier* entitled 'Tales from the Crypt' has the eponymous lead get involved in a convoluted series of practical jokes, culminating in a 'zombie attack'.

Episode three of British slacker sit-com *Spaced* acts as a precursor to *Shaun of the Dead*, with Simon Pegg's character dreaming that he's trapped inside a *Resident Evil*-style video game. Notably, a poster for *Dawn of the Dead* was prominently displayed throughout the series.

Zombies – in one form or another – have also turned up in shows like *The Man From U.N.C.L.E* (season two's 'The Very Important Zombie Affair' sees agents Solo and Kurayakin up against voodoo, zombies and corrupt politicians on a Caribbean island), *Alias* (the episode 'Before the Flood' has *28 Days Later*-style living zombies) and *Supernatural* (the *X-Files*-

Zombie fun for kids in *Zombie Hotel* (left) and for adults in *Alive* (right).

inspired show had a 2006 episode entitled 'Children Shouldn't Play with Dead Things', where a lovesick girl is revived as a vengeful zombie using necromancy).

To show just how mainstream zombies had become by the turn of the century, kids' cartoon *The Angry Beavers* even had an episode called 'Open Wide for Zombies', in which the beavers battle the living dead in a spooky bayou. Similarly, *Zombie Hotel* was, as the title suggests, an animated show about a family of zombies who run a hotel and centres on Fungus and Maggot, two children who pretend to be human so they can attend school.

Hidden-camera shows have become increasingly outrageous in recent years, so it's no surprise that a couple of these have featured zombie spoofs. 2001's *Spy TV* had a segment where a security guard took his first nightshift watching over a construction site that used to be a cemetery. His reaction when 'zombies' suddenly start to crawl from the grave and attack his colleague is priceless.

Scare Tactics also had a zombie skit, with a newly hired cemetery worker finding himself battling a particularly irate-looking zombie. It's easy to mock the people on these shows, but who wouldn't freak out if they saw 'corpses' rising from their coffins?

After years in the shadows, at last zombies seem set to take centre stage on TV, with producers finally seeing the sub-genre's potential. The first attempt, sadly, fell at the first hurdle.

Babylon Fields was a pilot commissioned by CBS for their autumn 2007 season – however, the show wasn't broadcast and it's now highly unlikely that it will be taken forward, despite an internet campaign. A pity, as this had the potential to be a unique and fascinating show.

The pilot opens with the dead literally clawing their way out of their graves. For reasons unknown, the dead of Babylon are returning to life – families come home to find deceased family members waiting for them, the cemetery is packed with the wandering dead and the population is thrown into panic, with visions of brain-eating zombies taken from movies dancing in their heads.

But these zombies are not movie monsters. They retain their memories and personalities, and want nothing more than to pick up where they left off. For some people, this is a dream come true – we see one woman in post-coital bliss with her dead husband (autopsy scars still visible on his chest) – while others see it as the end of the world and arm themselves to the teeth.

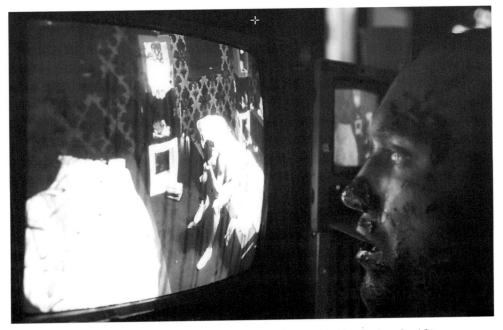

It seems that the critics are right — *Big Brother* is watched by mindless zombies! A scene from *Dead Set.*

The pilot is similar in plot to French film *Les Revenants* (2004), although presumably it would have developed a distinct identity as it continued — and that is the depressing thing, because it never got the chance.

Watching the *Babylon Fields* pilot is a frustrating experience. The show establishes its premise, introduces the characters and then leads into story strands that will never be followed up. For instance, one zombie — a former cop who was seemingly killed by the wife and daughter he'd been abusing — reports his own murder to the police and demands an investigation. And then it ends.

One of the great lost TV shows, *Babylon Fields* may have failed to make the airwaves, but a more traditional zombie theme was adapted to the small screen in *Alive.*

At the time of writing, *Alive* has yet to air, but an effective viral marketing campaign — with original video clips on the website *fightingthedead.com* in the form of news reports and Civil Defence broadcasts — has already created a buzz about the series. Created by *Star Trek* writers Judith and Garfield Reeves Stevens alongside Matt Vancil, the show is set in a military bunker called Falcon Rock, where survivors of a zombie apocalypse are holed up, having sought shelter there after zombies took over the world in just six days.

If the teaser clips are anything to go by, this looks to be an intense, exciting series, very much in the Romero tradition — though with a few interesting twists, such as the zombies' apparent ability to adapt to their surroundings. One clip shows them wearing helmets to protect themselves against bullets in the head.

Trash-TV queen Davina McCall becomes a flesh-hungry zombie in *Dead Set*.

The teasers also address an issue that is conveniently ignored in other zombie films where the infection is carried in the blood – namely that it's not just bites you need to worry about. A prime example of this can be found in *House of the Dead 2*, where the protagonists are frequently hit in the face by zombie blood splatter with no ill effects. This raises questions about infection through the mouth, nose or eyes. *Alive* would seem to take that into account.

While the world waited for *Alive* to premiere, Britain's Channel Four – or more precisely its digital spin-off channel E4 – stole a march on everyone with *Dead Set*, a five-part shocker aired in the week leading up to Halloween 2008.

Written by *Guardian* columnist Charlie Brooker, the show offered a neat twist on the traditional zombie film theme of survivors under siege. In Brooker's story, contestants taking part in Channel Four reality show *Big Brother* find themselves the only apparent survivors after an unexplained zombie outbreak.

The idea of a bunch of mismatched people stuck in a self-contained house is scary enough on the real *Big Brother*, and Brooker's script cranks up the tension and paranoia effectively as the various misfits argue and fret about what to do. Unfortunately, the show suffers from being a little *too* true to life – the characters are every bit as unpleasant as those seen on the real show, and with no one to root for – even the lead character, production assistant Kelly (Jaime Winstone), is

Online serial *Dead End Days* saw zombies trying to fit into society.

less sympathetic than she ought to be – the viewer is left to simply wait for these annoying people to die rather than become engaged with their plight.

That said, anyone who is repulsed by lowest-common-denominator TV will be amused to see its patron saint Davina McCall having her throat torn out and head caved in.

Director Yann Demange is over-influenced by *28 Days Later*, copying the film's high-speed cinematography, and the 'documentary' style grates – this isn't a pseudo-documentary like *The Blair Witch Project*, and so there's no real excuse for the camera going out of focus. It's a pointless conceit that simply doesn't work.

However, *Dead Set* has a lot going for it. It's pretty full-throttle stuff once it gets going, and the humour is kept sensibly in check. Although billed as a comedy horror, it's actually fairly straight, any humour coming from the absurdity of the situation and stupidity of the characters.

In fact, the series becomes increasingly grim as it progresses, and has a suitably bleak conclusion. It's also unquestionably the goriest programme ever seen on TV – exploding heads, eviscerations, and more, make this a blood-soaked match for any zombie movie.

Brooker clearly knows his zombie culture, and his show is a flawed but exciting production. Its success – the first episode set a new record for E4's ratings – will hopefully encourage more horror TV production in the UK.

It's not just television broadcasters who are using the internet to expand the reach of the zombie. There are several websites featuring original video and animation, much of it superior to the shot-on-video DVD films that continue to proliferate.

Even the zombies have fun in *Dead End Days*.

A good example is the Canadian *Dead End Days*. This forty-eight-episode serial first appeared in 2003, and deals with the problems of the 'previously deceased' who have returned to life and are struggling to fit into society. The battles between the living and dead are long over and now the two groups live side by side – despite the latter still harbouring a hunger for brains.

In *Dead End Days*, the zombies don't simply co-exist with humans – they've become a social demographic, even to the extent of being targeted by advertisers. But, as their numbers grow, will they finally make the living into an oppressed minority – and how long will it be before their cannibalistic tendencies run rampant again?

Dead End Days mixes horror, humour, comedy, social satire and romance in equal measure. It's better than the vast majority of shot-on-video zombie films, proving that it is possible to do something innovative with a minimal budget. The idea that zombies would be a powerful consumer lobby is interesting (apparently, they are easily impressed by any product which uses the word 'brain') and the series out-Romeros Romero when it comes to critiquing modern society.

More interestingly, the idea of humans and zombies having to co-exist – zombies holding down jobs, the living torn between leaving well alone and killing off the undead – is handled well, and predates *Babylon Fields*, *Shaun of the Dead* and other productions which explore similar themes. The whole series is now available as a four-disc DVD set from *www.deadenddays.com*.

Ten-part animated series *Xombie* [*www.xombified.com*] is a nicely designed work that has also spun off into comic books and even a novel. Set in 2042, it follows the adventures of a little girl called Zoe and her zombie friend Dirge as they make their way through Destiny City following a plague which has brought the dead back to life. Dirge is a 'variant' – a zombie who has maintained his intelligence, unlike the majority who are bloodthirsty maniacs.

With decent characterisation and a strong plot, this is a lot better than most animated shows, and is well worth checking out. Creator James Farr continues to flesh out his undead world in a variety of formats, and hopefully *Xombie* will eventually be made available to a more mainstream audience.

More traditional is *War of the Dead – Z.E.R.O.* [*www.warofthedead.com*], an ambitious high-definition series that seems to have stalled after a couple of episodes in 2007.

Set ten years after a zombie outbreak that has been successfully put down, the series follows the adventures of the Zombie Emergency Response Operations task force, whose job it is to eliminate any remaining zombies and prevent fresh outbreaks. Ambitious in scope, *War of the Dead* unfortunately suffers from many of the problems that befall shot-on-video productions – namely, terrible acting and clichéd characters. The Z.E.R.O. squad are particularly unpleasant, and the short episodes seem to be padded out with needless material setting the scene.

Writer and director Mike Disario seems too attached to traditional film and television formats to be willing to explore the narrative freedom that a web-based serial allows, to the detriment of the project. There are plus points – the production values are good and this is one of the best-looking web video streams around. But the story – even after two episodes – seems to be going nowhere.

Several one-off zombie films have appeared online. Unfortunately, most of them are little more than shorter versions of the trashy video productions already clogging up the genre. Often shot in black and white (because *Night of the Living Dead* was) the likes of *Zombie Muffin Munchers*, *Zombie Party*, *The Survivor*, *Gay Zombie* and others are pretty forgettable. *Amid The Dead* is slightly more ambitious, but no more appealing, being a messy mix of bad acting, zombie attacks and existentialism.

More interesting is the silent black and white short *Le Retour du Zombie*, which features a particularly effective resurrection scene, and *Zombie Tales*, which offers a spoof ad for 'Zombie Fresh' – a spray for anyone having to share their lives (or their beds) with a member of the living dead.

Several filmmakers have taken advantage of *Night of the Living Dead's* public domain status to remix the film into a variety of projects. The most novel is *Nocturnal Emissions*, which mixes the Romero footage with clips from 1950s sex-education films to create an interesting experimental short.

Elsewhere on the internet, several web comics deal with zombies – Eric Maziade's *Zombies?* is fairly humorous if inconsequential, while *My Living Dead Girl* is a hugely entertaining strip about preteen schoolgirl Courtney, who just happens to be a zombie. *The Zombie Hunters* is more action and horror oriented, as the eponymous hunters battle the undead in a weekly strip series. Other strips include the excellent *Kristy vs. the Zombie Army*, *Hockey Zombie*, *Marv the Zombie*, *Zombie Panic*, *Tales from Suburbia*, *Rex Target: Freelance Zombie Hunter* and doubtless many more.

There are also a number of 'zombie survival guide' sites, offering guidance and advice for people facing a zombie holocaust, as well as a large number of fictional blogs that offer an episodic zombie story. Fans of undead erotica can check out *Zombie Pin Ups* and *The Living Dead Girlz*.

In fact, the sheer amount of zombie-related material online – everything from review sites to social networking – is impossible to calculate. One thing is for sure – zombie fans are not short of online resources to check out.

12. Zombie Renaissance
The Living Dead Devour Pop Culture

Once a horror character becomes established, it's never very long before they are absorbed into popular culture. When Frankenstein's Monster first appeared on screens, audiences screamed with terror; within a few years, he could be seen in comedy films like *Hellzapoppin'*, and would turn up everywhere from ice cream wrappers to comic books and toys.

So it has been with the zombie. And while the living dead have maintained their ability to terrify and horrify audiences – primarily because, unlike other horror archetypes, zombies are a faceless mass that evoke our darkest fears about death (and more pointedly the dead returning to attack the living) – zombies have also become figures of fun.

Just as every kid in the 1960s and Seventies knew how to affect a Dracula pose or a Frankenstein walk, now everyone knows how to shuffle along like a zombie (or at least they think they do – anyone who has suffered through the glut of shot-on-video zombie films could tell you that it's clearly not as simple as it looks).

Say 'brraaaiinns!' and everyone knows what you're talking about – zombies have become part of the popular consciousness. The living dead are – alongside serial killers – truly the entertainment world's favoured bogeymen.

Zombies have likewise made their mark in the world of music – and not simply as a 1960s band (Rod Argent and Colin Blunstone's beat combo the Zombies were none too horrific). Songwriters and bands have long found the living dead to be fertile subject matter.

The 1950s and Sixties saw an explosion of interest in horror from kids, who were eating up classic horror movies on TV and enjoying a whole slew of shockers in the cinema (in the USA at least; in Britain, the 'X' certificate kept most of them locked out). Horror Hosts like John Zacherle and Ghoulardi introduced a whole new generation to the genre, and it wouldn't be too long before horror combined with the other new teen obsession – rock'n'roll. In particular, Cleveland-based Ghoulardi mixed the two together in his show, and would later prove to have been a formative influence on Lux Interior of the Cramps.

Several gimmicky 'horror rock' and 'shockabilly' songs of the time featured zombies. 1953 calypso number 'Zombie Jamboree' was recorded by Lord Intruder, and has subsequently been covered by several acts, interpreting the song as everything from reggae to folk to rock'n'roll.

1960 saw the Crewnecks record 'Rockin' Zombie', a light-hearted tale of a chap meeting a feisty female zombie while walking past the cemetery, and attending an undead party. It wasn't a hit, but remains a popular Halloween tune to this day.

Girl Group the Magics tried – and failed – to start a new dance craze with the infectious 'The Zombie Walk', while the Revels combined doo-wop and zombies in 'Dead Man's Stroll', and the Poets mixed zombies with just about every other monster in the bluntly titled 'Dead'.

In Britain, Screaming Lord Sutch took the horror trip (and referenced voodoo in his dramatic, pre-Alice Cooper horror stage show) while Screaming Jay Hawkins did likewise in America.

A collection of terrifying creatures in Michael Jackson's 'Thriller'.

ORIGINAL MOTION PICTURE SOUNDTRACK STEREO

THEY'RE BACK!..
AND THEY'RE HUNGRY...

THE RETURN OF THE LIVING DEAD

THE CRAMPS
THE DAMNED
ROKY ERICKSON
THE FLESHEATERS
45 GRAVE
THE JET BLACK BERRIES
SSQ ● TSOL
TALL BOYS

The soundtrack to *Return of the Living Dead* featured an impressive collection of mid-Eighties punk and goth acts.

It's in more recent years that zombie music has become more mainstream, thanks largely to metal and punk bands. As early as 1983, comedy punk band Peter and the Test Tube Babies released 'Zombie Creeping Flesh' as a single (though the cover image was taken from *Zombie Flesh Eaters*), and the soundtrack of *Return of the Living Dead* in 1985 offered a selection of punk horror tunes, including the Cramps' 'Surfin' Dead', 'Dead Beat Dance' by the Damned and songs by 45 Grave, Roky Erickson (though sadly not his classic 'I Walked with a Zombie') and others. Ex-New York Dolls Arthur Kane and Rick Rivets formed the Corpse Grinders and wore zombie make-up on stage, and the goth sub-culture referenced the zombie look with cadaverous bands such as Alien Sex Fiend.

Bands like Necrophagia display their horror-movie influences on songs such as 'And You

Will Live in Terror' (complete with a video featuring footage from Lucio Fulci's *The Beyond*) and 'Embalmed Yet I Breathe'. Send More Paramedics took matters a step further – not only did this thrash band take their name from a line in *Return of the Living Dead*, but the band actually dressed as zombies on stage.

Horror punk band the Misfits also dabbled with zombiedom, particularly in the video for 'Scream', directed by George Romero, and songs like 'Astro Zombies'. Former Misfits frontman Glenn Danzig subsequently extended his horror obsession, not least though his involvement in the Verotik comic-book imprint and the 2005 movie *Grub Girl*.

Japanese band Electric Eel Shock recorded 'Zombie Rock'n'Roll', while Recently Vacated Graves label their output 'true zombie metal', and, with songs like 'Forever to Hunger for Brains', who can argue?

Other acts that have used zombie imagery or sung about the living dead include Sum 41 (the cover of their album *Does This Look Infected?* has the band made up as the living dead), Peaches and Iggy Pop (using zombies in the video for 'Kick It'), Eurovision Song Contest winners Lordi, Alien Sex Fiend, the Fleshtones, Phantom Planet and many, many more. Special mention must go to Jonathan Coulton for his amusing song, 'Re: Your Brains', an impassioned plea from a zombie to a co-worker who is being unreasonable about sharing his brain. You can find the video for this (and various alternate versions) on YouTube.

Future horror director Rob Zombie wore his genre influences on his sleeve with both his band White Zombie and his solo work.

Electro punks Zombie Girl also make their interests clear on their 2007 debut album *Blood, Brains and Rock'n'Roll*, which includes songs like 'Jesus Was a Zombie' and 'Living Dead Superstar'. The band struggled to get the original album art – featuring singer Renee C. Komor, blood and brains – printed, and seem to revel in horror, death and gore, mixing spooky sounds with their dark lyrics.

White Zombie also wore their horror influences proudly, and frontman Rob Zombie

An interesting offshoot of the burlesque revival has been the birth of 'gorelesque' with groups like this.

(Robert Cummings) kept up the good work in his solo projects, with songs like 'Living Dead Girl'. Zombie is now one of the more impressive new horror movie directors, directing *House of a Thousand Corpses*, *The Devil's Rejects* and the reimagining of *Halloween*. It remains to be seen if he'll make a living-dead movie.

The biggest zombie hit came from the unlikely source of Michael Jackson. The title track from his multi-million-selling album *Thriller* (1983) was pretty insipid stuff, but when it came to shooting the music video, Jackson went all out.

With John Landis directing, the promo is a mini-movie that first features Michael transforming into a werewolf, and then has a lengthy dance routine with a bunch of zombies. It's pretty embarrassing stuff – very 1980s in all the worst ways and with a dismal acting performance from Jackson ('I'm not like other guys…').

The singer insisted on having a statement disavowing interest in the occult attached to the video, lest anyone would mistake his musical horror romp for a hymn to Satan. However, in its day, it was seen as revolutionary stuff, and the fifteen-minute promo and 'Making of' video briefly became the bestselling home video release of all time.

Jackson isn't the only person to present all-singing, all-dancing zombies to the world. The living dead have trodden the boards on stage in a handful of shows. *Zombie Prom* was a musical that sought – and generally failed – to capture the spirit of *The Rocky Horror Picture Show* with deliberately kitsch, 1950s-styled characters and plotline. First performed in 1993, it was adapted into a short film in 2006.

More bizarre was *Evil Dead: The Musical,* which debuted in Canada in 2006. Audiences are handed coveralls before the second act, and warned that they *will* be drenched in blood – a gimmick that seems to be as much of a draw as the actual performance. In 2007, *Night of the Living Dead: The Musical* was staged in Illinois, which had much the same sort of splatter warning (an unrelated movie with the same name is in production as we go to press).

Zombies don't seem ideally suited to the world of advertising but, in the last few years, the living dead have been used to sell an unlikely variety of products. An ad for glucose drink Lucozade saw people fleeing a zombie attack in a shopping centre and was pulled from prime time in Ireland after causing a minor moral panic. After failing to catch their victims, the zombies instead have a drink and enjoy a game of basketball.

JC Penney sold clothes with an ad that had students attacked by 'zombie clothing' that stripped them of their fashionable togs – the

Zombies have now joined the more traditional horror characters by appearing on a wide variety of products from sweets to board games to toys like the gruesome *Attack of the Living Dead* series.

Living Dead Dolls — cuddly characters for spooky kids.

message apparently being that you shouldn't be a fashion victim.

In the UK, Specsavers also featured zombies in their push to sell more eyeglasses, while the Samaritans used zombies to promote a suicide hotline, and Mini Coopers were sold as zombie-proof. Given the determination that advertisers have to push brands as being a mark of individuality, it seems that zombies have become established as a handy advertising motif for the mindless mass.

Anyone looking to introduce their kids to zombie culture can now do so with a range of toys, although the *Attack of the Living Dead* series might well traumatise them more than a Lucio Fulci film. Aimed at the collectable market, these detailed — and extremely gory — figures have their own zombie story (it's pretty much the standard bio-infection tale) and there are a wide variety of characters available. Fans can also buy *Land of the Dead, Shaun of the Dead* and other movie-related figures.

These gory toys — based on adult movies — went more or less unnoticed by any self-styled moral arbiters until a collection was released to tie in with *Planet Terror*, at which point all hell broke loose. The problem? A doll based on Quentin Tarantino's character, with the less-than-subtle name of 'Rapist Number One'. Despite the fact that this was simply the character's 'name', and the fact that these 'toys' are not really aimed at kids anyway, shops banned it while feminists raged.

Zombie walks have become something of a phenomenon in recent years, taking place across the world.

Their apparent belief was that a single toy would actively encourage the trivialisation of rape (it wasn't the first such moral outcry against such a toy; a few years earlier, the *Sin City* Marv figure – strapped to an electric chair – was also 'banned').

Less gruesome and extreme are the popular Living Dead Dolls, which offer an alternative to regular dollies for gothically inclined kids. This ongoing series of collectables are both cute and creepy, though possibly no more so than dolls that wet themselves.

Other toys on the market include the Animated Crawling Zombie (a talking, legless green monster who is described as a 'giggle-inducing ghoul') and several board games, including *Zombies!!*, *Zombie Town* and *Last Night on Earth*. Model-makers can choose from a variety of zombie model kits, including tie-ins to *Zombie Flesh Eaters*, *Night of the Living Dead* and *Plague of the Zombies*, while zombie masks range from the generic to the specific (such as a none-too-realistic looking Bub from *Day of the Dead*, the cemetery zombie from *Zombie Flesh Eaters* and Flyboy from *Dawn of the Dead*).

One of the more unusual zombie cultural crossovers in recent years has been the rise of the zombie walks and flashmobs. These are organised gatherings of people, dressed and acting as zombies, in public places – sometimes to promote an event, sometimes just for the hell of it. This phenomenon is indicative of the zombie's pre-eminence among horror archetypes – no one is organising vampire walks, werewolf walks, or even space monster walks.

The first zombie walk seems to have been in 2001, in Sacramento, where a 'zombie parade' took place to promote a local film show. By 2005, zombie walks were taking place across America. In San Francisco, some two hundred 'zombies' gathered, while over a thousand turned up to the Monroeville Mall in Pittsburgh (where *Dawn of the Dead* was shot) in 2007. Not to be outdone, Brisbane in Australia held a march where fifteen hundred 'zombies' took part. On Halloween 2008, your author joined 1227 people in Nottingham's Market Square to set a new world record for the number of 'zombies' in one place.

Variations on the theme have included zombie pub-crawls (where presumably the shuffling, staggering walk becomes easier with each successive pub visited), zombie yoga and charity fundraisers where the 'undead' raise money for assorted worthy causes.

Of course, not everyone is happy with this. Just as we can guarantee that, every Halloween, some vicar will start preaching about trick or treating being the first step towards Satanism, so zombies are frowned upon by those that have an agenda to further, insist on taking matters literally or simply lack a sense of the absurd. In May 2008, the BBC reported that 'a procession of devils, ghosts and zombies through the historic Spanish city of Toledo [in fact this was a street performance by actors from the Morboria Theatre Company] had been branded blasphemous by the Catholic Church'.

Religious objections aside, it would seem that the zombie is now an intrinsic part of popular culture, and is destined to remain so for some time. While other monsters have faded, the zombie seems as relevant as ever – perhaps even more so, given the increasingly uncertain world we live in, where the idea of humanity being wiped out by a biological, nuclear or chemical attack seems ever more feasible – an apocalypse is at the back of everyone's mind.

Who would bet against the zombie dominating 21st century horror in much the same way it shuffled to pre-eminence across the previous century?